Flickers of Desire

STAR
★★★★★★★★★★ AMERICAN CULTURE / AMERICAN CINEMA
DECADES

Each volume in the series Star Decades: American Culture/American Cinema presents original essays analyzing the movie star against the background of contemporary American cultural history. As icon, as mediated personality, and as object of audience fascination and desire, the Hollywood star remains the model for celebrity in modern culture and represents a paradoxical combination of achievement, talent, ability, luck, authenticity, superficiality, and ordinariness. In all of the volumes, stardom is studied as an effect of, and influence on, the particular historical and industrial contexts that enabled a star to be "discovered," to be featured in films, to be promoted and publicized, and ultimately to become a recognizable and admired—even sometimes notorious—feature of the cultural landscape. Understanding when, how, and why a star "makes it," dazzling for a brief moment or enduring across decades, is especially relevant given the ongoing importance of mediated celebrity in an increasingly visualized world. We hope that our approach produces at least some of the surprises and delight for our readers that stars themselves do.

ADRIENNE L. McLEAN AND MURRAY POMERANCE
SERIES EDITORS

Jennifer M. Bean, ed., *Flickers of Desire: Movie Stars of the 1910s*

Patrice Petro, ed., *Idols of Modernity: Movie Stars of the 1920s*

Adrienne L. McLean, ed., *Glamour in a Golden Age: Movie Stars of the 1930s*

Sean Griffin, ed., *What Dreams Were Made Of: Movie Stars of the 1940s*

R. Barton Palmer, ed., *Larger Than Life: Movie Stars of the 1950s*

Pamela R. Wojcik, ed., *New Constellations: Movie Stars of the 1960s*

James Morrison, ed., *Hollywood Reborn: Movie Stars of the 1970s*

Robert Eberwein, ed., *Acting for America: Movie Stars of the 1980s*

Anna Everett, ed., *Pretty People: Movie Stars of the 1990s*

Murray Pomerance, ed., *Shining in Shadows: Movie Stars of the 2000s*

Flickers of Desire

Movie Stars of the

1910s
★☆★☆★☆★☆★☆★★

EDITED BY

JENNIFER M. BEAN

RUTGERS UNIVERSITY PRESS

NEW BRUNSWICK, NEW JERSEY, AND LONDON

LIBRARY OF CONGRESS CATALOGING-IN-PUBLICATION DATA

Flickers of desire : movie stars of the 1910s / edited by Jennifer M. Bean.
    p.   cm. — (Star decades : American culture / American cinema)
  Includes bibliographical references and index.
  ISBN   978–0–8135–5014–5   (hardcover : alk. paper)
  ISBN   978–0–8135–5015–2   (pbk. : alk. paper)
  1. Motion picture actors and actresses—United States—Biography.   I. Bean, Jennifer
M., 1968–   .   1006479114
  PN1998.2.F5585   2011
  791.4302'80922—dc22
  [B]
                                                        2010035281

A British Cataloging-in-Publication record for this book is available from the British Library.

This collection copyright © 2011 by Rutgers, The State University

Individual chapters copyright © 2011 in the names of their authors

Visit our Web site: http://rutgerspress.rutgers.edu

Manufactured in the United States of America

For my students

CONTENTS

☆☆☆☆☆☆☆☆☆★★★

debated here in a different context. It is in the context of the classroom, however, where my aims for this collection have taken particular shape, often angling against prevailing trends in history textbooks and developing alongside what my students were willing—or determined—to think about. I dedicate this collection to them, and to the brilliant light their every question has cast.

Flickers of Desire

INTRODUCTION

☆☆☆☆☆☆☆☆☆★

Stardom in the 1910s

JENNIFER M. BEAN

Nothing—*nothing*—like this had ever existed before. Stage stars were
known only to those who could afford to see their plays. . . . The movies
offered amusement to the masses.

—William J. Mann, *The Biograph Girl*

Desire is not simple.

—Ann Carson, *Eros: The Bittersweet*

There are a number of ways one might go about discussing
the origins of American film stardom and the inestimable impact of stars on
the growth of a domestic industry through the course of the 1910s. One
might feasibly begin by questioning whether or not it is even proper to
speak of an origin for film stardom when a theatrical star system, similar in
some formal properties although different in tendencies, preceded the
invention of motion pictures by at least a century. The answer to this question of origins is both no and yes. No, because before there could be movie
stars there had to be a conception of the film *actor*; and the flourishing of a
predominantly narrative cinema after 1906, followed by the practice of hiring a stock troupe of regular players in 1908 and 1909, fostered an understanding among both the public and the motion picture producers that the
people appearing on the screen were professional performers. Yes, because
the unprecedented intensity of feeling that audiences expressed for their
favorite "picture personalities" in 1910, and the rapid acceleration of a multimedia system shaped by mass technologies of communication and representation, hint that film stardom flaunts a difference at once qualitative and
quantitative.

I begin with this wobble between yes and no in order to flag the complexity of a phenomenon impossible to pinpoint as a locatable or knowable
event, a definite point in time, for it is an origin deeply implicated in a constellation of transformations. Such an approach refuses a dubious thesis
much bandied about, still, among those who talk about film and where it
came from (most notably, perhaps, in David Cook's introductory textbook,

A History of Narrative Cinema), that "the star system was born" by virtue of a publicity stunt engineered by Carl Laemmle, supervisor of the Independent Motion Picture Corporation (IMP), in the spring of 1910. The story pivots on Laemmle's coup in hiring the "Biograph Girl," Florence Lawrence, circulating "anonymous reports of her death" and "using her real name in public for the first time." Laemmle then "undertook an extensive advertising campaign to denounce the story as a 'black lie' spread by the Patents Company to conceal the fact that Miss Lawrence had come over to IMP" (Cook 36). Admittedly, in the spring of 1910 independent companies like IMP were struggling to compete with the near monopoly over distribution, production, and reception systems that the licensed members of the Motion Picture Patent Company (among them Edison, Kalem, Vitagraph, Essanay, and Biograph) had created in late 1908. And it is certainly true that Laemmle's stunt labored to undermine public opinion of the MPPC while flaunting the "real" name of a favorite "picture personality." But as with so many textbook approaches to the telling of history, a temptation for neatness denies complex historical variables in favor of a sensational event that can hardly account for the "how," "what," and "why" of a nascent star phenomenon.

Why, for instance, did anyone care about the fate of a figure they knew only as the "Biograph Girl"? Why, when this new species lacked even an agreed-upon definition or set of advertising policies and principles, did fans express an electrifying proximity to their favorite players that amounts to a relationship at once imaginary and deeply felt? It is telling, for instance, that in April 1910 *Moving Picture World* reported "an extraordinary demand throughout the country by exhibitors for photographs of the actors and actresses. The patrons say they want to get a closer view of the people" (9 April 1910, 559). One month later, another writer for the same magazine trumpeted his astonishment at "the interest the public has taken in the personality of many of the picture players," exclaiming: "Managers all over the country are *begging* the manufacturers to furnish them with photographs of their players so that they may be displayed in the lobbies of their theaters, and the people who are *craving* to see and meet the originals may be in a measure consoled" (21 May 1910, 825, emphasis added). Whether or not the flurry of photographs, postcards, lobby displays, and lantern slides circulating in the latter months of 1910 "consoled" viewers in lieu of "originals" is up for speculation. But there is no question that the articulation of public desire—an intensity of feeling conveyed through verbs like "begging" and "craving"—plays a fundamental role in the lexicon of early film stardom. As the *New York Dramatic Mirror*, a relatively prestigious periodical traditionally devoted to news of theatrical and vaudeville circuits, announced in early 1912: "By devoting to portraits of players so much of the extra space allotted to motion pictures in this annual number, *The Mirror* is merely responding to the desires of the picture public" (31 January 1912, 51).

By titling this collection *Flickers of Desire*, my intent is not to grant un-fettered agency to fans as stardom's prime determinant, nor do I believe that any representation—in early film culture or in our own day—"merely" responds to a perceived craving. Rather, viewer desire and representational strategies each produce and disquiet the other in a contagious, spiraling, multimedia phenomenon refracted through ever-mounting palimpsests of texts: images in films, photographs, portraits, caricatures, etchings, im-printed objects, and sketches; a flurry of stories, rumors, allusions, imita-tions, advertisements, press books, interviews, and eyewitness testimonies; a series of jokes, limericks, songs, dances, and so on. If this list looks messy, so be it. This is the prerogative of desire conceived in terms that implode normative regimes of signification, adamantly defying the logic of linearity and expediency, aggressively rerouting, protracting, and intensifying a kind of affect and ensuing effects often difficult to explain. This desire is the pre-rogative of a mass-cultural phenomenon that promiscuously migrates across media forms, fragmenting the unity of any single author or author-izing agency. It is also the methodological prerogative of contributors to this volume, who take early stardom's multiple meaning-making sites as a scin-tillating challenge and render the relation between industrial ideology, cul-tural mores, and the circulation and consumption of cinema's first decade of stars a productively difficult one.

☆☆★★★ Rebellious Humbug

Twenty years have passed since the publication of Richard deCordova's now classic study *Picture Personalities: The Emergence of the Star System in America*, which remains (until the publication of the current vol-ume) the only book-length consideration of stardom through the course of this decade. Beginning with the pioneering premise that grasping the impli-cations of the actor's performance in early narrative cinema demands a "dis-cursive analysis" of extra-filmic factors, deCordova broke with formalist approaches dominant at the time and turned to a careful examination of trade journals such as *Moving Picture World*, primarily addressed to exhibitors, as well as to monthly magazines like *Motion Picture Story Magazine* and *Photo-play* that addressed a larger public. Importantly, the latter two periodicals were launched in 1911. Both were primarily designed to relay stories from the films, and both initially included a small section that carried anywhere from a half dozen to a dozen photographs of screen players. Although *Motion Picture Story Magazine* (based in New York) favored the licensed companies and *Photoplay* (based in Chicago) favored the independents, the remarkably similar trajectory of the two begins within a few months, as both journals expanded their photo-based sections and carried columns titled "Answers to Inquiries" in response to fan letters requesting information about their favorite players (*Photoplay* shortly retitled its section "The Question Box," perhaps as a means of distinguishing itself). But "these questions led to and were answered by a name, an identification in a quite literal sense," deCordova claims, while stressing that the identity of early "picture personalities" was restricted to a discourse on acting and to information (at once sparse and repetitive) concerning their *professional* lives, their existence in films. It is not until 1913–1914 that a "marked expansion" of knowledge privileging the player's *personal* life became the primary focus of discourse and "brought into existence the star" (98).

By now, we have grown so accustomed to consuming the personal lives of film stars—individuals whose eating habits, fashion choices, marriages, divorces, affairs, childhoods, politics, and drug habits are flaunted as a matter of course—that the origins of such a phenomenon may appear inevitable in retrospect. That inevitability may have been felt from the very start, given what film historian Sumiko Higashi calls the insatiable "curiosity of devotees" plaguing editors with questions, the likes of which prompted *Motion Picture Story Magazine* to add a "Chats with the Players" department in 1912 and "Greenroom Jottings: Little Whispering Room from Everywhere in Playerdom" in 1913 ("Vitagraph Stardom" 270). That same year *Photoplay* retitled their "Notes on the Players" section as "Photoplayers' Personalities: Little Glimpses Behind the Screen as It Were." It is relatively easy to see that the lure implied by "glimpsing," "chatting," or "whispering" hints at an illusive depth, a phantasm of access to interiority that must be accorded a special place in the history of early stardom. But to claim, as deCordova does, that the "private lives of the players were constituted as a site of knowledge and truth" (98) raises serious doubts, insinuating as it does a rather naïve readership and overlooking entirely the playful and often ironic tones assumed by studio-originated publicity as well as the promiscuous replay of star materials in other media outlets.

In 1914, at the very moment that this "truth" about stars as persons allegedly crystallizes, for instance, the Fox Company introduced an unknown actress, Theda Bara, at a legendary press conference in Chicago. As Gaylyn Studlar explains in her chapter for this volume, the event "strained the boundaries of credulity," participating in a "discursive context of skepticism" surrounding the industry's systematic exploitation of stars by that time. Born Theodosia Goodman in Cincinnati, Ohio, the daughter of a lower-middle-class Jewish family, Bara shimmered into the limelight as a "well-known actress from Paris," albeit one born not in Europe but "in the shadow of the Sphinx." As Studlar recalls, press agents eagerly pointed out that their new star's name formed an anagram for "Arab Death," and she teases out an equally fantastic array of monikers that proliferated in fan magazines, newspaper articles, and studio publicity following Bara's stunning debut in *A Fool There Was* (1915) as a sexually aggressive and destructive "vamp": "The Arch-Torpedo of Domesticity," "The Queen of Vampires," "The Wickedest Woman in the World," "Purgatory's Ivory Angel," "The Ishmaelite of Domesticity," "The Devil's Handmaiden," and the "Priestess of Sin."

Given the astonishing "humbug" surrounding Bara's ascension to superstardom, might we not concur that the public's desire to know *more*, to draw closer to the "real" self of the star, mingles from the very start with an equally passionate interest in the phenomenon of spectacular delusion? Although not unique to film stardom by any means, the modern publicity stunt has distinctively American roots, largely pioneered by P. T. (Phineas Taylor) Barnum in the 1840s and 1850s. As cultural historian Neil Harris has shown, Barnum recognized that the curiosities, wonders, and freaks that he featured in his exhibits would not have been successful if they had not been extensively, hyperbolically, and fallaciously advertised. When audiences discovered they had been duped by, say, the "Feejee [Fiji] Mermaid," they expressed interest in what Harris terms an "operational aesthetic," in the intricate means through which Barnum had engineered such spectacular deceptions (61–89). That Barnum's capacity to entice and deceive became the crucial ingredient in his self-cultivated reputation as the "presiding genius" of American showmanship affords an intriguing "origins" for thinking about the formation of modern celebrity culture, not least because any legacy routed through Barnum returns us to the stage, specifically to Sarah Bernhardt, the Western world's most prestigious theatrical diva at the turn of the century. "By adopting Barnumism," argues theater historian Susan Glenn, "Bernhardt ushered in a new cultural phenomenon: the egotistical female artist who not only promotes her plays but actively constructs, exhibits, and advertises her own curious and flamboyant personality" (29).

Glenn's exquisitely detailed account of Bernhardt's widely publicized "personality"—including repeated proclamations and recantations of her Jewish heritage, her noisy endorsement of the suffragette movement, and her passion for collecting exotic objects as well as lovers—is of inestimable import to histories of stardom in America where Bernhardt's fame attained especially acute status in the press. In the most general and obvious way, the circulation of materials referring to Bernhardt's personal life, and hence the public perception of an individual who transcends each performed role, interrupts the premise that film historians have long enshrined as the distinguishing mark of *film* stardom. Nor is it coincidental that Bernhardt appeared in several film versions of her stage roles, most famously *Camille* (1911) and *Queen Elizabeth* (1912). Billed as "features" or "specials" imported from Europe, these two- and three-reel films circulated through innovative distribution strategies that highlighted a film's ability to sustain audience interest as a single entity, rather than as one entry among many in a fast-changing eclectic variety program (comprising one- and split-reel films running ten to fifteen minutes in length) that formed the U.S. industry's dominant mode of production and distribution in 1910–1912.

Whether or not these highly publicized and often imported "feature" films—showcasing well-known stage stars like Rejane, Mrs. Fiske, James K. Hackett, Miss Mildred Holland, and James O'Neill as well as Bernhardt—represent the first moment that filmgoers knew they were "seeing stars," as Janet Staiger argues, depends on how one understands the identity of those performers achieving recognition at the same moment as "picture personalities," known only by virtue of their appearance in films ("Seeing Stars" 14–15). We return to this point momentarily, but it bears stressing for now that by 1913, as Elaine Bowser sums up, "the era of star exploitation was only just beginning: Theda Bara had yet to be invented" (119). More emphatic still, as Studlar reveals, the Fox company's laborious construction of Bara as a decadent embodiment of feminine evil directly affiliated her star persona with the thespian credentials and sensual, orientalized, exotic roles of Bernhardt, whose 1916–18 U.S. tour of her stage role as Cléopâtre (in French) conspicuously coincided with the anticipated release of Bara's epic film vehicle, *Cleopatra* (1917).

☆☆★★★ Modern Womanhood

I have belabored the triangulated histories of Bara, Bernhardt, and Barnum in order to pry open a genealogy of celebrity culture in America ripe with balderdash, a sort of sensational ballyhoo eagerly consumed by a mass public intrigued with fantasies of rebellious otherness. I have also done so in order to foreground the close association of these fantasies with female performers who emblematized a defiant selfhood and formed an important crucible for modern feminism. It is in this spirit that

Sarah Bernhardt as Cleopatra.

Anne Morey and Kristen Hatch approach the feature film extravaganzas that respectively showcase Geraldine Farrar and Lillian Gish. In the case of Farrar, Morey highlights the opera-turned-film-star's "ability to unite two apparently incompatible aims: she permitted film to make a claim for the upper-middle-class carriage trade at the same moment that she helped to domesticate a cadre of risqué 'brothel play' roles." While only one of the fourteen films Farrar made with Famous Players in the second half of the decade directly adapted an opera (*Carmen*, 1915), the majority reiterated a variation on the reformed or fallen woman theme, the *ne plus ultra* of prestige soprano roles since the nineteenth century. At first glance, the case of Gish might suggest Farrar's dire opposite. As Hatch explains, the star's blond hair, blue eyes, and pale skin embodied middle-class ideals of white womanhood onscreen, and her characters in film vehicles—almost all directed by D. W. Griffith—emit an ethereal and luminous innocence in a world threatened by interracial mixing, masculine brutishness, and the turmoil of war. But Hatch shows how Gish's offscreen persona increasingly undermined the logic of her films. Fan magazines like *Photoplay* and *Motion Picture Magazine* marshaled her pale coloring and slender features into the image of a "cool" and businesslike woman, a professional immersed in a serious study of the science of acting. In like manner, Farrar's status as a professional actor, a woman dedicated to her work, anchored her offscreen identity to respectability, while her appearance in films enabled the widespread circulation of her sinfully exotic operatic persona. In both cases these stars helped forge, to borrow Hatch's phrase, "a new vision of modern womanhood."

Other female film stars became prototypes of a new physical culture, their identities constructed and supported by a discourse that promoted steady nerves and athletic prowess—a phenomenology of performance radically distinct from stage traditions in which the performers' emotional range or acting skill attain paramount status. None were more visible than serial adventure stars like Pearl White, Grace Cunard, Ruth Roland, Cleo Madison, Kathlyn Williams, and Helen Holmes, whose global popularity flaunted the "modern girl" as a daring creature immune to the anxieties of urban culture, eager to experience the thrill of the unknown, and capable of feats that would put grown men to shame. As Mark Cooper reveals in his chapter on White and Cunard, a number of national industries translated and modified these icons of modern femininity, while U.S. fan discourse reveals a capacious appetite for playing with their offscreen identities, a juggernaut through which the meaning of the character appearing onscreen is intensified or rerouted. He draws attention, for instance, to the rhetorical strategies whereby a female reporter initially poses as a "naïve fan who mistakes fiction for real life" and enters the "fearless" star's home with trepidation, as if expecting the nefarious thugs populating serials like *The Perils of Pauline* (1914), *The Exploits of Elaine* (1914), and *The Broken Coin* (1915) to suddenly appear with knives, ropes, and perhaps even a poisonous gas or death-ray device in hand. "This is a ruse," he notes: "The author playfully disavows her knowledge that villains do not infest the star's . . . home in order to allow readers the satisfaction of believing they can tell the difference between fiction and real life." In so doing, such interviews reveal "what real life is and offers the star, rather than her character, as a point of identification." But if we ask what "real life" means, then the answer shimmering through any number of interviews, publicity reports, behind-the-scenes photographs, and testimonials stresses the degree to which "uncertainty and danger define [the serial stars'] daily routine." In short, the labor involved in staging and performing the feats that appear onscreen surfaces in star discourse as far more risky, daring, and difficult than that represented by the fictional heroines.

The lexicon of physical risk was hardly idiosyncratic to serial stars. Interviews with Mary Pickford, as Christine Gledhill observes in her chapter here, "often includ[ed] snippets about Pickford's feats of endurance while filming, suggesting competition with her serial-queen rivals." Other rivals included Annette Kellerman, the former Olympic swimming champion who became the Fox Company's featured star in spectacular underwater fantasy films like *Neptune's Daughter* (1914) and *A Daughter of the Gods* (1916), and, perhaps most notoriously, comedians like Mabel Normand. The era's indisputable queen of comedy, Normand's roguish personality and daring persona were first established in Biograph films during the picture personality era. In *Tomboy Bessie* (1911), for instance, she rides a bicycle sitting on the handlebars, robs a chicken coop, and uses a slingshot, and in *A Dash Through the Clouds* (1912) she rescues her sweetheart by ascending in an open-door airplane. By 1914 Normand featured as the leading female star and oftentimes as director at the Keystone Film Company, while publicity touted her as "one of the swimming champions of the Pacific Coast, an expert horsewoman, athletic, and fond of all outdoor sports to a degree which permits of her being thrown or dragged about in some of the more strenuous comedy work in a way that would put most women in the hospital" ("A Champion Swimmer Who Swims for Plays," *Blue Book Magazine*, July 1914, n.p.). Most women, that is, but emphatically *not* female stars whose laborious physical exertion registered with innumerable fans, honored in tributes like "Mademoiselle Film vs. Mademoiselle Stage," the award-winning essay of a 1914 write-in contest sponsored by *Motion Picture Magazine*. Written by Helen Mar of

Annette Kellerman in *A Daughter of the Gods* (1916). Courtesy of the Museum of Modern Art Film Stills Archive.

Rochester, New York, the subtitle of the essay headlines the question: "Are the Demands on a Film Actress More Exacting and Strenuous Than Those on Her Stage Sister?" The response, "Emphatically Affirmative," is supported throughout the piece, leading the writer to assay her belief that "Mademoiselle Film" is entitled to "the high and loyal esteem in which she is held by us, the solid and discerning regiment of Film Fans" (August 1914, 128).

The vocal presence of female fans in the decade is commensurate with the rising presence of women in every facet of American life. Although the Nineteenth Amendment giving women the right to vote would not be ratified until 1919, statistics clarify that in the course of the first two decades of the twentieth century female enrollment in colleges and universities "increased by 1000 percent in public institutions and 482 percent in private ones." Women employed as "clerks, saleswomen, stenographers, typists, bookkeepers, cashiers, and accountants" soared from "9.1 percent in 1910 to 25.6 percent in 1920" (Ammons 82). "Never before in civilization," wrote Jane Addams as early as 1909, "have such numbers of young girls been suddenly released from the protection of the home and permitted to walk unattended upon city streets and to work under alien roofs; for the

Mabel Normand, playing opposite Roscoe Arbuckle in *He Did and He Didn't* (1916), demonstrates the daring athleticism that "permits of her being thrown or dragged about in some of the more strenuous comedy work in a way that would put most women in the hospital." Courtesy of Photofest.

first time they are being prized more for their labor power than for their innocence, their tender beauty, their ephemeral gaiety" (Lant, *Red Velvet* 5).

It would be a mistake to romanticize the freedom of many such young girls, especially those who were among the fifteen million Italian, Jewish, and eastern European immigrants arriving in the United States between

1890 and 1915. Providing a ready pool of "labor power" for sweatshop factories, teenage immigrants worked in unsanitary and often life-threatening
conditions. A lack of familiarity with English may have prohibited many
such girls from reading and responding to early fan discourse, but their
presence in nickelodeon theaters has been amply documented, part of a
broader recognition by recent historians that women increasingly composed
the industry's primary target audience through the course of the 1910s (see
Higashi "Vitagraph"; Stamp; Fuller; Studlar "Perils"). "By the 1920s," writes
Antonia Lant, "popular wisdom had it that films were *for* women, and that
they formed the majority of audiences. These regular filmgoers further
shaped cinema's fortunes in their buying of, and written responses to, film
magazines" (*Red Velvet* 1).

Women writers also shaped cinema's fortunes in their capacity as
screenwriters, a tradition including the prolific output of Sonya Levien,
Anita Loos, Jeanie Macpherson, June Mathis, and Frances Marion. As Giorgio Bertellini recalls in his chapter here on the Anglo-American actor George
Beban, whose performance as a sympathetic Italian immigrant in *The Sign of
the Rose* (alternately titled *The Alien*), as well as in *The Italian* in 1915, drew
from a picturesque imaginary of New York tenement life, female script-
writers played an important role in altering common perceptions of oceanic
migration and immigrant life. "While many of these stories highlighted the
trip to New York as a journey toward a better life, and represented social ties
within the ghetto as less oppressive than those experienced in the homeland, these films often departed from the drama of immigration. They also
repeatedly addressed issues germane to mainstream American culture by
venturing, without pedantry, into questions of social freedom, sexual
expression, and gender and interracial relations." As Bertellini teases out,
Beban played a prominent role in generating a sympathetic portrayal of
immigrant "others" and creating a racialized star profile, the likes of which
paved the way for the next decade's notorious "Latin Lover," the exotic and
sensual Rudolf Valentino. He also reminds us that Valentino's persona was
discovered and profiled by screenwriter June Mathis in her scripts for *Four
Horsemen of the Apocalypse* (1921) and *Blood and Sand* (1922).

Perhaps even more critical for the history of stardom in the 1910s,
women writers shaped cinema's fortunes in their capacity as journalists and
critics, preeminent among them Louella Parsons, Adele Whitely Fletcher,
Colette, Kitty Kelly (*Chicago Tribune*), Grace Kingsley (*Los Angeles Times*),
Alice Hall (*Pictures and the Picturegoer*), and Mabel Condon (*Motography* and
Photoplay). As Richard Abel argues in his chapter on G. M. Anderson and the
picture personality era, this genealogy arguably begins when Gertrude Price,

a self-professed "Moving Picture Expert," inaugurated a syndicated series of "personality sketches" of popular film players for the Scripps-McRae newspaper chain in late 1912. Emphatically, Abel's recovery of Price's "personality sketches" reveals that the euphoria of proximity to film players' personal lives circulates on a mass scale well before industry-oriented publications like *Motion Picture Story Magazine* and *Photoplay* indulged public curiosity. This revelation amounts to more than a mere fiddling with dates, since Price's exposés in a vast newspaper chain that catered to the working class reveal two distinct emphases. On one hand, a distinctively modern fantasy dominates at least "two-thirds" of Price's stories, all of which promote female players described as "athletic young women, carefree but committed to their work, frank and fearless in the face of physical risk. . . . [usually] unattached, and without children." Such female "picture personalities," Abel concludes, "would have been especially appealing to young female movie fans as active, attractive, independent workers or professionals and, therefore, successful role models to emulate." On the other hand, the prevalence of stories dealing with western subjects and the "good bad outlaw" character type embodied by Anderson's "Broncho Billy" suggests that nostalgic fantasies of an America in which the pursuit of happiness depended on rugged individualism and the settling of an untamed frontier played a prominent role in the national imaginary fostered by early stardom.

☆☆☆☆★ Democratizing Fame and Magnetizing Bodies

"America," writes Leo Braudy, "pioneered in the implicit democratic and modern assumption that everyone could and should be looked at. This it seemed was one of the privileges for which the American Revolution was fought" (506). Whether or not we agree that a "democratization of fame" begins when Americans toppled Britain's monarchical rule in the late eighteenth century, a pseudo-discourse of democracy, of opportunity available to all, attained governing status in early star discourse. Neither kings nor queens, gods nor goddesses, many stars were touted as resembling more ordinary people, just "like you and me."[1] They were our friends. It is telling, for instance, that in late 1919 reporter Randolph Bartlett virulently attacked the machinations of the "star system," by which he meant the kind of publicity stunts geared to "create" stars in the manner established by Fox's publicity department for Theda Bara. But he vociferously defended the "star idea" that would sustain itself regardless of advertising ploys since "the principal interest of the majority of normal human beings is their friends. . . . So we are attracted to personalities upon the screen. No matter what they do, we are interested" ("The Star Idea versus the Star System," *Motion Picture Magazine*, August 1919, 107).

The idiom of friendship emerged early. In January 1913, the *New York Dramatic Mirror* provided portraits of players as diverse as Florence Turner, John Bunny, Kathlyn Williams, Gene Gauntier, G. M. Anderson, and Alice Joyce, claiming that "the faces are as familiar as those of old friends and as welcome" ("Personality a Force in Pictures," 15 January 1913, 44). If a good friendship takes time, then so too with early picture personalities whose weekly appearance in one- and split-reel films in rapidly changing variety programs across the country enabled "the spectator" to "gradually . . . know such a player as he knows a friend and the more complete the acquaintance, the more thorough the enjoyment to be gained from a film performance." The public's "acquaintance" with these personalities was also shaped by production practices increasingly geared toward serialization, or what Abel in his study of G. M. Anderson calls the "seriality" of the "single-reel fiction film." Known for western action films as early as 1909, Anderson's role as "Broncho Billy" in over fifty one-reel films produced between 1910 and 1913 demonstrates that "a series based on a recurring 'picture personality' who embodied a more or less consistent character 'type,' could successfully attract mass audiences to return again and again to picture theaters." But repetition alone could hardly lure and attract. Moreover, as Abel quips, Anderson "would have been the first to admit that his range as an actor was limited." Even so, his stocky, taciturn, tight-lipped performance as a "good bad man" generated "an unexpectedly strong screen presence," a phenomenological appeal regularly referred to in the press as "magnetism."

Although I can only touch on the array of semantic meanings attached to the concept of "magnetism," its ubiquitous use in the period encourages a reorientation of the concept of "attraction," a term widely associated in film historical discourse with a fin-de-siècle cinema's technological prowess and the earliest moving-image machine's euphoric proximity to modernity. It bears stressing that stars would be marketed as the preeminent motion picture *attraction* in publicity and advertisements by the mid- to late 1910s, but the meaning of "attraction" in this context derives not from the spectacular lure of the fairground or the magic show. It stems instead from a tradition of philosophical and scientific assessments of the invisible forces affecting or linking spatially discreet material bodies. It is this invisible "contact" that Isaac Newton raised, by way of speculation, in the final query of his *Opticks* (1717): "Have not the small Particle of Bodies certain Powers, Virtues, or Forces, by which they act at a distance . . . ? For it's well known that bodies act upon one another by Attractions of Gravity, *Magnetism*, and

Electricity" (375–76, my emphasis). Newton's theory of the invisible laws of gravity, in concord with the seemingly miraculous discovery of electricity by Benjamin Franklin and the more dubious but wildly popular theory of "animal magnetism" proselytized by Franz Anton Mesmer in the eighteenth century, fed a western world's fascination with the idea of invisible emissions that could literally "move" other bodies and things. In the 1820s, for instance, the German novelist Johann Wolfgang von Goethe formulated a theory of "attraction," explaining: "We have all some electrical and magnetic forces within us; and we put forth, like the magnet itself, an attractive or repulsive power" (Asendorf 156). A belief in the electromagnetic fluids of the body pervaded most every philosophical, scientific, sociological, and artistic movement in the nineteenth and early twentieth centuries. To take one curious and yet illustrious example, in 1913 the *New York Times* published a special cable from Paris, "Hands Are Magnetic Poles." Here readers learned that a French scientist, M. Fayol, had built an instrument consisting of a "delicate metal cylinder" that "swings in a perpendicular position between ball bears" on an adjustable oak board that could measure the "vital magnetic fluid emitted by the body" (13 April 1913, C2).

Less exacting devices tallied the magnetic appeal of film players. But it was generally agreed that "the most popular actors [in film] may not be the most skillful," as Frank Dyer observed in 1913: "The popular actors seem to have the indefinable quality of taking a good photograph, and making appeals by reason of their inherent *magnetism*" (Bowser 106, my emphasis). However "indefinable," the logic that equates a player's drawing power with the allure of "magnetism" prevailed in headlines such as "Personality—Box-Office Magnet," as the *New York Dramatic Mirror* trumpeted in 1914, citing Kathlyn Williams, "Broncho Billy" Anderson, Flora Finch, John Bunny, and Mary Fuller among others as "examples of players with personality—individuality that has value, that is a magnet in the box-office" (14 January 1914, 52). That same year, shortly after the eighteen-year-old Blanche Sweet signed a contract with Famous Players–Lasky, one writer for *Motion Picture News* struggled to explain the "screen magnetism" of her appeal. "The man doesn't live," he sighed, "who could watch a good Sweet picture without feeling a sense of her actual presence—without almost believing that he could touch flesh if only his hand could come in contact with the figure on the screen" (19 December 1914, 34). For those who did have the privilege of coming into contact with the figure on the screen, as when reporter Mabel Condon ventured to the Edison Company's New York studio to interview Mary Fuller in the spring of 1914, "the first clasp of [Fuller's] hand" appeared wholly explanatory. "There is magnetism in this experience," Condon informed her readers, "and you continue to feel it long after" ("'True Blue' Mary Fuller," *Photoplay*, May 1914, 61). Arguably, the notion that certain personalities emit a magnetic charge capable of "touching" and "moving" others even at a distance may be *the* phantasm explaining the chiasmic relation between fans and early film stars, an electrifying proximity at once imaginary and literally felt. Insofar as "magnetism" simply belongs to a person, emerges from the shimmer of their very *being*, the concept synchronized neatly with a pseudo-democratic discourse encouraging the conception of film stars as "ordinary" folks—ordinary, that is, and yet exceptionally magnetic.

The underlying complexities implicit in such a discourse emerge sharply in Scott Curtis's detailed study of Douglas Fairbanks, a star generally understood as one of the decade's most magnetic personalities. In 1915, as Curtis explains, when Fairbanks left the stage to sign a contract with the Triangle Film Corporation, he was only one of approximately sixty actors that Triangle "wooed" from the stage in an attempt to build a company associated with prestige pictures. The project of making films "for the masses with an appeal to the classes," however, failed miserably, in part because Triangle directors "found themselves relying on static long takes and sluggish editing" in order "to accommodate hyperbolic, mannered theatrical acting styles." Fairbanks's startling popularity, beginning with his first film vehicle *The Lamb* (1915), proved an exception to the rule, largely due to his "savvy cinematographic presence," his willingness to adapt his persona to film, and a comedic wit that played to the film's many "medium shots." Fairbanks's strenuous athleticism also enabled a rousing tempo that appealed to filmgoers, and Curtis neatly parses the mounting discourse through which the actor's enthusiastic, rugged, and adventurous physical feats formed a synecdoche for filmic realism—a "real" associated with on-location shooting, a newly formed "Hollywood" frontier in the west, and hence an idealized American imago distinct from the civilized effeminacy of the east coast as well as the artifice of the Broadway stage. Ultimately, each of these representational and discursive techniques reinforced the "authenticity" and "magnetism" associated with Fairbanks. As Curtis puts it, Doug "just plays himself."

The state of simply being oneself, rather than playing a part, had far-reaching implications for the fledgling film industry's promotion of their stars' personal magnetism, and undoubtedly fostered fans' sense of intimacy with their favorite players. In contrast to the elusive dignity associated with prestigious stage performers—such as Madame Sarah Bernhardt or Miss Maude Adams—the majority of film stars throughout the decade were known quite simply as "Doug," "Charlie" (Charles Chaplin), "Mabel" (Mabel Normand), "Pearl" (Pearl White), "Bunny" (John Bunny), or by monikers associated with physiological traits like "Fatty" (Roscoe Arbuckle) and "Dimples" (Maurice Costello). In the case of Mary Pickford, as Christine Gledhill's shrewd analysis reveals, the simple appellate "Little Mary" was "more than a studio brand name." As she observes: "'Mary' generically designated 'every girl,' while 'little' encapsulated both her diminutive stature and ingénue roles. In combination 'Little Mary' Pickford encouraged identification of actress with roles—frequently also named 'Mary'—making the star available for audience possession."

Gledhill's sustained scrutiny of the different meanings Pickford's iconic stardom assumed when it crossed the Atlantic and developed in Britain frames the American embrace of a magnetic selfhood in sharp relief. While British commentators consistently hyped Pickford's acting talent and oriented her wild popularity within a lexicon of theatrical traditions, the American press increasingly separated performer from role, inscribing the screen's fairy-like, will-of-the-wisp, pathetic, wistful, charming, tomboyish, altogether lovable girl figure as an emanation of Pickford's unique personality. What Gledhill terms the "mystery of personhood" at the heart of stardom, however, was promulgated on both sides of the Atlantic where audiences registered an intense, even overwhelming emotional cathexis to the "girl." While the camera's intimate probe of Pickford's every movement and gesture afforded an illusion of proximity for the individual viewer, the cinema's capacity to annul geographical and cultural difference generated another illusion of proximity, a sort of democratic incursion. The popularity of the girl with the "golden curls," as Gledhill tallies, was "initially registered in numbers, computed in 'millions.'" By 1914 those millions—both within the United States and across the globe—were understood as united in their common relationship to "Our Mary."

The world's familiarity with "Charlie"—or "Charlot," as the French dubbed him—proved equally ubiquitous, and the comedian's rapid ascent to global superstardom in 1915 competed only with that of Pickford and Fairbanks. Unlike "Doug" and "Mary," however, Chaplin's offscreen self— the soft-spoken, decidedly "serious," and even "shy" man busily immersed in his work—differed widely from the iconic "Tramp" figure he invented for the screen. A bit grotesque, and lacking the coordinates of geographical and cultural identity we so often associate with selfhood, the Tramp figure— replete with baggy trousers, oversized shoes, bowler hat, short mustache, and limber cane—could be anyone. More to the point, anyone could *be* the Tramp, and an overwhelming number of men, women, and children tried.

Dubbed "Chaplinitis" in 1915, the compulsion to imitate "Charlie" stunned a public for whom the very ideation of mass culture, as I argue, took shape through "Charlie's" omnipresence in soldier barracks and on street corners, schoolrooms and dance halls, amateur stages and motion picture screens. It is hardly surprising that the undifferentiated appeal and near pandemic spread of a funny yet vulgar figure like the Tramp worried social commentators, among them Walter Pritchard Eaton, who decried what he perceived as a semi-hypnotic religious cult fed by "you worshipers of Charlie Chaplin" ("Actor-Snatching," *American Magazine*, December 1915, 36).

Even as self-professed social guardians like Eaton lamented the magnetic power associated with film stardom, a fascination with American stars and the peculiar strength of the star-spectator bond developed in France where an emergent generation of film critics launched one of the first sustained attempts to grapple with the implications of the new medium and its peculiar species of celebrity. In 1916, the preeminent prewar music critic, Emile Vuillermoz, launched a biweekly column, "Devant l'écran," in *Le Temps*. As Richard Abel clarifies elsewhere, Vuillermoz's thinking followed two paths. One of them resonates with this discussion insofar as he believed that the camera "turned certain actors into 'astral bodies'" whose essence was delivered up to the spectator in a direct, intimate, and profound encounter—"as absolute gift." This intimacy was comfortable for the masses, Vuillermoz believed, because these stars became "'friends' to follow through different adventures" ("Photogénie" 108). At the same time, Vuillermoz became increasingly interested in the camera's capacity to transform and reveal aspects of the world around us, including the very concept of self, an idealist position he shared in part with Louis Delluc, a young drama critic and novelist who became editor-in-chief of *Le Film* in June 1917 and who attempted to account for the phenomenon of the American film star in essays on Sessue Hayakawa, Charlie Chaplin, and William S. Hart, among others.

In his chapter on Hayakawa, Daisuke Miyao takes a cue from Delluc's lyrical rendering of the Japanese star's intense screen presence as something other than "talent," something that was a "natural force," a beauty that was "painful": "Few things in the cinema reveal to us, as the lights and silence of this mask do, that there really are *alone* beings." Miyao's aggressive reading strategy posits a rich tension between the American film industry's laborious attempts to manage the meanings of the Asian body, to assimilate Hayakawa as an all-American and morally refined man on the one hand; and viewers' sensational, phenomenological responses to the sheer carnal presence of the actor onscreen on the other. Ironically, the

Japanese media, which refused to acknowledge Hayakawa when he emerged as a sudden superstar following his performance as an Asian villain in *The Cheat* (1915), altered course as Hayakawa's career flourished and his self-sacrificial characterizations in films like *The Hidden Pearls* and *The Man Beneath* elaborated tropes of sympathy for the Asian "other." The ongoing idolization of the star in the western world encouraged the Japanese press, as Miyao concludes, to promote Hayakawa's body as an emblem of what the Japanese body could become, if westernized, thus reinscribing a racial logic that Hayakawa's films labored to explore and transcend.

Biology indeed proves a determining factor in early film stardom as it continues to be today. Quite frankly, democracy has never been all it is cracked up to be, as the conspicuous absence of African American, Native American, and Chinese American stars, or even the presence of racial and ethnically marginalized "magnetic" personalities, makes noisily clear. At the same time, curiously odd biological characteristics—like Ben Turpin's perpetually crossed eyes and wildly engorged Adam's apple—could enable a unique appeal. And Turpin, who deserves acclaim as arguably the first screen player ever named or discussed in the media (as early as 1909, according to Anthony Slide), achieved distinctive status throughout the decade, even among an array of clowns whose undersized, oversized, twitching, stumbling, pot-bellied, wand-like, adroitly clumsy, and altogether *unusual* physiologies determined the near surrealist and decidedly sensational antics of slapstick comedy's finest performances in these years.

As Rob King argues, however, the drive to assimilate comic bodies, to curtail such wildly non-normative figures and feats, accelerated as well. And by the early 1920s, the meanings associated with comedian Roscoe Arbuckle's biological features—most specifically his "fatness"—formed a guarantee for those who would turn the 275-pound comedian into a "scapegoat" for the "massive" and apparently uncontrollable growth of the film industry and of the spiraling, unprecedented, and unparalleled power of film stars to influence public perception by the end of the decade. King's intricate analysis scrutinizes Arbuckle's rising prominence as both director and star after 1915, during which time the comedian labored to overcome the perception of his "fatness" as a determining factor that relegated the meaning of his "self" to sheer "body." Arbuckle also sought to transform perceptions of slapstick comedy as commonplace knockabout fun by incorporating elements of a pictorial tradition and a logic of simple rural pleasures tinged with a bit of good-hearted fun. "Body versus brain, performance versus direction, 'Fatty' versus 'Roscoe': these were the contradictory coordinates from which would emerge new parameters for comic stardom,"

Ben Turpin, undated photo. From the author's collection.

King writes, while also revealing how these coordinates reflect conflicting cultural registers, a hybrid of genteel tastes and embodied sensations, of "high" and "low" cultures, of a both/and logic that liquidates traditional distinctions and forms the basis of the movies' emergence as "mass entertainment." The scandal that terminated Arbuckle's career in the early 1920s, however, and which altered the currency associated with film stars more generally, retreated to the easy economy of the biological body. As King puts it with characteristic flair, "Arbuckle's fatness became polluted and obscene, at once the dead weight that allegedly crushed Virginia Rappe's bladder and a symbol of moral disorder whose expulsion permitted the 'normalization' of the movies."

Whether or not any norm was secured by stardom, or by an American film industry more generally in the decades to follow, remains the task of the subsequent volumes in this series. Frankly, I have my doubts. What remains vividly certain, however, is one simple fact: as a new breed of historians, vitalized by the broader reach of archival materials available in the digital age, set off roaming through the messy, mass-mediated phenomenon shaping modern celebrity culture, we must agree to disagree on certain counts. By embracing just this spirit, *Flickers of Desire* aspires to the fully contradictory status of a "collection of essays." The result is a study of stardom's genesis that is whole enough, at moments, to cohere in an identifiable set of concerns, but partial enough, at other or even the same moments, to frustrate any totalizing assessment. What becomes evident in the pages that follow is that contributors share a powerful sense of commonality in confronting cultural and historical issues—about politics, identity, nationalism, consumerism, economics, and aesthetics—and in insisting that stars are central rather than peripheral to the constitutive matrix of film history. In so doing, we hope this collection prompts further explorations as to how and why, in the course of the ten years covered by this book, a cinema without stars, one lacking even the habit of crediting names on the screen, developed into a cinema in which stars became the American film industry's gold standard, its determining economic and aesthetic factor—and consequently its greatest risk.

NOTE

1. I borrow the phrase "like you and me" from Richard Dyer, with a touch of irony intact. The most common error marring general scholarship on film stardom has been the tendency to treat the silent era as a homogenous "early period," a time, according to Dyer's oft-cited study, when "stars were gods and goddesses, heroes, models—embodiments of *ideal* ways of behaving" (*Stars* 24). Dyer erroneously pinpoints a "paradigm" shift, somewhere near the end of the 1920s and the beginning of the 1930s, when stars transformed from "gods to mortals" and became "identification figures, people *like you and me*—embodiments of typical ways of behaving" (24, my emphasis). Taken together, the first two volumes in this Star Decades series offer an important correction to this historical generalization. Compare, for instance, Scott Curtis's discussion of Douglas Fairbanks's rise to stardom in this volume with his subsequent chapter on Fairbanks, "King of Hollywood," in *Idols of Modernity: Movie Stars of the 1920s*. In the latter, Curtis traces the emergence of a discourse around 1920 that granted stars like Fairbanks the status of "royalty," and hence altered the democratic rhetoric that suffuses these earlier years in which stars were understood as "identification figures, people like you and me."

G. M. Anderson

"Broncho Billy" among the Early "Picture Personalities"

RICHARD ABEL

Among the "picture personalities" who increasingly assumed a crucial role in promoting motion pictures between 1910 and 1912, G. M. "Broncho Billy" Anderson certainly was one of the more remarkable. In the fall of 1911, for instance, in the industrial heartland of northeastern Ohio, the *Canton News-Democrat* ballyhooed Anderson as "the best known motion picture actor living . . . his face [as] familiar to the people of this country as that of President Taft's" ("This Man's Photo Seen Every Day by 300,000," 5 November 1911, 15). By the following spring, Essanay

G. M. Anderson, Essanay Photoplayer, circa 1913.

was boasting that Anderson was now famous worldwide for the character he often played, "Broncho Billy" (Essanay ad, *Moving Picture World*, 30 March 1912, 1123). In Great Britain, several months later, *Bioscope* made an even more extravagant claim for what it called this "magnetic man": he "can be 'felt' photographically on a screen, just as Irving was 'felt' in actual life" on the English stage ("The Pick of the Programmes," 1 August 1912, 367). Anderson arguably demands attention as a pioneering cowboy movie star, whose popularity as "Broncho Billy" offers some insight into why westerns became such an "American subject" in the early 1910s. His regular weekly appearances onscreen also suggest why audiences were so attracted to other early "personalities" as well—for example, Florence Lawrence, Florence Turner, Marion Leonard, Alice Joyce, Mary Pickford, Maurice Costello—and how that attraction registered not only in the trade press but also in local newspapers. Moreover, the unusual fame that his cowboy character quickly enjoyed abroad can be taken as an early sign of the U.S. film industry's heady opportunistic aims to expand its reach beyond the borders of the USA.

The "Broncho Billy" Brand

> I love to watch the cowboys
> And see the horses run,
> I wish I had a hundred votes
> For Gilbert Anderson!
>
> (Buster Trishy, a Texas boy, "Popular Player Contest,"
> *Motion Picture Story Magazine*, April 1912, 137)

So who was G. M. Anderson prior to his starring role as "Broncho Billy"? Born Max Aronson in Little Rock, Arkansas, on 21 March 1880, and raised in St. Louis, Missouri, the man who would become "Broncho Billy" was an unsuccessful New York stage actor and sometime model for magazine illustrators before he Anglicized his name to George M. Anderson in 1903, was hired by the Edison Manufacturing Company, and played several minor roles in *The Great Train Robbery* (1903). After learning as much as he could about the new motion picture business, Anderson convinced the Vitagraph Company to let him write and direct more than a dozen comedies and dramas between the summer of 1905 and the spring of 1906. Refused a partnership at Vitagraph, he went to work for Selig Polyscope in Chicago and, in the winter and spring of 1907, joined H. H. Buckwalter in Denver to make several profitable westerns, among them *The Girl from Montana* and *The Bandit King* (both 1907). Refused a share of Selig's business as well, in the summer of 1907 he teamed up with another Chicago exhibitor/distributor, George K. Spoor, to found a new film production company, Essanay (S & A), and changed his name one last time to Gilbert M. Anderson. During the next several years, as Essanay became a member of the MPPC, Anderson wrote, directed, and sometimes acted in one film on average per week and, leading a peripatetic production unit (its headquarters shifted from Southern California to Colorado to Texas and back to Southern California), gradually began to specialize in "school of action" western films such as *The Road Agents* or *The Indian Trailer* (both 1909) and *Under Western Skies* or *Broncho Billy's Redemption* (both 1910). The last title would be the first in a series of increasingly numerous Broncho Billy one-reelers, in all of which Anderson starred: three in 1911, nineteen in 1912, and thirty-four in 1913.

Anyone seeking more detailed information about G. M. Anderson's pioneering career, his construction in 1912 of a permanent studio in Niles, California, and the fortunes of Essanay have several excellent sources from which to choose (Kiehn; Smith). The task here, however, is to locate traces of Anderson's early stardom, sketch a portrait of the actor as a movie cowboy, especially as "Broncho Billy," and account for that figure's phenomenal appeal in the early 1910s. References to Anderson in the trade press prior to 1911 focused on the reputation he had gained from building and managing Essanay's western production unit and from turning out a steady schedule of noteworthy films. That spring, the *New York Dramatic Mirror* in particular also began to take notice of him as an actor, printing his "leading man" photo among the first "picture personalities" that would regularly mark its weekly pages and acknowledging that he was "known to thousands of picture lovers, with whom he is a favorite" ("'Spectator's' Comments," 16 April 1911, 28–29). By the summer of 1911, Anderson was so well known that exhibitors everywhere could use his name—along with a few others—to promote their frequently changing programs in local newspapers. In Ada, Oklahoma, for instance, the Majestic Theater put his name above the title of its featured Essanay western and advertised in the *Ada Evening News*: "G. M. Anderson in 'A Pal's Oath'" (11 August 1911, 3). In Mansfield, Ohio, the Arbor Theater lauded *The Puncher's Law* (September 1911) as another one of those "famous western pictures by the Essanay Co. in which they feature the very popular actor G. M. Anderson" (*Mansfield News*, 3 October 1911, 5). In Canton, Ohio, the Odeon assumed that its clientele would want to know that *The Sheriff's Brother* (July 1911) had "Mr. Anderson, everybody's favorite, in [the] leading role" (*Canton News-Democrat*, 9 September 1911, n.p.) That fall, in nearby Youngstown, the Princess Theater arranged with the local newspaper to print Essanay's publicity photo of Anderson and a brief story calling him "one of the most popular motion picture actors of the day" ("Today's Entertainments," *Youngstown Vindicator*, 15 October 1911, 15). For months thereafter, all of its Sunday program ads featured an Essanay western starring Anderson, now locally nicknamed "Bullets" (*Youngstown Vindicator*, 15 October 1911, 15, and 7 January 1912, 17). By early 1912, many exhibitors could count on a large, steady audience for "Broncho Billy" stories with G. M. Anderson in the title role.[1]

A stolid, rather stocky man with a full, heavy face and prominent nose, Anderson would have been the first to admit that his range as an actor was limited. A reviewer once wrote of his acting that he played with "the usual sturdy vigor" (*New York Dramatic Mirror*, 10 January 1912, 30). Yet he came off well if a shot required him to look taciturn, or to glower tight-lipped at an antagonist, or to appear uncomfortably quiet while facing a young woman, or even to smile at a lone child, and he projected (much like the aging John Wayne would in later decades) an unexpectedly strong presence onscreen. Although he had to learn to ride horses, handle revolvers and rifles, and wear lived-in cowboy gear comfortably, Anderson was clearly convincing and accepted by audiences as "true to life": in May 1911, an experienced cowhand claimed that his "movements, his dress and, more than anything else, that smile of his and his facial expressions make him . . . the best cowboy character delineator of any film concern" ("Letters to 'The Spectator,'" *New York Dramatic Mirror*, 24 May 1911, 33). Trade press reviews consistently praised his "gripping characterization," whether as "Broncho Billy" or another cowboy figure, as in *The Bandit's Child* (March 1912) (*Moving Picture World*, 2 March 1912, 768). Local exhibitors more and more featured his name in their ads: in Lowell, Massachusetts, Anderson was the Voyons' "favorite western actor"; in Fort Wayne, Indiana, his name assured the Gaiety's fans that *Broncho Billy's Bible* (June 1912) was "a big, vital, powerful picture"; in Hamilton, Ohio, the Jewel perhaps inadvertently misnamed his character "Broncho Billy" in advertising *The Dead Man's Claim* (May 1912); in Sheboygan, Wisconsin, the Princess called Anderson the "king of Motion Picture players" (*Sheboygan Journal*, 5 April 1912, 8; *Hamilton Evening Journal*, 11 May 1912, 2; *Fort Wayne Journal-Gazette*, 2 June 1912, 9; *Lowell Sun*, 6 June 1912, 10). The title of "king" was not all that inappropriate, for, in *Motion Picture Story Magazine*'s first "Popular Players Contest," he was among the top five actors receiving more than "one million and a half votes" from fans ("Winners of the Popular Players Contest," July 1912, 34). By June 1912, Essanay could offer enthusiastic fans, like the Texas boy quoted above, "4 sepia-tone lithographed posters and postal photos of G. M. Anderson . . . the World's Greatest Photoplay Star" (see the Essanay ads in *New York Dramatic Mirror*, 29 May 1912, 29, and *Moving Picture World*, 1 June 1912, 787).

Well before committing to the "Broncho Billy" series, Anderson already had developed the recurring kind of cowboy figure that would make him (and others later, from William S. Hart to Clint Eastwood) a star: the "good badman." In *Under Western Skies* (August 1910),[2] for instance, he plays one of three drunken cowboys who attack a young woman left alone at a ranch and make her the stake in a poker game and then in a gunfight; in desperation the woman agrees to marry the survivor (Anderson) but refuses to accept him. Her fiancé, who has been away on a trip east, tracks the couple down and gets her to flee with him but eventually abandons her when they lose their way in the desert. When Anderson, now a respectable miner, finds her, she finally pledges to love him and then persuades him not to shoot the coward who once promised to marry her. An even more telling instance of this "good badman" appears in *A Pal's Oath* (August 1911).When a doctor refuses to tend to his badly injured "pal," Anderson robs a pony express rider whose money pouch he has spotted so he can pay for what turns out to be a successful treatment—and the "pal" promises to keep the robbery a secret. Later, however, he arranges Anderson's arrest and imprisonment so he can marry the woman his friend has been courting. Released from jail several years later, Anderson plans his revenge. Now a disheveled figure, he peers through a ranch house window (much like the one through which the "pal" first saw the courting couple) and discovers the "pal" embracing his wife and young daughter (a portrait of Lincoln hangs prominently on the back wall). Startled and saddened, he slowly holsters the revolver he has aimed through the window, shakes his head, and quietly steals away.

This redemptive character increasingly had the benefit of similarly strong stories, most notably in one of the earliest "Broncho Billy" films, *Broncho Billy's Christmas Dinner* (December 1911). This film begins with a town sheriff receiving news about the outlaw Broncho Billy, his daughter preparing to take a stagecoach off to college, and Broncho Billy himself planning to rob the stagecoach—and smiling as he rips a wanted poster off a tree. Drunken cowboys spook the stagecoach horses, and the daughter, who has been sitting in the driver's seat, struggles vainly to rein in the out-of-control horses. Surprised by the stagecoach that races past him, Broncho Billy rides after it, climbs on board, and gradually brings the horses to a halt. Recovering from a faint, the young woman thanks him by inviting him home for Christmas dinner; after eyeing the cash box he intended to steal, Broncho Billy reluctantly accepts. When he discovers she is the sheriff's daughter, Broncho Billy decides to confess his identity and the sheriff offers him immunity. Although he tries to leave, the daughter draws him back to the dinner table where everyone accepts him with a handshake and all (but Billy) bow their heads for a blessing by the local parson—who, ironically, had been buying drinks earlier for the drunken cowboys. In reviewing this film, the *New York Dramatic Mirror* found the "thrilling ride on [the] stage coach . . . as exciting and realistic as anything of its character ever shown in pictures" ("Reviews of Licensed Films," 3 January 1912, 30). Indeed, the surviving film print reveals some deft framing and editing, including an unusual high angle midshot/long shot taken from a camera mounted behind Broncho Billy as he struggles with the horses' reins. Yet the *Mirror* also was impressed by his acting "in the quieter moments" of the film, such as when, near the end, a pensive Broncho Billy is washing up in the foreground space of a small room while, in the larger adjacent space, the family and other guests cluster around the festive dinner table.

Throughout 1912 and into 1913, Anderson's "Broncho Billy" character often appeared initially onscreen as an outlaw or else as a cowboy between jobs, and almost never as a rancher, entrepreneur, or any kind of property owner. Provoked by one or more twists of plot, the character then usually underwent a transformation through "moral and psychological conflict" into a respectable "ethical role model" (Smith 58, 134, 149). That transformation could involve an unexpected love interest, as in *Broncho Billy and the Girl* (April 1912) and *Broncho Billy's Escapade* (August 1912); a heroic sacrifice in which he is fatally wounded, as in *Broncho Billy's Last Hold-Up* (August 1912); or a confession of guilt, before dying, to a woman whose husband he had long ago killed, as in *The Reward for Broncho Billy* (December 1912). By incorporating Christian themes of moral uplift, self-sacrifice, and redemption—most explicitly expressed in *Broncho Billy's Bible* (June 1912)—the films often evoked the ideals of evangelical Protestantism (Smith 145–46). Yet "Broncho Billy" as a character was never entirely fixed or stable. In *Broncho Billy's Narrow Escape* (July 1912), for instance, he is a ranch hand falsely accused of stealing a horse, and it is the ranch owner's daughter who has to "make a hard ride"—ending with her successful return framed by a silhouetted doorway, not unlike a much later famous shot in John Ford's *The Searchers* (1956)—to save him at the last moment from being lynched ("Critical Reviews," *New York Morning Telegraph*, 14 July 1912, 4:2, 4). An even more surprising variation on his usual character occurs in *A Wife of the Hills* (July 1912), where Anderson plays an outlaw whose own wife and pal conspire to get him arrested and jailed. He escapes, intending to take revenge on his unfaithful wife and her lover, and a posse pursues him to the illicit couple's isolated cabin. In the gunfight that ensues outside the cabin, a stray shot from the posse strikes the lover, who dies in the woman's arms. Once again looking through a window, Anderson now smiles in gratification and gladly gives himself up to the posse.

Although never strictly a parent, "Broncho Billy" sometimes served as a surrogate father figure to one or more children. In *Broncho Billy's Gratitude* (June 1912), for instance, he is wounded and tended by a woman whose young daughter he befriends. Later the woman's estranged husband kidnaps the girl and flees in a stagecoach; when Billy holds up the coach, he discovers the girl and returns her to her mother; his good deed, however, does not keep him from being arrested by a posse. This ingratiating, protective attitude toward children, especially girls, also affected the character's actions in *Broncho Billy's Heart* (November 1912), where a family man steals a horse for his covered wagon and is saved from arrest when Billy exchanges his own horse for the one stolen and manages surreptitiously to return it to the owner, and in *Broncho Billy's Ward* (February 1913), where he agrees to serve as the guardian for a dying friend's young daughter and later consents to her request to marry, although he himself has come to love her. Arguably, this behavior made "Broncho Billy" an appealing figure to audiences that could include mothers as well as children, both boys and girls. Although the films may have had Anderson's character repeatedly appear at the outset as "a stoic, isolated male," they consistently embraced "traditional, middle-class ideals of morality, manhood, and character" (Smith 134, 149, 151–52). As immigrant boys like Harry Golden would later admit, Broncho Billy taught them "New World" attitudes and instilled in them their "first ideals of American manhood" (Levin 67).

That Essanay, and probably Anderson himself, promoted "Broncho Billy" as a "character-creation" may have had special significance within the U.S. film industry, for Anderson's recurring character was unique and uniquely popular in 1911–1912. This was the first and most successful American attempt to create in motion pictures what was then assumed as a defining characteristic of print fiction and stage plays: a "character" with at least a relative sense of psychological, emotional, and moral "depth," and one that was also "original" and did not depend on a prior literary antecedent, adapted or translated onto film. In this case, of course, "originality" came from Anderson himself as a "picture personality": his embodiment onscreen was necessary for "Broncho Billy" to exist and to circulate as a recurring fictional character to admire and even emulate. At the same time, however, as a serial figure, "Broncho Billy" was not unlike Buffalo Bill, Deadwood Dick, Jesse James, Young Wild West, and others on whom earlier dime novel series had been constructed. The name functioned much like a brand that could guarantee repeated spectatorial satisfaction. In "Broncho Billy," therefore, Anderson created (he also wrote many of the scripts) a remarkable figure that served to redefine what would keep audiences returning to motion picture theaters, regularly and frequently. The appeal would come not so much from company trademarks, as before, but from a series of film stories that involved a single recurring character (already characteristic of French comic films) within the popular "American subject" of the western or, more specifically, the cowboy picture. And the appeal would come equally from a single popular "picture personality," G. M. Anderson, who, along with half a dozen others, played such a crucial role in establishing the nascent movie star system.

☆☆☆★★ "Star Performers" on Parade

It is notoriously difficult to date the beginnings of public interest in motion picture actors, but traces of it can be found at least by early 1910. In February of that year, in his "On the Screen" column in *Moving Picture World*, Thomas Bedding (Lux Graphicus) noted what he had once predicted, the arrival of "star performers": "It is common talk in moving picture circles now that the success of a particular film or of a particular company's films are traceable to one or two performers. . . . The outcome of all this of course is that the public interest in the picture heightens on account of its personalities" (5 February 1910, 167). Three months later, the writer of another column, "Observations by Our Man About Town," was stunned to realize that "the interest the public has taken in the personality of many of the picture players is astonishing. . . . Managers all over the country are begging the manufacturers to furnish them with photographs of their players so that they may be displayed in the lobbies of their theaters, and the people who are craving to see and meet the originals may be in a measure consoled" (*Moving Picture World*, 21 May 1910, 825).

Although the trade press initially was far from certain that "star performers" would benefit its principal priority—"elevating" motion pictures—both the *World* and *New York Dramatic Mirror* took hesitant steps to satisfy this public craving by running a few photo stories of what it decided were favorite "picture personalities." Local newspapers showed far less hesitancy, however, as the early stories that touted Anderson's popularity suggest. Indeed, daily newspapers arguably took the lead in responding to the public craving for "picture personalities," ensuring that newspapers would play a crucial role in what was fast becoming a multimedia system of movie stardom.

As is well known, Florence Lawrence, the former "Biograph Girl" (and teenage vaudeville performer), was the first to receive much attention, largely due to an infamous publicity campaign engineered by Carl Laemmle for the independent film company, IMP (deCordova 56–61; Bowser 112–13). That campaign included several "events," from a faked news story of Lawrence's death in an auto accident—quickly picked up and debunked even in small-town newspapers—to her surprise visit to St. Louis in late March (see, for instance, "Rumor Hands a Hot One," *Iowa City Press*, 8 March 1910, 8). The latter was especially significant in that Lawrence was explicitly labeled a "film star" in an extensive series of articles, with accompanying photos, in the *St. Louis Times*. Advance stories prepared the paper's readers for the special two-day appearance of "the girl with a thousand faces" (IMP's own hyperbolic phrase); thousands of fans greeted her with an ovation when she arrived by train (the reception allegedly rivaled that for either Commodore Perry or President Taft); and hundreds heard her speak at the Gem Theater, where she signed photographs for up to "500 women." At the same time, the Empress Theater in downtown Washington, D.C., was promoting Lawrence to the level of a stage actor in IMP's *Mother Love* (March 1910), naming her "The Maude Adams of Moving Pictures" (Empress Theater ad, *Washington Post*, 21 March 1910, 4). In early May, an unusually prominent photo story in the *Des Moines News* featured Lawrence as the most popular of four female "star performers," with this ditty as an epigraph: "This is the girl of the wondrous faces, / Whom you meet in a hundred places; / Each time she told a story to you, / Then vanished like magic when it was through" ("On the Moving Picture Stage: Have You Seen These Faces?" 6 May 1910, 16). As a sign of her continuing popularity with audiences over the next few years—from the time she left IMP for Lubin and then, in 1912, founded her own company, Victor Films, which released through Universal—theater managers across the country consistently cited Lawrence in their newspaper ads, often placing her name above the title of any film in which she was starring—and in larger typeface. As late as 1913, she still was such a fan favorite that she placed fifth in *Photoplay Magazine's* "Great Popularity Contest" (July 1913, 61).

Laemmle's campaign had the effect (probably intended) of boosting the status of his and other "independent" companies, and Vitagraph, another leading MPPC firm, quickly countered by mounting its own promotion of the "Vitagraph Girl," Florence Turner. That promotion included personal appearances in the New York City area (not far from the company's studio in Brooklyn), and Vitagraph even commissioned a special "waltz song" for Turner who would perform it herself to "wild applause"—and the sheet

Florence Lawrence,
Motion Picture Story Magazine,
March 1911.

music cover was printed in *Film Index* ("Vitagraph Notes," *Moving Picture World*, 2 April 1910, 515; "A Vitagraph Night for the Vitagraph Girl," *Film Index*, 23 April 1910, 3; "The Vitagraph Girl," *New York Dramatic Mirror*, 23 April 1910, 20; and "Vitagraph Girl Feted," *Moving Picture World*, 23 April 1910, 644). Both the *World* and the *Mirror* featured Turner in their first photo stories that summer, the one as a "picture personality" but the other, perhaps more boldly, as a "motion picture star" ("Picture Personalities. Miss Florence E. Turner: The Vitagraph Girl," *Moving Picture World*, 23 July 1910, 187–88; "A Motion Picture Star," *New York Dramatic Mirror*, 18 June 1910, 17). Reading either magazine, exhibitors would have learned that Turner was a "blend of nationalities" (Spanish, Italian, Scottish, and American), "*petite*, dark, slender, vivacious, full of life and go, just as we see her on the

Florence Turner,
Motion Picture Story Magazine,
July 1911.

stage [screen]," and that she had come to Vitagraph while rehearsing the role of an Italian street gamine for the European tour of an Italian pantomime company. With fan letters pouring into the company, she agreed to give out photos of herself at public appearances (Bowser 113). Much like Lawrence, and unlike Anderson (by 1911), Turner played a wide range of roles—"pathetic, grotesque, humorous, sentimental"—from *The New Stenographer* and *A Tale of Two Cities* (both February 1911) to *Auld Lang Syne* (July 1911) and *Cherry Blossoms* (August 1911). Intriguingly, when the Newspaper Enterprise Syndicate began to include "picture personalities" in the "daily birthday feature" it released to newspapers in early 1911, Turner's photo story was one of the few actually printed in papers from Fort Wayne, Indiana, to San Antonio, Texas ("Florence Turner in Notable Gallery," *Moving Picture World,* 14 January 1911, 73; "Our Daily Birthday Party," *Fort Wayne Daily News,* 6 January 1911, 14; *San Antonio Light and Gazette,* 6 January 1911, 8). Much like Lawrence, she too would later draw on her popularity as a star to found her own company, Turner Films, but in England, where she produced half a dozen films before the outbreak of World War I.

The tipping point that convinced the film industry to embrace and exploit the emerging star system probably came during the first six or eight months of 1911. The publication of *Motion Picture Story Magazine* early that year certainly was influential because, from its initial appearance, each month's issue came with full-page photographs of the "picture players"— among the first were both Lawrence and Turner ("Personalities of the Picture Players," March 1911, 1–6, 57). But there were other signs of intense audience demand. Beginning in February, letters to "The Spectator" in the *New York Dramatic Mirror* increasingly asked to know more about the actors, and one fan listed his favorites, all but two of them women: Florence Lawrence, Mary Fuller, Marion Leonard, Pearl White, Gene Gauntier, and the unnamed Mary Pickford (1 February 1911, 30). In late March, *Motography* even included a short piece titled "The Value of Stars": "They constitute one of the most valuable assets in the film maker's treasury. . . . It is doubtful if the film-maker has any other resource so potent to attract the public" (25 March 1911, 322). From then on, the trade press cooperated with manufacturers to invest in "picture personalities" for promotional purposes. *Motion Picture Story Magazine* expanded what was called its "Gallery of Picture Players" photos to a dozen per month. The *New York Dramatic Mirror* began printing up to half a dozen smaller publicity photos of such picture players, including brief stories on these "subjects of illustration."[3] In April, the second story on G. M. Anderson described him as "known to thousands of picture lovers, with whom he is a favorite, as may be seen by the many inquiries regarding him from MIRROR readers" ("Subjects of Illustration," 26 April 1911, 28–29). Exhibitors perhaps even more quickly saw the advantage of naming favorite "picture personalities" in their local ads. In early January, in Sandusky, Ohio, for instance, the Theatorium urged its clientele: "Don't Miss Seeing MISS MARY PICKFORD, formerly the Biograph Girl but now an IMP" (*Sandusky Star-Journal*, 10 January 1911, 6). About the same time, in Bismarck, North Dakota, the Gem featured *The Gray of the Dawn*, "in which Marion Leonard, the star performer of all companies, plays probably her heaviest role" (*Bismarck Daily Tribune*, 3 January 1911, 4). A month later, in Hawarden, Iowa, the Electric Theatre placed a puzzling bit of newspaper copy for *Rachel*, a Kalem "melodrama with a strong appeal to the Jews of America, with Miss Alice Joyce in the title role" (*Hawarden Independent*, 23 February 1911, 4).

The second of the three women who became so well known as the Biograph Girl, Marion Leonard (much like Lawrence) successfully advanced her career in late 1910 by moving to an independent company, Reliance, and then a year later founded her own production company, Gem Motion

Pictures. Throughout much of 1911, exhibitors consistently used Reliance's publicity material to alert their audiences to Leonard's appearances and the range of characters she played. In New Castle, Pennsylvania, Herbold's Acme noted that *The Little Avenger* "afforded Miss Marion Leonard, in the character of an unfortunate girl whom the policeman's wife befriended and took her home when arrested, an opportunity to do some clever acting" (*New Castle News*, 24 February 1911, 9). In Butte, Montana, the Orion Theater informed "admirers of Marion Leonard" that they could see her one evening in "another of those beautiful Reliance productions called *Till Death Do Us Part*" (*Anaconda Standard*, 7 April 1911, 9). In Oshkosh, Wisconsin, "the Colonial's favorite actress" starred in *The Gloved Hand* as a woman who "by indomitable will, ris[es] from the sordid dance halls of a western mining town to a state of dramatic bliss as the wife of a wealthy man" (*Daily Northwestern*, 8 April 1911, 11). In Benton Harbor, Michigan, the Bell Opera House placed her name above the title of its featured film, *The Seal of Time* (*News-Palladium*, 30 April 1912, 8). The trade press ads for Gem productions, Richard deCordova rightly argues, were "the most clever of the period": one framed a photo of Leonard's face in a diamond ring, with the caption that she was engaged; another was a full-page letter from Leonard, announcing that she indeed was engaged—to Gem (deCordova 68–69). Internal conflicts at the Sales Company, the only independent distributor at the time, apparently prevented the Gem productions from being released until they were sold to the Rex company (Mahar 63). By February 1912, in Fort Wayne, the Lyric could announce the "reappearance," in *Under Her Wing*, of that "most popular motion picture leading woman . . . Marion Leonard of the Rex-Gem pictures" (*Fort Wayne Sentinel*, 1 February 1912, 12). Although Leonard herself would abandon filmmaking for several years, she remained a favorite even after Universal took over distribution of Rex films: in July, in Hamilton, the Grand, promoting *A Mother Heart*, described her as "the greatest of moving picture actresses" ("Amusements," *Hamilton Evening Journal*, 26 July 1912, 5).

Among the "Famous Kalem Beauties," there were two that the firm particularly promoted ("Ten Famous Kalem Beauties," *New York Dramatic Mirror*, 31 January 1912, 53). The writer, director, and actor Gene Gauntier was best known early on as the "Kalem Girl" and for her "girl spy" roles in Kalem's Civil War films, but she gained even more prominence in 1911–1912 when she took a production unit to Ireland and then Egypt to make heavily publicized "Irish features" from *Arrah-Na-Pogue* (November 1911) to *You Remember Ellen* (March 1912) and "exotic" films such as *A Tragedy of the Desert* (July 1912) (Orpheum ad, *Titusville Herald*, 6 April 1912, 5; Opera House ad, *Mansfield News*, 25 May 1912, 16; Jewel ad, *Hamilton*

Evening Journal, 5 June 1912, 8).[4] Kalem's most popular "picture personality," however, was a former "Gibson Girl," Alice Joyce ("Alice Joyce, Kalem Beauty, Will Appear in Higher Class Photoplays," *Fresno Morning Republican,* 27 September 1912, 9). As early as March 1911, "a beautiful photogravure, hand-colored in France," of Joyce was on offer to exhibitors—and, in turn, fans—and by the summer she was being heralded as a "bright little star" (Kalem ad, *New York Dramatic Mirror,* 8 March 1911, 31; "Shea Theater," *Fitchburg Daily Sentinel,* 10 July 1911, 7). That fall, in Gettysburg, the Pastime Theatre began placing her name above the title of Kalem films such as *The Branded Shoulder* (August 1911); in Coshocton, Ohio, the Luna warned Joyce's "hundreds of admirers in the city" not to miss *For Her Brother's Sake* (October 1911); and that winter an eleven-year-old girl ended her doggerel tribute with the line "the fascinating, captivating, charming Alice Joyce" (Pastime Theatre ad, *Gettysburg Times,* 7 October 1911, 1; "Costello at Luna," *Coshocton Daily Age,* 15 November 1911, 5; "The Popular Player Contest," *Motion Picture Story Magazine,* March 1912, 164).

When, in July 1912, *Motion Picture Story Magazine* began inserting a free color portrait in each issue, the first star chosen was Joyce. Also that summer, in an unusual ad, the manager of the Bijou Theatre in Benton Harbor noted that Joyce was "among the first to win fame as a portrayer of the silent drama. . . . We have seen her in all sorts of parts and whether dressed in the rags of a mountain maid or in a spangled gown at a ball, her charming ways and sweet face always win the heart of her audience" ("The Theatre," *News-Palladium,* 16 August 1912, 2). In one of her more intriguing films, *"Rube" Marquard Wins* (September 1912), Joyce plays a fan of the New York Giants; before a crucial game, the team's leading pitcher, Marquard, is lured away from the Polo Grounds and locked in a nearby high-rise building; in the stands, Joyce uses her binoculars to spot him yelling out a window and then races in her automobile to his rescue—so he can win the game ("'Rube' Marquard Great Twirler, at the Fairy To-Day," *Fort Wayne Journal-Gazette,* 4 September 1912, 8; City Opera House ad, *The News,* 27 September 1912, 1). She also was one of the few "picture personalities" before Anderson to have a newspaper photo story in print, and, when the City Opera House in Frederick, Maryland, advertised a special Christmas program in late 1912, she was first on the list of six "all star players" (City Opera House ad, *The News,* 24 December 1912, 1).[5] Yet, unlike most early female stars, Joyce also remained popular with audiences well into the decade, as evidenced in Kalem's *Alice Joyce* series of two-reel films (1914–1915).

Although Mary Pickford, the third "Biograph Girl," is the subject of the next essay in this volume, she too, upon leaving Biograph for IMP, quickly

Alice Joyce,
Motion Picture Story Magazine,
August 1911.

became one of the first major "picture personalities" ("Mary Pickford," *Billboard*, 24 December 1910, 11). The sobriquet "Little Mary" that IMP pinned on Pickford was circulating by late 1910 ("The Lyric," *Fort Wayne Daily News*, 23 January 1911, 4); three months later in Greenville, Mississippi, David Crocket Himier took his "picture fan" brother to task with a bit of doggerel that included only two names—Florence Lawrence and "Little Mary Pickford . . . his greatest joy in life" ("Hard on Henry," *Daily Democrat*, 19 May 1911, 9). When she left IMP that fall for a new independent company, Majestic, the *Cleveland Leader* printed an unusual photo story of the "blonde and petite" eighteen-year-old "star" ("Moving Picture Star Tells of the Thrill of Her Art," 22 October 1911, S:5), and stories of her new affiliation reached rural areas like Humeston, Iowa, where "Little Mary" was described as "a great favorite of the patrons of the Princess" ("Princess Notes," *Humeston New Era*, 25 October 1911, 1). Majestic mounted an extensive ad campaign for Pickford, whose film characters often shared her first name, and the *Mirror* even consented, in early December, to make her the first motion picture actor to grace its front cover (Majestic ad, *New York Dramatic Mirror*, 29 November 1911, 27; "Mary Pickford—Little Mary," *New York Dramatic Mirror*, 6 December 1911, 29). Pickford soon returned to Biograph, where she remained (uncredited) throughout 1912, but exhibitors across the country continued to promote her appearances because she was such a familiar attraction for audiences. In Oelwein, Iowa, for instance, the Dreamland placed her name above its featured film title, *The Mender of Nets* (February 1912) (*Oelwein Daily Register*, 26 April 1912, 8). That fall, in Fresno, a photo of Pickford accompanied an unusual, highly favorable review of *A Pueblo Legend* (August 1912) ("Aztec Portrayal Pleasantly Greeted," *Fresno Morning Republican*, 19 September 1912, 13). When, in December, David Belasco hired Pickford to perform a leading role in *A Good Little Devil* on Broadway, the threat of her disappearance from picture screens prompted much newspaper comment. In Waterloo, Iowa, a large photo story tried to claim her for "'movie' enthusiasts" as the "charming little 'movie' actress who has captured the hearts of thousands who do not even know her name" ("Happy Christmastide for Popular Little Heroine of Moving Pictures," *Waterloo Reporter*, 28 December 1912, 8). Pickford would return to motion pictures the following year, but as a crucial star for Famous Players feature films.

In February 1911, a *Moving Picture World* article on acting noted that "feminine stars, of the Florence Lawrence caliber, seem[ed] much more numerous than their male vis-à-vis" (C. H. Claudy, "Too Much Acting," 11 February 1911, 289). That observation generally seemed to hold, not only in the trade press but also in newspaper ads and photo stories. A number of male "picture personalities" other than Anderson did emerge during the early 1910s, however—that is, John Bunny (the Vitagraph comic), King Baggot (IMP's "leading man"), Francis X. Bushman (the main lead in Essanay's Chicago production unit), and Arthur Johnson (often paired at Lubin with Lawrence). The earliest and most prominent of these most likely was Maurice Costello at Vitagraph. In October 1910, the *New York Dramatic Mirror* began to print a series of photo stories about Vitagraph actors, and the first (after Turner) was devoted to Costello ("Maurice Costello," 5 October 1910). *Motion Picture Story Magazine* also included his portrait—along with those of Lawrence, Turner, and Joyce—in its initial set of "personalities of the picture players" photos. So attractive for audiences was he that, in May 1911, in Warren, Pennsylvania, the Theatorium announced that it would give away, with each admission to *His Mother*

(May 1911), "a beautiful photo of Maurice Costello" ("A Vitagraph Feature," *Warren Evening Mirror*, 26 May 1911, 2). That fall, in Coshocton, the Luna highlighted Costello as "the most popular player" in *A Western Heroine* (September 1911) ("Costello at Luna," *Coshocton Daily Age*, 15 November 1911, 5); a month later, in Oakland, the Camera topped that praise with this claim: "no photoplay actor has reached or will reach the height of popularity and the hearts of the picture lovers as Maurice Costello has" ("Costello Seen in Photo-Play at Camera," *Oakland Tribune*, 14 December 1911, 4). In late January 1912, in Greenville, Mississippi, the Princess Theatre chose to make Costello rather than his film, *An Innocent Burglar* (November 1911), "the feature tonight" (*Daily Democrat*, 25 January 1912, 9). When, in March, Vitagraph placed an ad in *Motion Picture Story Magazine* for "Souvenir Postal Cards of the Vitagraph Players," only one card needed to be shown—Costello's (March 1912, 151). The relatively easy winner of the *Magazine*'s first "popular player contest" that summer, Costello also incited fans to outdo one another with doggerel tributes: one hailed Costello as "the king of the Photoplay, / Handsome and manly, our hero and friend"; another, linking actors' names with alphabetical letters, wrote "C for Costello, with his dimples and smile, / He's really an actor, the girls think, worth while" ("The Popular Player Contest," *Motion Picture Story Magazine*, March 1912, 160, and April 1912, 134; "Winners of the Popular Players Contest," *Motion Picture Story Magazine*, July 1912, 34).

★★★★★ Movie Stars and Their Audiences: At Home and Abroad

Evidence of the emerging star system's success as a marketing strategy is hard to miss by the end of 1912. Early that year *Motion Picture Story Magazine* instituted a gossip column, "Chats with the Players," that interviewed three or four "picture personalities" each month.[6] That fall *Motography* introduced "Sans Grease Paint and Wig," an interview column written by Mabel Condon that profiled a single "picture personality" in each issue, and the subject in late December was "'Broncho Billy' in Real Life" ("Sans Grease Paint and Wig," 12 October 1912, 287, and 21 December 1912, 481). Evidence in local newspapers is even more telling. In November 1912, for instance, the *Anaconda Standard* (Montana) printed a lengthy "Theatrical" column, partly based on an article in *Theater Magazine*, arguing that "the astonishing success" of motion pictures was due in large part to each leading player's "magnetic personality" (24 November 1912, 3). The column astutely observed that patrons of the "movies" . . . now watch for announcements of the photoplays in which their particular favorite appears and endeavor to see all of that player's characterizations. There are matinee idols of the "movies" as well as of the legitimate stage. While admirers of a star of the real theater may have an opportunity to see their favorite once a season and in one part, the popular motion picture players may be seen every week in different roles, and during the course of a year they play many parts.

The column concluded with a list of "the most popular favorites," in which each of those "picture personalities" already singled out is named, along with Mary Fuller and Marc McDermott of Edison.

That same month the Scripps-McRae newspaper chain proclaimed that its "moving picture expert," Gertrude Price, would be entertaining readers with stories about the "MOVING PICTURE FOLKS" because "'the movies' [were] the biggest, most popular amusement in the world" ("The Movies," *Des Moines News*, 11 November 1912, 2). These stories soon turned into a syndicated series of "personality sketches" (illustrated with line drawings) that could appear up to several times a week, not only in Scripps-McRae newspapers located in the Midwest but also in many others that subscribed to the United Press Association. Consequently, they may have been more widely read, especially by moviegoers, than anything in the trade press and perhaps even in the new fan magazines. Price wrote exclusively about American "moving picture folks," and her choices were striking. One out of four or five actors, for instance, was described as acting in westerns; indeed, Anderson was the subject of the fourth story printed ("Alkali Ike and Broncho Bill Tear Things Up Something Fierce," *Des Moines News*, 16 November 1912, 3). At least two-thirds of Price's stories, however, were devoted to women, from obvious stars such as Pickford and Joyce to lesser-known personalities, whether working for large or small production companies. The one on Pickford was quite characteristic in its colloquial language and summary take on star power: "Stunning Mary Pickford—Only 19 Now—Quits $10,000 'Movies' Career to Shake Her Golden Locks as a Belasco Star" (*Des Moines News*, 9 January 1912, 7). The general readership of Scripps-McRae newspapers suggests that Price's extensive "gallery of picture players" may well have assumed a gendered audience. The texts, with their elaborated, punchy titles, and the images of countless female stars certainly could have appealed to male readers, just as many "Broncho Billy" films could have appealed to mothers and girls. Yet overall, Price's stories seemed to target working women. Most of the movie stars she promoted were described as "athletic young women, carefree but committed to their work, frank and fearless in the face of physical risk. . . . [usually] unattached, and without children" (Abel, *Americanizing* 245). Such female "picture personalities," arguably, would have been especially appealing to young female movie fans as active, attractive, independent workers or professionals and, therefore, successful role models to emulate.[7] Although never named as such, most could be considered "popular, influential figures of a specifically American 'New Woman'" (Abel, *Americanizing* 246).

Finally, although public interest in "picture personalities" such as Pickford and Lawrence soon extended beyond the United States (see Gledhill in this volume), it was through the "Broncho Billy" cowboy pictures that the American star system first really took hold in the motion picture markets of Europe and elsewhere. In Great Britain, according to *Bioscope*, "Indian stories, cowboy subjects, or Western dramas," especially those of Essanay and Selig, already were very popular by late 1910 ("Topics of the Week: The Popularity of Western Films," *Bioscope*, 18 August 1910, 4–5; "What the People Want," *Bioscope*, 27 October 1910, 73). In its ads, Essanay quickly began distinguishing the films "'Made in the West' by Westerners" from its other releases there (Essanay ad, *Bioscope*, 16 February 1911, 37). By March 1911, *Nickelodeon* was taking note of what the British were calling a "welcome . . . invasion," singling out in particular the success of Essanay's "wild west dramas" in London ("London Likes Essanay Western Photoplays," *Nickelodeon*, 18 March 1911, 311). That summer *Motography* (formerly *Nickelodeon*) repeated what was then well known: throughout England, "phases of cowboy and Indian life are the most popular subjects for American films" ("Moving Picture Business Abroad," June 1911, 142). And the *New York Times* (which rarely noticed motion pictures) reprinted *Motography*'s article under a headline that neatly summed up the westerns' commercial and ideological function: "Exporting an Imaginary America to Make Money" (30 July 1911, 5:4). At the same time, in Germany, where Essanay opened a sales office in Berlin, the "Broncho Billy" films, according to censorship records, were being distributed widely throughout Central Europe (Götkürk 96). By 1912, in its *Bioscope* ads, Essanay was extolling Anderson as "the ever popular 'Broncho Billy,'" which soon became "the World Famous Role of Broncho Billy" (Essanay ads, *Bioscope*, 25 January 1912, xxii, and 6 June 1912, 734). In reviewing *Broncho Billy and the Bandits* (May 1912) and *Broncho Billy's Narrow Escape*, *Bioscope* praised the character's "irresistible charm of personality and . . . breezy, easy, infectious humor" and concluded, "He can be fierce and terrible too, when there is cause as the bandits find to their cost, but, in spite of his moments of stern menace, he is essentially the great, good-humoured 'Billy,' of whom we have all learned to grow fond. His overflowing geniality, the twinkle in his humourous eye, as well as his sure, sober strength in times of peril, are magnetic" ("The Pick of the Programmes: What We Think of Them," 13 June 1912, 819, and 1 August 1912, 367). By July, as for exhibitors in the United States, so too in Great Britain: Essanay was taking orders for "photogravure portraits" and posters of Anderson to satisfy fans (Essanay ad, *Bioscope*, 18 July 1912, 1705). All this gave credence to Essanay's boast, also taken up in U.S. newspaper ads, that "Broncho Billy" was the first American "world famous character-creation" (Essanay ads, *Moving Picture World*, 29 June 1912, 1187, and *New York Dramatic Mirror*, 4 September 1912, 31).[8]

At least two points are worth stressing by way of a conclusion. First, that G. M. Anderson was hailed as the country's "most photographed man" in 1911 testifies to the importance of both "Broncho Billy" as a "good badman" figure of moral redemption and social assimilation and the western as an emerging genre of imagined national origins and manly character. No less significant is this: the "Broncho Billy" films demonstrated that seriality in the single-reel fiction film, especially a series based on a recurring "picture personality" who embodied a more or less consistent character "type," could successfully attract mass audiences to return again and again to picture theaters. Moreover, the European fascination with Anderson's "character-creation" alerted the industry that American stardom could be profitably exported abroad. Second, that Anderson and other early picture personalities were promoted not only in the industry's trade press and new fan magazines but also in hundreds of daily newspapers testifies to the latter's significance in establishing the marketing viability of the emerging star system. Indeed, newspapers were unusually crucial because their broad, frequent circulation of images and stories about picture personalities in the public arena served as a recurring stimulus, luring more and more people into the growing fan culture for motion pictures. Perhaps most important, this newspaper discourse strongly suggests that, by the early 1910s, the marketing of movie stars already was becoming dependent on a synchronic, multimedia system that has proved especially persistent over the past century.

NOTES

1. The trade press did not take note of Essanay's publicity scheme until late 1911—see, for instance, "The Most Photographed Man," *New York Dramatic Mirror*, 22 November 1911, 26.

2. As of this writing, surviving 35 mm prints of the Anderson films discussed in this essay can be found as follows: *Under Western Skies, Broncho Billy's Christmas Dinner, Broncho Billy's Last Hold-Up, Broncho Billy's Narrow Escape*, and *A Wife of the Hills* at the Nederlands Filmmuseum, Amsterdam (*Under Western Skies* is also at the National Film and Television Archive in London), and *A Pal's Oath* at the Library of Congress (Washington, D.C.).

3. *Moving Picture World*, of course, had printed "picture personality" photo stories of Pearl White and Mary Pickford even earlier, in December 1910.

4. Gauntier did appear in the early photo story that highlighted Florence Lawrence: "On the Moving Picture Stage: Have You Seen These Faces?" *Des Moines News*, 6 May 1910, 16.

5. The *New York Dramatic Mirror* later offered free color portraits of Joyce and Gauntier to its subscribers (14 June 1911, 30).

6. "Chats with the Players" first appeared in *Motion Picture Story Magazine* in February 1912 (135–38).

7. See, for instance, Price's story about Selig's emerging star, Kathlyn Williams—"'Miss Billie Unafraid'—Torn by a Tiger but Nervy as Ever to Act the Most Daring Things Ever Seen on the Stage!—Heroine of the Movies" (*Des Moines News*, 17 November 1912, 7).

8. A similar boast can be found in a wide range of daily newspapers: Gaiety ad, *Fort Wayne Journal-Gazette* (2 June 1912, 9); Royal ad, *Mansfield News* (13 July 1912, 16); "Among the Theatres," *Charleroi Mail* (10 August 1912, 3); Colonial ad, *Fort Wayne Journal-Gazette* (25 August 1912, 8); and *Ada Evening News* (4 December 1912, 3).

2 ☆☆☆☆☆☆☆☆☆☆☆
Mary Pickford
Icon of Stardom

CHRISTINE GLEDHILL

"Dawn, over a daisy-filled meadow: the spirit of spring imprisoned in woman's body: the first child in the world" (*Photoplay*, July 1918, 111). Thus, with Mary Pickford emerged the world's first experience of full-blown *film* stardom. Others, notably Florence Turner and Florence Lawrence, had marked out the path a few years earlier; and others, for example, Mary Fuller, Mabel Normand, the Gish sisters, and serial queens Pearl White and Helen Holmes, emerged alongside her. But through the 1910s it was around Mary Pickford in particular that star practices were consolidated and star discourses woven. Through Pickford, studio executives and publicists, cultural commentators, newly constituted film critics,

---

Mary Pickford, 1914. Courtesy of the Library of Congress.

and fan-magazine journalists confronted a novel phenomenon, exploring its economic, ideological, cultural, and aesthetic possibilities.

Cinema gave "America's Sweetheart" to the world and with her a model—an imaginary horizon of "starriness"—to be competitively emulated in different film cultures from country to country, for example in Britain with the promotion of Alma Taylor as the "English Mary Pickford," or the naming of Ermeline as the "Indian Pickford." Accordingly, this chapter engages with the circulation of "Mary Pickford" in a British as well as an American context. Central, however, to both arenas is the inauguration of film stardom through the figure of *"The Girl."*

☆☆★★★ Naming and Numbers

The story repeated endlessly as the need to tell it grew with her fame was that Pickford—then known by her birth name, Gladys Smith, and living in her home town, Toronto—was thrust onto the stage at age five after her father died, leaving her mother to bring up three children and Mary to become the family breadwinner.[1] This story echoes the popular account of the equally fatherless Florence Turner's first stage appearance, supposedly at age three. In both cases the child performer spontaneously upstages the adults, much to the merriment of the house and chagrin of parental guardians. The absence of the father, the strong maternal household, and the precociousness of the child in both stories suggest the power of the girl-child as the imaginary locus of growing social and emotional stirrings that would be intensified with the phenomenon of film stardom. However, playing minor child roles in minor traveling theatrical companies would not turn "Baby Gladys," as she was billed, into a national icon. Echoing Turner's theatrical advancement with Henry Irving's company, the turning point for Gladys Smith was winning a child role in David Belasco's production of *The Warrens of Virginia* (1907). When this closed in April 1909, she—initially reluctant—goaded D. W. Griffith at Biograph into giving her a trial. In retrospective stories about these encounters, charismatic paternalistic directors bow with some amusement but shrewd calculation to the demands of an adolescent girl, whom they then mold for future fame (Gordon Gassaway, *Motion Pictures*, September 1915).[2]

Stardom required not only visibility but crucially a name. However, given Biograph's reluctance to identify actors, it was, her story says, the public who named her after her characters: "Little Mary." How this came about became a matter of fascinated retrospective speculation in her later publicity (*Moving Picture World*, 29 July 1911, 216; *Nashville Democrat*, 29 December 1912).

Between 1909 and 1910—when Pickford appeared in over eighty short films—invented names were circulated for popular female players: the Vitagraph Girl (Florence Turner), the Biograph Girl (Florence Lawrence). When Lawrence left Biograph, Pickford took her place as "Little Mary." However, on her move at the end of 1910 to IMP, Pickford's stage name, established by the publicity-canny Belasco, was announced beneath her portrait as part puff for the studio's coup in *Motion Picture World*: "Miss Mary Pickford (Independent Moving Pictures Company)" (24 December 1910, 1462). An early attempt to analyze Pickford's appeal while claiming the artistic status of the film actor, the accompanying article suggests that by the end of her first twenty months in filmmaking, Pickford's rise to notice was an established fact: "Miss Pickford is an artiste of the highest rank in a field where there are few of her kind. . . . Her success with another picture company [Biograph] was so pronounced that she became known to millions as 'Little Mary'" (1264). IMP, recognizing the commercial value of a brand name, advertised their acquisition under the banner "She's an Imp," announcing "'Little Mary's' First Appearance in IMP Films!" Another advertisement proclaimed of *Her Darkest Hour* (1911), "Exhibitors who know the drawing power of 'Little Mary' will be delighted to learn that she appears in almost every foot of this splendid reel" (*Motion Picture World*, 4 February 1911, 280). The development of star exploitation was, however, an uneven process, with both IMP advertising and *Motion Picture World* reviewers continuing to focus on story, often without naming actress or even characters, while IMP collapsed Pickford's individual identity into its production brand, the "Little Mary" series.

Pickford's second move to the newly formed independent company, Majestic, at the end of 1911 produced another flurry of advertising trading on her iconic identity, reinforced by the film title *The Courting of Mary*, which reflexively merged Majestic's coup with plot and performer with character (*Motion Picture World*, 25 November 1911, 669). Pickford quickly abandoned Majestic after only five films, exchanging publicity and a higher salary for a return to the anonymity of Biograph, compensated not only by the artistic direction and developing cinematic expertise of Griffith, but also by the consequent increasing attention given to films by dramatic critics (*Moving Picture World*, 2 December 1911, 761).[3] Astutely, her next move in 1912 returned her to theatrical limelight and full public identification when Belasco cast her as the blind heroine of the fairy play, *A Good Little Devil*. Playing in the flesh, in a fixed location, gave a material reality to her reported popularity, since not only was she nightly named in the playbill, but crowds gathered at the stage door and now recognized her on the streets (*New Jersey Telegraph*, 27 January 1913).

"Little Mary" was more than a studio brand name, signaling, as the invariable quotation marks suggested, a collaboration in which publicity makers, studios, audiences, and Pickford herself participated to both liberate and contain a developing public icon. "Mary" generically designated "every girl," while "little" encapsulated both her diminutive stature and ingénue roles. In combination "Little Mary" Pickford encouraged identification of actress with roles—frequently also named "Mary"—making the star available for audience possession.

Once named, the significance of Pickford's popularity was initially registered in numbers, computed in "millions." Positive reviews of her performance in *A Good Little Devil* by noted drama critics not only extended awareness of her existence to a theatrical clientele, but invited awed comparison of her visibility as a film star with the lesser reach of the more prestigious theater actress and the greater social importance of statesmen. *Theatre Magazine* noted: "Not even the Divine Sarah has appeared before so many . . . in so many roles" (June 1913). *Cosmopolitan* pondered the paradox: "Mary Pickford is a pet of playgoers all over the country who don't even know her name. Her acting has thrilled hundreds of thousands of people who never heard the sound of her voice. The answer to this paradox is: the 'Movies'" (July 1913).

This fact intimated a new kind of wondrous power afforded by the cinematograph. A drawing of a cinematographer cranking his camera to release a fairy illustrates the text's comment that "Miss Mary Pickford . . . has been observed simultaneously by more than a million people . . . from coast to coast, from Alaska to New Orleans, from 'Frisco to New York" (*Nashville Democrat*, 29 December 1912). This roll-call of America's cities suggests the power of her numerical appeal to unify a nation—diversity and distance annulled in a common relationship with "Our Mary"—that was soon to become global. In April 1914, *Motion Pictures* noted, "In Paris, London, New York, or in strange nameless border settlements of Asia and Africa and Australia, this little figure has made friends. Millions have seen and applauded her." Throughout the 1910s the relentless growth and tenacity of her following suggested a strange reordering of social priorities. In 1915 the *Pittsburgh Gazette* somewhat acerbically noted: "Revolutions, wars have their day, but Mary Pickford and Tennyson's brook go on for ever. She is the paramount obsession of the pleasure-seeking populace" (5 June 1915).

The "pleasure-seeking populace" suggests the new visibility of the mass audience whom she drew together across social, state, and eventually national divisions. Initially, encouraged perhaps by Pickford's strategic decision to return to Belasco, her appeal was explained in terms of "acting," and theatrical precedents were in order. The *New Jersey Telegraph* (27 January 1913) reporting on *A Good Little Devil* noted "this clever little actress [is] intimately known" as "The Maude Adams of the Movies," a comparison reiterated through the next two years.[4] Her return to filmmaking to join Adolph Zukor's Famous Players, however, provoked democratic distinctions between film and theatrical stardom: "Mary Pickford has come to be the intimate possession of all the people, whereas the *great actress*, whether she be Bernhardt or a celebrity from Albion or The States, remains more or less a tradition, more or less a mere soulless name" (*Photoplay*, November 1915, 53). If ubiquitous visibility contributed to cinema's intensification of stardom, the cultural arena of the stage actress removes her from ordinary lives. In a *Blue Book* interview for August 1914, Pickford knocked the Maude Adams sobriquet on the head: "I'm just plain Mary Pickford and that's all there is to it!" Thus a struggle between traditional and new discourses for ownership of her fame initially marks the criss-crossing commentaries that probe its significance. *Photoplay*'s Estelle Kegler was equally blunt: "Out in Manhattan, Kansas, or Moose Jaw, they knew all about little Mary long before Mr. Belasco, dealer in highbrow drama, even considered offering her a prominent place in a Broadway production. And she burst upon the 'big way' with the acclaim of more than a million picture fans trailing her right up to the stage door" (1913, 34–35). Even the young Vachel Lindsay wrote a serenade aiming to "snatch her from Belasco's hand and that prison called Broadway" (unattributed clipping, December 1915). Locating her appeal in her commitment to both artistry and popular stories, *Theatre Magazine* noted that "she, unlike her co-actors, never saw the audiences as a 'joke'" (June 1913).

Pickford's millions also designated dollars. With each career move, her skillfully negotiated salary hikes became a matter of increasingly astonished comment, associating film stardom with new kinds of wealthy lifestyle and provoking a sometimes sour note from commentators. In January 1915, the *Los Angeles Times* announced, "Interview with Mary Pickford Costs Money," and detailed imaginary charges for time spent interviewing her: talking, losing her hanky, applying eye shadow (20 January 1915, 3:4). The same paper commented in May 1915, "Mary Pickford is a cute little motion picture girl with curls and a baby stare . . . [who] gets $2000 a week for staring" (11 May 1915, 3:1). In September 1915 *Photoplay* noted of her salary for the coming year that "she is about to receive a salary equal to that which our United States of America gives its President." If the *New Jersey Evening Mail* cheerily named her the girl with a "million dollar smile" (2 October 1915), *Motion Picture Mail*'s special Pickford issue for 1 January 1916 opened its otherwise appreciative dossier with "When a girl is only twenty-three . . . yet receiving a weekly salary that is the equivalent of two hundred and fifty working girls' wages, there is need of an explanation."

While gender attitudes contributed to astonished reactions at the discordance between Pickford's girlhood and business acumen, commentaries indirectly probed the meaning of the wealth spreading to a new class of film entertainers and its impact on the millions who followed them. Little Mary's acquisition of a cabriolet automobile or her flight from Los Angeles to New York for a five-day shopping trip endorsed the sheer enjoyment offered by consumer culture along with superb advertising for manufacturers (*Los Angeles Times*, 7 December 1913, 7:2; *Photoplay*, August 1917, 11–12, 54). But interview copy worked equally to mitigate the moral implications of a consumer identity that threatened to remove her from her audiences and undermine the democracy of her mass appeal. Thus many articles assure readers that wealth has not "spoilt" little Mary, that her tastes remain simple. As the *Los Angeles Times* commented, "This clever little lady is as simple and unassuming as the ordinary sweet school miss of sixteen summers" (7 December 1913, 7:2). One year and considerably more fame later, she is still "a very unassuming little person [who] prefers gardening and baking to state occasions" (*Los Angeles Times*, 24 January 1915, 3:3).

☆☆☆★★ "Little Mary" in Britain

While countless British stage actors had crossed the Atlantic throughout the nineteenth century, American cinema "virtually" reversed the trend. However, international following had to be created and was never certain. In India, for instance, while Pearl White and other serial queens appeared regularly in film advertisements during the 1910s, Pickford was almost invisible. Initially, promoting Mary to British audiences confronted geographic, temporal, and, to a certain degree, cultural distance. Nevertheless, the British film industry was closely connected to the American, imports from which increased exponentially with the impact of the Great War on home production. "Little Mary" had come to Britain as part of Biograph's output, supported by its Bulletins from which the two main trade journals—*The Bioscope* and *Kinematograph and Lantern Weekly*—derived their own, generally abbreviated, copy. Since Biograph suppressed the identities of actors, Pickford's name did not feature. However, *Motion Picture World*'s article on Pickford's acquisition by IMP was adapted by *Bioscope* under the heading "A Leading Picture Actress" (16 February 1911, 65). Substituting Bernhardt for Belasco, the paper assured exhibitors that Pickford's "work will receive as much warm commendation in England as in America." Guaranteeing a popularity already established elsewhere, it concludes: "'Little Mary,' as she is universally called in the States, is as charming a girl as can be found, and . . . she has real talent."

In the initial absence of fan publications, it is unclear how far and by what means Pickford's image penetrated the consciousness of British filmgoers between 1909 and 1912. A new "weekly independent newspaper for all interested in the photoplay," established in June 1912 with the unlikely title of *The Film Censor*, vacillated about her name—she was "Mrs Owen Moore [who is] none other than the ever-popular Mary Pickford" (11 September 1912, 2), "Miss Moore" (9 April 1913, 3), and "Miss Mary Pickford Moore" (28 May 1913, 6)—suggesting the cultural distance to be crossed in establishing a British public relationship with film stars. However, in the same year *Film Censor* noted, "'Little Mary' has endeared herself to the hearts of thousands in all quarters of the globe," and reproduced a photograph that "will be familiar to all picture-playgoers." While her image in films may have been familiar and even popular, the concept of her worldwide fame stemmed from her American publicity.

The years 1913–1914 were a key period in the development of film-star discourse in Britain with the emergence of film magazines. Most important was *The Picturegoer*, which, established in June 1913 (and later retitled *Pictures and the Picturegoer*), began the process of separating performer from screen performance necessary to fandom. From its inception, *Picturegoer* sought to bind readers simultaneously to picture players and to its own monthly appearance by instituting a version of the numbers game established by American magazines—the "Favourite Players" competition—helpfully supported by lists of names to choose from and short biographies. This ran teasingly over several months between 15 November 1913 and 30 May 1914, when it was finally announced that the American Florence Turner had polled the top number of votes among actresses, ahead of Mary Fuller and Alice Joyce. Mary Pickford, although included among the choices, was nowhere in the outcome. A second competition was staged in 1915, however, strategically separating "Greatest British Film Players" from the "World's Greatest Film Artistes." Now Mary Pickford topped the female poll of the latter with 250,545 votes to Florence Turner's 170,335 and serial queen Kathlyn Williams's 96,950 (*Pictures and the Picturegoer*, 6 November 1915, 112–13).[5]

In the meantime, the trade press began to register the impact of this particular actress on their fortunes. In October 1913, *Bioscope*, offering advance notice of Pickford's coming appearance in the film version of *A Good Little Devil* (1914), and reminding exhibitors of her "clever leading parts . . . with the A. B. Company," noted the effect of Pickford's filmic presence on attendance and audience response (9 October 1913, 135; 30 October 1913, 361).[6] Since wartime meant severe shortages of product for exhibitors, many of the old Biograph films were reissued several times over. Nevertheless, it was only when the last films of Pickford's 1912 period at Biograph were reissued for the first time toward the end of 1914 that her presence was acknowledged. By the time of the third reissue of her first Biograph films, running between 1915 and 1917, *Bioscope*'s copy suggested that she was the *only* attraction in crude or out-of-date stories, while the later 1912 films are characterized as accomplished star vehicles: "a charming Mary Pickford comedy," a "Mary Pickford drama."

Pickford's value to the trade was closely bound up with the enhancement of her artistic reputation following her Belasco engagement and subsequent contract with Famous Players, a company to whom *Bioscope* offers "undying gratitude" for establishing the feature film "as a solid, serious, dignified form of dramatic art" (12 March 1914, 1179; 19 November 1914, 711). Creating a popular mass market meant crossing entrenched class divisions to incorporate those values that would appeal to middle classes and allay nervousness about the democracy of millions. *In the Bishop's Carriage* (1913) is, *Bioscope* declares, "the sort of picture that is wanted more urgently every day, now that the cinematograph theaters are beginning to appeal to intelligent people, as well as to the lower classes" (13 November 1913, 667). It later notes that such patrons are also "wealthier" (16 December 1915, 1249).

Significantly, it was following her second Belasco engagement that the British trade press developed its own commentary on Pickford and her films, for the film trade's understanding of performance was rooted in culturally embedded theatrical values. From 1908 a lively relationship with stage actors had tended toward a theatricalization of British filmmaking and criticism (see Burrows, *Legitimate*). *Film Censor* greeted Pickford's Belasco engagement as the achievement of public (because theatrical) recognition: "Little Mary is to be nameless to her admirers no more. She is now seen in a Broadway Theatre" (26 March 1913, 5). *Pictures and the Picturegoer*'s "Greatest British Film Player Competition" warned its readers that they must vote according to "artistic merit, not popularity or good looks," and proceeded to list different character types in which an actor might excel (17 April 1915, 50). Drawing on British theatrical precedent, *Bioscope* suggested that "the power of Mary Pickford's personality draws people to cinemas as Ellen Terry did to the theatre" (6 May 1915, 563, 565), and British reviewers frequently noted the good performances of supporting actors, requesting that they be named alongside Pickford as star (*Bioscope*, 20 August 1914, 715, and 26 November 1914, supp. v). By the time of *Mistress Nell* (1915), the cultural gravitas of a new Famous Players–Lasky/Pickford release led *Bioscope* to comment that J. D. Walker's trade shows "are rapidly assuming an importance in film circles comparable, let us say, with a first night at His Majesty's Theatre" (6 May 1915, 563).

Thus Anglicization initially incorporated Pickford into a theatrical framework. However, her stardom, sent from America, required cultural recognition of a performance mode quite different from the foregrounded acting of Florence Turner's impersonations which, supported by her personal presentation of her films to British audiences, made her so popular here (see Gledhill, "Screen Actress"). If Turner's tour-de-force mimicry—supported by her U.K. public appearances—ultimately impeded the development of the consistent personality necessary to stardom, Pickford's presence had to be established from afar. Thus advertising copy played with capitals, bold and normal type, and brackets to foreground intimate first name over formal surname and to dramatize the approach and eventual arrival of the star with successive films, exclaiming, for example, "**YES! MARY** PICKFORD **IS COMING!**" (*Bioscope*, 13 August 1914, xi), later followed by a *Pictures and the Picturegoer* cover declaring "**MARY PICKFORD** is **HERE!**" (29 May 1915). Meanwhile, *Illustrated Films Monthly* informed readers that it was "Little Mary's dearest wish to visit the United Kingdom . . . and arrangements had been made," but wartime conditions prevented it (November 1914, 191).

Such advertisements were supported by longer trade press reviews and by the new fan magazines that kept American news stories about Pickford circulating while offering illustrated novelizations of new films in anticipation of future releases. Pickford is drawn closer to the British public through repetitive advertising of her life story—ambivalently titled "The Film Life of Mary Pickford" (*Film Flashes*, 13 November 1915, inside cover)—and the circulation of the pet names devised in America. Significantly, "America's Sweetheart" is rarely used, while the diminutive "Little Mary" of the early years is gradually displaced toward the end of 1914 by recognition of her growing authority as the "World's Sweetheart."

By 1917 the trade recognized Pickford's stardom as an economic force. *Bioscope* noted that "she is almost an institution" (17 February 1916, 733), while J. D. Walker's advertisements bluntly trumpeted "official" box office figures, naming her "the showman's mascot and sure money-maker" (9 August 1917, 657; 29 September 1917, 58). However, British trade and fan press commentators and fans themselves also worked to appropriate

Pickford's Americanness. Shifts from "World's Sweetheart" to "Everybody's" or "People's Favourite" effectively localized the star's celebrity (see *Film Censor*, 10 December 1913, 8). And *Pictures and the Picturegoer* boldly challenged readers with its front cover question "Is there an English Mary Pickford?" below a portrait of the Hepworth star Alma Taylor (12–19 May 1917), to which readers responded in the affirmative (2–9 June 1917, 206; 9–16 June 1917, 224).

☆☆★★★ **Girl-Child**

Pickford's film career, as we know, did not last beyond the 1920s. Her stardom was in one key respect rooted in the popular imaginary of the 1910s and early 1920s in America and Britain: its investment in the girl-child and the fantasy world of child's-play. Contrary to the usual career progression of the theatrical actress toward ever more "heavy" or "emotional" parts, Pickford's filmography shows a staged reduction in age from the ingénue roles of the Biograph era to the "Growing Girl" roles identified by John Tibbetts and finally to where she began onstage: at twenty-five years of age playing the child in *Poor Little Rich Girl* (1917). *Rebecca of Sunnybrook Farm* (1917), *Daddy Long Legs* (1919), *Pollyanna* (1920), and *Little Lord Fauntleroy* (1921) followed. Although, as Tibbetts points out, Pickford played the literal child relatively late in her career and rarely throughout the film, the combination of Victorian child-woman injected by Griffith into her Biograph roles and her own diminutive childlike appearance and previous stage experience playing children meant that the child haunted her ingénue and girl characterizations (Tibbetts "Mary Pickford"). When IMP cast her in *The Dream* (1911) in the dual roles of virtuous wife and the husband's dream transformation of her vamping in a public bar, *Motion Picture World* was surprised: "Our feelings . . . were somewhat sentimental when we saw 'our Mary' as a wife arrayed in the evening gown and dining with swells. . . . We have always considered 'Mary' as a child. It has never occurred to us that she might grow up and be a woman some day" (28 January 1911, 182). Much of the Pickford publicity continued to perceive her as child-woman, which her own reported activities with children both on and off the set, including adopting a 400-strong orphanage, reinforced (see *Los Angeles Times*, 24 January 1915, 3:12; *Photoplay*, September 1915 and January 1918; *Cleveland Leader*, 22 October 1916). Commentary emphasized her childlike features, such as her ready ability to cry (*Vanity Fair*, 25 January 1913); her "piquant pout of the lips" (*New York Dramatic Mirror*, 19 March 1913); and her "ingenuous face" (*St. Louis Globe*, 20 August 1916).

While her girl-child roles demonstrated acting skills and interviews detailed her techniques of child impersonation, this also enabled her to maintain the persona by which she had become beloved—"Little Mary" (*Moving Pictures*, February 1917; *Vanity Fair*, December 1917). Some "sweetheart" manifestations were too much for realists on either side of the Atlantic, and sarcasm directed at cuteness and curls could be cutting. But while much of the publicity—photographs of "Mary" holding her skirts, or caressing flowers or kittens—promoted a public image of chocolate-box simplicity, her films, their more considered reviews, and even lengthier examinations of her stardom suggest that the girl-child cued into a cultural imaginary working between a Victorian past and coming modernity, social change and a world at war.

The "Girl" was a ubiquitous figure in the 1910s and into the 1920s—a figure shared by Britain and America not least through literary and cultural sources (see Burrows "Girls"). The Girl cued back into Victorian middlebrow culture's "child-woman" but also forward into the adventurous girl/boy of the transitional, cross-century period's investment in the fantasy world of child's play for grown-ups.[7] The ingénue roles of Pickford's romantic and domestic comedies and melodramas were imbued with immediately recognized "girlish" qualities: there are references to "girlish emotions" (*New York Dramatic Mirror*, 11 September 1913, of *In the Bishop's Carriage*); "budding girlish figure" (*Cosmopolitan*, July 1913); "girlish beauty" (*Motion Picture World*, January 1916); "unassuming girlishness" (*Photoplay*, August 1917, 12). Girlishness, however, meant more than adolescent quirks. To the interviewer Katherine Synon, Pickford appeared "a girl standing on the threshold" ("The Unspoiled Mary Pickford," *Photoplay*, September 1915). If psychologically the "threshold" implies a state of transition, the Girl is its archetypal representative: her culturally assigned femininity open to empathic feelings; her youth to mutability; her body and psychology to physical and emotional change; her cultural position veering between the carefree irresponsibility of childhood and idealism of the young adult. Pickford's "girl" roles, therefore, enabled her to exercise her much admired capacity for conveying fleeting, often contradictory emotions or passing thoughts made available as aesthetic experience, with pathos and comedy, laughter and tears the most frequently cited combinations. If Pickford's increasing adoption of child roles intensified this combination, her source materials opened up the more fantastical terrain of childhood fictions, connecting their investment in magical transformations and mutability with cinematography's capture of fleeting moments of liminal being and transient feeling. An identification of Pickford with the fairy world of Belasco and Barriesque whimsy runs through her publicity in the 1910s, from the cameraman cranking his machine to release a Pickford fairy (unattributed cutting, December 1912) through the *Fort Wayne Journal*'s "deliciously whimsical sprite of a girl" (7 February 1915) to the fan declaring "Mary Pickford is a fairy . . . not of this world" (*Motion Pictures*, May 1918). While descriptions of Pickford as a "will-o'-the-wisp" link the liminality of the fairy world to the mutability of Pickford's Girl (*Evening Mail*, 13 November 1915; *Motion Pictures*, January 1916 and May 1918), her invocation in both the American and British press as a "female Peter Pan," "never grow-up Mary," or "the Girl who never Grows Up" underscores her hesitation at the threshold (*New York Review*, 11 September 1915; *Syracuse Post Standard*, 28 September 1918; *Bioscope*, 17 December 1914, 1197).

Comedy, however, renders Pickford's girl more robust. Thus the British *Bioscope* argues of *Cinderella* (1914), this "is no ordinary Cinderella—for she is Mary Pickford. . . . The lonely little kitchenmaid becomes, in her hands . . . a figure of childish dreams, gloriously young and natural, and marked by that humanising grace of humour of which Mary Pickford so thoroughly understands the secret" (17 December 1914, 1197). Yet humor, while injecting a robustness into Pickford's girl, also intensified her underlying fragility, a combination invoked in recurring, double-edged terms: "whimsical," "winsome," and the endlessly repeated "wistful."[8]

Wistfulness, ameliorating loss through tenacious hope, attached to the many orphan or bereaved child roles in which the "Girl" appeared. As an orphan Pickford became available to everyone, while loss of a parent and childhood hardship was often read back into her biography. Orphanhood literally clothed her in rags—to her own frequent discomfort and some complaints from the fan press. More significant, it tapped into an aesthetic structure of feeling that resonated for a period caught between acculturated Victorian values and the aporias of a modernizing world. The pathos of Pickford's girl-child produced acute pleasures. In *A Good Little Devil* she is "winningly pathetic" (*Baltimore American*, 24 December 1912); *Tessibel of the Storm Country* (1914) offers the "beauty of pathos" (*Photoplay*, September 1915) and *The Foundling* (1916) "exquisite pathos" (*Chicago Tribune*, 3 January 1916), while for *Photoplay*'s Julian Johnson her performance was "soul-wrenching in its quaint piteousness" (February 1916, 51).

While British commentators are cooler, less addicted to "girlishness," and more interested in Pickford's ingénue and "girl-wife" roles as performed *types*, they too succumbed to the "pathos" of her girl-children, particularly as mediated by humor. Thus *Picturegoer* promises of the film *A Good Little Devil* "pathos galore and rollicking pantomime to drive away the tears"

(27 December 1913, 367); *Bioscope* argues, "It is only Mary Pickford . . . who can create . . . just that particular kind of sentiment . . . almost unbearably heartbreaking in its tender pathos . . . mingled with enchanting humour" (14 May 1914, 753); while the president of a British film club writes to *Pictures and The Picturegoer* of "humour that had with it a pathos that was at times almost heartbreaking" (14 June 1919, 596). *Photoplay's* Julian Johnson sums up the piquancy of this combination as "that precious stage jewel: a laugh set in a tear" (February 1916, 51).

For many commentators, pathos explained Pickford's power over audiences. In an interview for the *Toledo Times*, Pickford herself suggested that seeing "'Little Mary' weep, smile and express various emotions . . . they come to have a sort of proprietary interest in this little figure, as they share in its experience" (4 June 1916). As a participatory structure, pathos enables spectators to perceive what is withheld from characters—reinforced by the distance between adult audience and child protagonist and the distancing perspective of humor—and so to look beyond the child to the oppressive forces against which she struggles. In this sense pathos educates the feelings. Pickford's Girl, positioned between an "old-fashioned" Victorian past and an evolving twentieth-century modernity, confronted a threshold of social change. The Girl's ready sympathies for the underdog aligned her with the Victorian "true woman." Emphasis on feeling drew on the same impulse by which nineteenth-century melodrama shifted moral legitimation from church to personally lived social relationships.[9] In this sense Pickford's roles, clothed in her girl persona, were received as manifestations of absolute good. "Whether comic or sad, a fairy or tom-boy she is always sweet, lovable, wholesome, suggesting good, never evil . . . Paramount estimate 10,000 people a day . . . benefit by the happy influence of this sunshiny little movie girl" (*Ohio State Journal*, 27 June 1915). Nevertheless, as "tomboy summer-girl" (*Motion Picture World*, 25 November 1911, 619), "tantalising, roguish girl" (*Chicago Herald*, 30 June 1915), or "carefree little madcap" (*Daily News*, 7 September 1915), she opened up space for mocking mimicry and emotion-fueled rebellion against injustice. As Delight Evans suggests in her *Photoplay* article "Mary Pickford, The Girl," she "upsets a few pet traditions" (July 1918, 91).

In tension with "old-fashioned" virtues, the signs of changing times in Pickfordian "fun" were recognized early. *Motion Picture World*, evaluating her career before moving to IMP, declared: "Miss Pickford is a veritable queen of comediennes: and back of that there is a thoroughly modern and progressive spirit unrestrained by worn out conventions" (24 February 1910, 1462). Trade journals' comments on her late Biograph, IMP, and early Famous

Pickford as "love-pirate" counters her "cute" stay-at-home wife in *The Dream* (1911).

Players films sense the emergence of a new type. Of the IMP-produced *Her Darkest Hour* (1911), *Motion Picture World*'s reviewer sagely explained "a prepossessing young woman . . . must . . . earn a living by being associated with men in public office" (11 February 1911, 323). Taking clever advantage of this tension, *The Dream* pitched that "well-known love-pirate, the female stenographer" against Pickford's initial stay-at-home little wife, characterized variously as "simple," "timid," and "demure," whose dreaming husband, tiring of her "cute little ways," imagines her a vamp and then cannot handle the result (*Motion Picture World*, 28 January 1911, 182; 21 January 1911, 152). In *A Girl of Yesterday* (1915), Pickford's own script develops this doubling strategy not as a feat of performance but in order to play the ends against the middle. While the sketchy plot has Jane Stuart and brother John escaping the repressive upbringing of Aunt Angela, a series of "vaudeville sketches" enables Pickford's Jane to test the modern pleasures of a "golfer," "equestrian," and "aviatrice" to which they are introduced by the modern family living next door. Playing the Girl's rebellious self against doubles representing her virtuous self, as in *Poor Little Rich Girl* (1917) and *Pollyanna* (1920), or herself doubling roles as in *Stella Maris* (1918), became a key device of Pickford's major features, scripted by her close collaborator and friend, Frances Marion. By this means Pickford's films maintained the Girl's function as a dual sign of virtue and rebellion.

About this time interviews on both sides of the Atlantic also explored the more unusual physical requirements of film acting, often including snippets about Pickford's feats of endurance while filming, suggesting competition with her serial-queen rivals (see Bean "Technologies," and Cooper in this volume). However, a prize-winning review submitted to the British fanzine *Film Flashes* suggests that doubling roles allowed Pickford to achieve a "great triumph as the prim maiden of long ago, and later, as the modern society girl" (12 February 1916, 14). If, as the *Spokane Review* argued of *Amarilly of Clothes-line Alley* (1918), the Pickford Girl's old-fashioned values privileged "simplicity, kindness and honesty" over those of her "so-called social superiors" (27 April 1918), her mix of slapstick, comedy, and pathos summoned up comparisons with that other child of misfortune, Charles Chaplin.

In February 1916, *Photoplay* identified Pickford's role in *Rags* (1915) as a "Keystone farceur." Later the *Cleveland Times* named her a "feminine Charlie Chaplin." While, like Pickford, Chaplin is associated with Victorian pathos, the *Cleveland Times* suggests the greater irreverence of the Girl's physicality: whereas Chaplin gains laughs subtly "by facial expressions anticipating events," hers is "more robust buffoonery" (11 February 1918). Thus, if her construction as child seems to halt the forward thrust of girlhood's threshold, regression to the child's acerbic look at the adult world counters Pickfordian "sweetness." Pickford's growing girl-child legitimated a use of slapstick that provided scope for staging moments of rebellion by stealth—for example, her famed improvisation debunking the "glad-girl," Pollyanna. Asking a fly if it wants to go to heaven, she grants the wish: she swats it. In her later films, slapstick cushioned her characters' acts of increasingly violent resistance: witness the shooting of her abusive stepfather in *Heart o' the Hills* (1919), which the British *Bioscope* found so shocking (1 May 1920, 68), and the murder of her former employer in *Stella Maris* (1918).

Pickford's persona of good-heartedness expressed in knockabout defiance of life's "hard knocks" suggested to American commentators that she represented a "type of American girl . . . widely followed in this country and recognized in others" (unidentified clipping, c. 1918). For *Photoplay* "America's sweetheart . . . is a girl of all girls, a real live American girl" (August 1917, 11). At Paramount, Laemmle had advocated her impersonation of diverse ethnic roles—British, Japanese, Italian, Dutch, Anglo-Indian—often not to her taste nor well received. It was as an American girl that she circulated abroad. *Mistress Nell* (1915) provoked from *Bioscope* humorous recognition of a reversal of cultural power: "Mary Pickford is now so very much more important a personage in English history than the second King Charles's . . . favourite" (6 May 1915, 565). American stardom's democratizing tendency partly explained Pickford's appeal. Thus the cinema house magazine, *Talbot Tattler*, reviewing *Such a Little Queen* (1914), noted "the American idea of the uselessness of thrones and all such regal nonsense" (16 December 1914, 30), while *Bioscope* suggested that "Americans see royalty through democratic eyes" (19 November 1914, 711). More cautiously, *Picture Show* commented that since "these pictures reach almost everyone from the poorest to the richest, it is a big moral responsibility" (31 May 1919, 17).

However, Pickford's representation of a specifically American, modernized femininity spun off from the American screen in 1917, when the United States entered World War I, and Pickford, along with Chaplin and Douglas Fairbanks, launched a series of Liberty Bond campaigns around the country, undertaking a number of patriotic acts: adopting a company of soldiers, organizing letters and presents to be sent to the trenches, and so on. "America's Sweetheart" eclipsed "Little Mary"—a national identification consolidated in *The Little American* (1917), in which Pickford plays an ingénue, Angela Moore, courted by both a German American and a Frenchman. Crossing the Atlantic after war is declared, Angela is rescued from the torpedoed *Veritania* and arrives in France where she turns the chateau she has just inherited into a hospital for wounded French soldiers. Compared to Allied propaganda of the time, the film was off-beat, not only in having the Pickford Girl confront the German military and cope with hysterical women in scenes of rape and pillage, but also in providing a conclusion that ended with the death of her French suitor and a kiss between Angela and her now chastened German lover through the wire mesh of a prison camp. The film was received positively by the American press, responding to Pickford as a figure capable of balancing patriotism with a humanism that rose above the "eagle-shrieking variety" and uniting a population of immigrants including those whose original countries were now at war. The *New York Dramatic Mirror* found it "singularly appropriate that Mary Pickford . . . almost a national figure in herself, should be presented as representing America's womanhood in one of the most powerful war pictures yet produced" (14 July 1917).

The Little American was largely well received in Britain, if with a changed ending that had Pickford back in America awaiting her French sweetheart (*Kinematograph and Lantern Weekly*, 10 January 1918, 47). If the American press recognized in the figure of Pickford's Angela Moore a revival of past American national pride (*Cleveland Plain Dealer*, 3 July 1917), the two main British trade press journals split between humanist sentiment and modern skepticism. *Bioscope* responded to Pickford's restraint: "There is nothing of the flag-waving jingoist about her. She is never a platitude. . . . She is a perfectly normal little human being whose first impulse is to avoid discomfort, but who faces danger, not through theatrical courage, but because . . . her kindness and her good heart are more strongly developed" (10 January 1918, 40). *Kinematograph and Lantern Weekly*, on the other hand, declared the film outright propaganda. Admitting the "gripping" realism of its war scenes, the review subjects the imaging of German atrocities and Pickford's Little American to sarcastic parody for its national presumptions: "Angela Moore is Mary Pickford, and July 4th is her birthday. We all know what that day means to loyal Americans." Later confronting the "beastly" Germans, "Angela finds that no one listens to her—despite her American citizenship; it is not worth a cent. She even has to take off their boots" (10 January 1918, 47). In this respect Pickford's combination of Victorian sentiment and American modernity brought to the surface shifting and conflicting currents in British culture, negotiating nationalism's association with the past and modernity with America that frequently divided the stances of the two papers. *Pictures and the Picturegoer*, however, writing on behalf of fans, was quick to take possession of Pickford's "Little American" as "'Our Mary' . . . the heroine of a tremendous story of the great war. Nothing more realistic has ever been staged" (19–26 January 1918, 80).

☆★★★★ Being Mary Pickford, Cinema Star

It is in the inflection of the discourse of film acting toward the notion of personality that the aesthetic of film stardom itself is realized. As Gordon Gassaway, writing in *Motion Picture Magazine*, declared, "Today, from the manager of a Moving Picture theater to the actor appearing upon the screen, personality is without doubt the prime factor which is putting the 'move' into Moving Pictures" (September 1915). British response cautiously concurred, attributing Pickford's appeal to "an indefinable 'something' . . . Personality" (*Pictures and the Picturegoer*, 27 October–3 November 1917, 463). *Kinematograph and Lantern Weekly*, while skeptical about the credibility of *The Heart o' the Hills*, declared, "Mary succeeds in putting it over somehow—just 'how' is a mystery; doubtless the genius of her personality" (1 April 1920, 98). Efforts to define film acting negotiated two different approaches. One, invested in traditional understandings of acting as the skill of impersonation, emphasized the technical requirements of performing for a camera in a silent medium. The second, stronger in America, separated personality from acting, articulating a sense of encounter with the person beyond technical skills. Thus *Motion Picture World* concludes its 1910 attempt to analyze Pickford's acting: "The essence of Miss Pickford's charm is born in her . . . and carries over into the audience a sympathetic interest in all she does. 'There she is,' means we are glad to see *you*, Little Mary, no matter what part you are playing" (24 December 1910, 1462).

These two approaches battled it out through the 1910s as reviewers and commentators sought to define star appeal. Thus in 1916, against the *Chicago Tribune*'s claim that "we love her not because she is Mary Pickford but because she is a gifted purveyor of charming personalities" (3 January 1916), the *St. Louis Globe Democrat* declared, "She has no method, no secret process, no formula. Her business in life is being Mary Pickford" (12 October 1916). But what did *being* Mary Pickford mean? Initially a Pickford personality is adduced from an amalgam of film roles, physical appearance, and behavioral traits—"rioting golden curls" (*Photoplay*, September 1915), "wistful violet eyes" (*Cosmopolitan*, July 1913). A similar merging occurs between actress and role in reviewers' persistent reference to "Mary" whatever the name of the character she is playing.

Richard deCordova argues of the emerging "picture personality" that while "acting" bestowed the prestige of theater, "personality" implied not a diversity of skillful characterizations but the existence of a stable identity rooted in the performer's offscreen everyday home life (Pickford endorsed this conception in an interview in *Photoplay*, August 1913, 34–35). "Ordinariness" not only created a sense of democratic sameness with the audience, but also mitigated the exoticism associated with theater's separation from normality. Moreover, "personality" itself was a changing concept to which film introduced a new dimension. At one end of the spectrum, deriving from the Latin "persona" denoting a mask or enacted character, personality invoked the public person displaying the typical characteristics by which a performer became widely known: Little Mary, America's Sweetheart. At another, more potently "starry" level, "person" denoted the "actual self" (*Oxford English Dictionary*) or "living soul, self-conscious being" (*Chamber's Twentieth-Century Dictionary*)—the inner self, supposedly hidden from public view.

The two meanings would eventually collide in those "not talked about" areas of private life the film industry was anxious to avoid, the boundaries of which, in the interest of sales, it was constantly pushing back. Early on, IMP allowed innuendo to spice its acquisition of Pickford by linking her image with Owen Moore within a heart-shaped frame, each half of the heart tagged respectively "She's An Imp!" and "He's an Imp!" while *Motion Picture World* speculated in their prerelease comments on Pickford's first IMP film, *Their First Quarrel* (1911, released as *Their First Misunderstanding*): "We would not be at all surprised if there was not something more than acting in the work of Miss Mary Pickford and Mr Moore in the pretty Imp comedy that bears the above title. The loves, jealousies, quarrel and make-up of the two newly-weds in the story are so perfectly portrayed that one cannot help feeling it is all real" (31 December 1910, 1540). However, initially the development of the discourse of personality largely steered clear of Pickford's romantic life. Although from 1915 onward interviews and feature articles begin to elaborate the details of her early childhood, theatrical career, and entry into filmmaking, these pieces remain respectfully distant and are often mediated by jolly interventions from Pickford's mother and siblings.

If Pickford's retreat to the anonymity of Biograph and the paternal shelter first of Griffith, then of the high-toned Belasco, and finally of Famous Players' protective Zukor held off the news media's increasing identification of personality with private life, there was little she could do about the intimate probe of the camera. Lacking spoken dialogue and verbal narration, the material conditions of silent film performance foregrounded the camera's relation to the performer's body as source of narrative intelligibility—in "the appeal of a glance . . . the crook of an arm . . . the twist of a smile" (Gordon Gassaway, *Motion Picture Magazine*, September 1915). Although in the theater the actor's body was subject to rigorous training, its collusion with cinematography made the least gesture a conduit to the fluid indeterminacy of self. In 1913, *Motion Picture World* urged its readers to go to see Miss Pickford in *Caprice*: "Mercy is a child of moods—we laugh with her, and as suddenly check ourselves as we see the cloud pass over her face. . . . It seems as if the heartstrings are under the influence of a hair-trigger control, and there is no foretelling a moment in advance on which side of the emotions the strain will lie" (15 November 1913, 718).

As the discourse of film acting merged into a discourse of personality, a cinematization of the performer took place, suggesting a symbiosis between mutable girl-child and cinema's power to capture the transient and liminal aspects of performing. Bringing to the screen "eyes that speak and light up in color and shade with her every emotion" (*St. Louis Globe Democrat*, 20 August 1916), Pickford's girl reveals "not one side but any number of moods and depths as well as surface emotions" (*Ohio State Journal*, 27 June 1915). At the same time, the struggle to reconcile personality with artistry clarified the distinction between theatrical and film stardom. The question was less whether the film star is "acting" or simply "being" than how the performer's body and feelings, interacting with cinematography, become revelatory instruments. As the British *Bioscope* argued, "Mary Pickford's is an art which is a part of herself. . . . Her art is herself, her only method to be just what she feels at the moment *according to the part"* (14 May 1914, 753; my emphasis). Conceptions of the film actor as an "artist's pallet [*sic*]" (*Motion Pictures*, September 1915) or "veritable Shakespeare's pen in human form" (*Motion Pictures*, May 1918) integrate the performer into the cinematic apparatus, dissolving the barrier between life and art. Thus Homer Dunne, observing Pickford at a charity event, suddenly sees her cinematic power: "It was while she was dancing that I saw a flash of the Mary Pickford with whom the public is so well acquainted. With a sudden sweeping swing of the arm and a roguish toss of the head, she removed her hat . . . in that instant the scene before me faded and there was a cutback to, say, *Fanchon the Cricket.*" Thus "the real Mary Pickford gliding at intervals before . . . [his] eyes" dissolves into "her phantom prototype, elusive and tantalizing, fluttering before . . . [his] mental vision" (*Motion Picture Magazine*, January 1916). In the *New York Review* an imaginary Pickford declares: "I am the delicate Feminism of Picturedom. The art seems to have culminated in me" (28 November 1914).

This attempt to define a cinematic mode of perception released through film stardom suggests a new form of performer-cinema-audience relationship—initially described in theatrical terms as "getting over." But early in the Pickford discourse, the *Minneapolis Journal* intuited a force that leaves the screen, compensating for the lack of theater's living presence: "There is a vivid spontaneity in her every move . . . which seems almost to bridge the gap between real drama and its pictured counterfeit" (11 November 1913). If cinema re-creates the actor's being as star personality, the personality reaches into the being of picturegoers: "We picture-patrons sit by and indulge our willing and elastic feelings in all the various pulsings of joy, sorrow, inquiry, fear, disappointment and expectancy while she pours them out to us thru that will-o'-the-wispy, camera-invented medium—her intangible personality" (Clara Louise Leslie, fan, writing to *Motion Pictures*, May 1918).

Thus the actor's bodily absence, her mechanical reproduction, and acting itself are no barrier between performer and audience. Their relationship is perceived as intersubjective, initiated by "a personality . . . that gripped the heart . . . reach[ing] out from the screens of a million picture theaters in every land on the globe" (*New York Dramatic Mirror*, March 1913). Through her film performances Pickford "worked her way into the hearts of her audience" (*San Francisco Post*, 13 September 1915), registering "intimate personal contact with every member" (*Cincinnati Star Times*, 17 November 1916). In 1919 the British *Pictures and the Picturegoer* asked retrospectively, "How it is that this slight little fair-haired girl has thus crept into the heart of the world?" (14 June 1919, 595). This emotional penetration produced an empathic response from audiences, men and women. Fredrick Wallace wrote in *Motion Pictures*, "I am a cold, calculating man . . . and as unemotional as a turnip (naturally), but when Mary Pickford smiles I sit in and grin into the dark like a Hindoo idol . . . and when she weeps—well . . . it's all I can do to keep from . . . wading right into whomever made her cry" (July 1916). Such commentary points to a cathexis between screen bodies and embodied viewers. The extra-cinematic power of this relationship became a cause for discussion when Pickford found she could no longer go shopping or travel in public without attracting a crowd.

Such visible demonstrations of public fascination suggested that the cinema was insinuating itself into everyday emotional and perceptual experience. Terms such as "magic," "hypnosis," "fascination," and "magnetism" are invoked to explain a new kind of "power" at work, extraordinary because invested in the figure of a girl. Thus the *New York Review*'s "Kindly Kritic" records Pickford's visit to a Broadway performance: "Mary Pickford sat in a box. Not all the King's horses and all the King's men of a typical first night could drag attention from her. It was wonderful to behold—this sure, unerring power to have and to hold. . . . EVERYBODY looked in Mary's direction—continued to look, fascinated—a species of hypnotism, drawn to the slip of a girlie by the marvelous power of Personality" (11 September 1915).

In the mid- to late 1910s, the Pickford commentary moved toward the auratic. As the *Ohio State Journal* noted, "Fans recognized stars long before the general critical press . . . but in course of time we all come to the shrine" (27 June 1915). Such perception structures the opening of many accounts of meeting Pickford, staging the moment of revelation and tone of veneration associated with stardom as well as a common narrative device for later star vehicles: "The spot where all these people wanted to stand was in the center of the room near a small table—a table on which stood a little golden-haired girl, who smiled and nodded brightly, and shook hands with as many as could fight their way up within hand-shaking distance. . . . The little girl on the table was Mary Pickford" (*St. Louis Globe Democrat*, 12 October 1916).

If the auratic suggests the mystery of personhood at the heart of stardom, the distinction between British and American conceptions of personality and acting articulated this differently. The shift from person as mask to "actual self" recorded in the *Oxford English Dictionary* maintains a distinction between outer role and inner being that persists in British culture's investment in "visible" acting. Play-acting, even of the "do-nothing kind," maintains a division between private and public, personal life and social role, that is vital to a culture embedded in social differences even as democratization was eroding them (see Gledhill *Reframing*). But American film stardom cuts

SOME REMARKABLE MARY PICKFORD
EXPRESSIONS AND MAKE-UP.

A study in happiness.
The Rich Little Girl.

A study in dirt.
The Slum Child.

A study in pity.
The Ragamuffin.

A study in severity.
The Schoolmistress.

Pickford demonstrates visible acting for her British commissioned pamphlet *How to Act for the Screen* (1919).

across the relationship between acted and "actual self," suggesting the American *Chambers's* integrated definition of "person" as "living soul, self-conscious being," seemingly accessible through film. If, for British culture, "visible acting" represents a powerful sociocultural value against which native would-be film stars would always struggle, Pickford's American stardom suggests the elision of performance and self that would underpin the Method. This is not to suggest that British audiences and reviewers did not fully embrace Pickford's star performances and Hollywood stardom in general. On the contrary, it is rather that explanations of her appeal are cast differently, veering away from the naturalism of personality to the thrill of performance. It was a London publisher that commissioned Pickford in 1919 to write a booklet, *How to Act for the Screen.*

Similarly, when the *New York Review* seeks to record the auratic experience offered by Pickford's girl-child, she pronounces directly from the page, a missionary voice enveloping readers: "I am the spirit of youth. . . . I move, like a Fairy of Childhood's Wonderland, across the white screen of the Universe. The very azure skies are not too far reaching for my silent drama" (28 November 1914). In contrast, British fanzine writers resorted to the storytelling voice, emphasizing the paradoxical combination of distance and intimacy in the auratic. One fictional story published in *Pictures and the Picturegoer*, entitled "She," is about a wimpish young man who one night is transformed: "I went to the pictures last night, and I saw—Her." Intrigued, the narrator accompanies his friend and is himself overcome: "A single figure occupied the screen, a figure of a girl. . . . Of the dignity and grace of her beauty I can and will say nothing, only this—a feeling of rest stole over me. . . . It was a glimpse of Paradise. . . . There she stood for a moment, and I will swear she nodded to Robbie and smiled. And her smile . . . remains with me yet" (7–14 April 1917, 37–38). In "Through Mary," a dour Scots minister, inspecting the evils of the picture-house, is converted to the movies: "Gradually an indefinable 'something' in the character of the heroine . . . caught and held his attention. Then the greatness of her acting, the wonder of her beauty, kept him enthralled. He was carried out of himself" (*Pictures and the Picturegoer*, 27 October–3 November 1917, 463).

★★★★★ Conclusion: Star Power

What, in the end, are we to make of the fact that the power of this new form of intersubjectivity is manifested through the figure of a girl-child? Arguably the mutability of Pickford's girl-child and the range of evanescent emotions it released meant she was never perceived merely as

"In the course of time we all come to the shrine." Auratic Pickford photographed by Baron Adolph De Meyer, *Vanity Fair* (1920).

child. Rather, the childlike generosity of her open collaboration with the camera promised intimate induction into experience significant to the adult. As already noted, emphasis in the Pickford discourse on "wistfulness" tapped into an undertow of sadness often remarked in her eyes and voice. This could be read back, as she frequently suggested herself, to her own loss of childhood. But to some commentators, her girl-child's transparent muta-bility of feeling hooked individuals into a broader sense of universal con-nection. The auratic tone of many responses suggests film stardom's role in filling the gap that Peter Brooks, writing about melodrama, argues marks the shift in Western society from a religion-based and hierarchal social order to the individual at its imaginary center.[10] A frequent term in Pickford discourse, "charm," may be devalued now, but its reiteration throughout the 1910s—"you are charmed with Little Mary, that's what is the matter" (*St. Louis Globe Democrat*, 20 August 1916)—suggests a sense of uncanniness in the star-viewer contact. Thus Alice Coon Brown noted that "in everything that she does there is the strange, unexplainable eerie quality" (*Ohio State Journal*, 21 June 1915). Peter Grindley Smith admits to "strange emotions . . . at the sight of Mary mothering an army of orphaned little ones" (*Photoplay*, January 1918). If the intersubjective relationship offered by stardom activates the liminality of personality, registration of the uncanny suggests encounter with the otherness at the center of selfhood that could be transformative. In this sense, following Brooks's account of melodramatic morality, the sacral dimension of stardom modernized morality in terms of the ethics of personality and personal relationships. The storyteller's overwhelming encounter with "She" arises from feeling that "here was one who knew life, and appreciated its difficulties as few have done . . . and had strength to spare for the support of her weaker brethren" (*Pictures and the Picturegoer*, 7–14 May 1917, 37–38), while the *New York Review*'s enshrined Pickford intones a veritable sermon: "I am all that is good and clean and innocent and wholesome in the fine art of Making Others Happy. . . . I bring to the darkness of side streets and the melancholy of desolate hearts and the bitter byways of Less Fortunate, a sudden majesty of peace that passes all understanding" (28 November 1914).

The shift from church to film stardom as source of ethical enlightenment is dramatized in the story of the Scots minister's conversion: "I have learned more in half an hour than the kirk has taught me in forehty [*sic*] years." His conversion is itself a melodramatic sign of the power of a new form of cinematized virtue: "Ah, he thought, surely a girl like that wields a power that kings might envy" (*Pictures and the Picturegoer*, 27 October–2 November 1917, 463).

The central values embodied in writings about Pickford's Girl are Beauty and Love, for which writers on both sides of the Atlantic felt the early twentieth century was starving. The Scots minister's "ugly cult of Bitterness was flung aside, forgotten, and for the first time he realised that a love of the Beautiful is necessary to man's welfare" (*Pictures and the Picturegoer*, 27 October–3 November 1917, 463). But it is perhaps the strength and novelty of the intersubjective relationship materialized in film stardom that centers Love at the heart of Pickford's stardom, amalgamating her offscreen activities—in particular her children's' charity work, public appearances, and later campaigning on behalf of overseas soldiers—with her films. Love is understood as a kind of practical empathy. Answering the question "Why

Do We Love Mary Pickford?" a fan writes in *Motion Pictures* that "most of all we love Mary Pickford because she loves us. We know she loves us because she seems to love everything around her. Her pulse beats in unison with the whole world" (May 1918). To Julian Johnson's euphoric invocation of Pickford that opens this chapter, Delight Evans replies: "What can I say? But one does not understand Mary Pickford. One loves her" (*Photoplay*, July 1918, 111).

These are difficult values to articulate in the twenty-first century, and at the time skeptical, satirical voices interrupted the adulation. However, the construction of the world's sweetheart demonstrates the formation of a cultural imaginary capable of recognizing loss and pain as a stimulus to renewed hope and interpersonal contact.

NOTES

I want to thank Jennifer Bean for her work as a patient and encouraging editor and in particular for her productive suggestions for restructuring the essay's different concerns.

1. In fact her father had already abandoned the family, and Mary was eight at her stage debut (Whitfield 11–12).

2. Most newspaper and some trade sources cited in this chapter were accessed in the Robinson Locke Scrapbooks housed in the New York Public Library, Performing Arts section. Scrapbook cuttings excise page numbers and in some cases are unattributed and/or undated. Any archival citation missing page numbers, dates, or source may be assumed to be from the Robinson Locke Scrapbooks.

3. Majestic announced Pickford's appearance on the front cover of the *New York Dramatic Mirror*.

4. Maude Adams was a beloved American actress for whom J. M. Barrie wrote the role of Peter Pan.

5. Figures were hyped since each coupon sent in counted as ten votes for first choice and five for second choice, thereby inflating the appearance of mass popularity.

6. It appears that Famous Players tested response by trade-showing the film in England before the American release on 1 March 1914. *Bioscope* reviewed it on 27 November 1913 (908) as did *Picturegoer* on 27 December 1913 (367), both warmly recommending it as a Christmas film and noting its release date as 1 December 1914.

7. The *New York Review* declared Pickford to be a "story book girl come to life" (11 September 1915). See also Wullschlager.

8. See *Photoplay*, "The Charm of Wistfulness" (August 1913, 35), and Alan Dale's interview, which notes her pensiveness three times (*Pittsburgh Leader*, 27 April 1914). In July 1918, *Photoplay* commented that Pickford has "the saddest eyes in the world" (111).

9. See Brooks. Eileen Whitfield suggests the impact of Pickford's early appearances in stage melodrama on the star's own outlook and later choice of film material (23–24).

10. See also Dyer "*Star.*"

3 ★★★★★★★★★★★★

Lillian Gish
Clean, and White, and Pure as the Lily

KRISTEN HATCH

In the summer of 1912, eighteen-year-old Lillian Gish wrote to her friend, Nell Becker: "We are going . . . to New York in a few weeks as mother has rooms engaged. I don't know what we are going to do when we get there. Dorothy [Lillian's younger sister] wants to pose for moving pictures, so watch the billboards" (Gish, letter to Nell Becker, undated, 1912).[1] Once the family reached New York, Lillian and Dorothy renewed their acquaintance with an old friend, Mary Pickford, whom they had met years earlier during their childhoods as itinerant stage actors. Pickford offered them an introduction to her director, D. W. Griffith, and later that summer the sisters starred in their first film, *An Unseen Enemy* (1912).

Lillian Gish, "The Lily Maid of the Cinema," 1919.

Despite the fact that she appeared in over thirty films in 1912 and 1913, Gish did not become a star through her work with the Biograph Company, which was the last of the film production companies to publicize its performers. Although fans wrote to *Motion Picture Story Magazine* clamoring to know the names of the actors who appeared in such films as *The Musketeers of Pig Alley* (1912) and *The Lady and the Mouse* (1913), both of which featured Gish, the magazine's "Answer Man" sternly scolded readers that questions about Biograph players would remain unanswered in accordance with the company's policy of keeping its actors anonymous. However, in May 1913, the same magazine announced the "joyful news" that Biograph had finally relented and agreed to share personal information about the actors who appeared in Biograph films ("Greenroom Jottings," May 1913, 166). The next month, *Motion Picture* readers were informed that Dorothy and Lillian Gish had starred in *An Unseen Enemy*, and in July, Lillian's photograph appeared in the magazine's Gallery of Picture Players, followed by Dorothy's appearance there in the August issue. After Gish left Biograph for the Mutual Film Company in 1913, she began to appear more prominently in film publicity. In August 1914 she was featured in an article in *Motion Picture Magazine*, and in December of that year she and Dorothy both appeared on the cover of *Photoplay*. However, it was not until the release of *The Birth of a Nation* in 1915 that Gish began to gain widespread recognition. Some journalists erroneously described this as her first film, though most remembered her as having been among the Biograph "pioneers." Readers of *Motion Picture Magazine* voted her performance in *Birth* as one of the year's best, though she ranked far behind Mae Marsh, whose performance in the same film received much more acclaim.

While Griffith devoted himself to directing the epic *Intolerance* (1916), in which she would play a small but pivotal role as the Eternal Mother, Gish appeared in a number of feature-length films that demonstrated her range as a performer. In *Daphne and the Pirate* (1916), for instance, she was a plucky French girl who manages to fight off the band of pirates that has kidnapped her en route to New Orleans, while in *Sold for Marriage* (1916), she played a Russian immigrant nearly forced into marriage with an older, wealthy man. By 1917, Griffith's leading actresses—Mary Pickford, Blanche Sweet, and Mae Marsh—had signed lucrative contracts with other production companies. However, Gish remained with Griffith for the remainder of the decade, assuming the ingénue roles that once would have gone to her more famous co-stars. In 1918, with her appearance in Griffith's *Hearts of the World* (1918), Gish emerged as a fully established star. That year she appeared in a Liberty Loan appeal directed by Griffith, as well as two other

Lillian Gish graces the cover of *Photoplay Magazine*, November 1919. From the author's collection.

Griffith films, *The Great Love* (1918) and *The Greatest Thing in Life* (1918). That year, her salary tripled, from $500 to $1,500 a week, and in 1919 her performances in *Broken Blossoms* and *True Heart Susie* secured her position as one of the screen's leading tragediennes (Affron 117).

Despite this critical success, Gish's future was uncertain. She wrote to Nell Becker: "I . . . don't know what I am going to do next. This business is in such a queer state now that no one seems to know where they are or what they are doing" (Gish, undated letter, 1919). That year, Griffith assigned her to direct *Remodeling Her Husband* (1920)—Gish's only foray into directing—and the *Toledo Times* announced that she would appear onstage in a "Griffith playlet," although this appears not to have been the case. One reviewer summed up the uncertain status of Gish's stardom:

> Miss Gish is a screen pioneer, commencing her career with Mary Pickford, Mabel Normand, and the Talmadges, yet she has never become definitely established in a place of public favor. We can estimate the popularity of Gloria Swanson, of Mary Pickford, of Norma Talmadge and Pola Negri, almost to the decimal point. But Miss Gish's remains a problem. She has given great performances in great pictures, and yet curiously we regard each new endeavor as a test of her. She appears as a wraith hovering on the borderland between oblivion and reality, a mystical creation whose power hypnotizes us momentarily and then leaves us wondering if it is not an illusion.
>
> (James R. Quirk, "What Does the Future Hold for Lillian Gish?" *Photoplay* 1919)[2]

To a certain extent, the "problem" of Gish's stardom stemmed from her ongoing association with Griffith; she was a "Griffith girl," which prompted a number of commentators to attribute her success to his direction. It may also be that Gish represented a different type of star than did Pickford, Negri, or the Talmadge sisters. While their stardom rested, to some extent, on the development of a respective character type that they enacted from one film to the next, Gish was celebrated for her ability to make each of her characters appear wholly unique. More important, Gish's offscreen persona destabilized the very ideology that informed her films with Griffith. In her most celebrated screen roles Gish embodied a civilized womanliness, driven by maternal desire and dependent on the protection of men. Offscreen, however, her persona reflected a very different image of modern femininity. Within the pages of such magazines as *Photoplay* and *Motion Picture*, Gish appeared to be ambitious and independent. These two aspects of her stardom were not merely contradictory; her star persona in fact undermined the ideological work of the films, making them seem outmoded while helping to forge a new vision of modern womanhood.

★★★★★ The Eternal Mother

It should come as no surprise that Gish came to national attention through her role as Elsie Stoneman in Griffith's *The Birth of a Nation* in 1915. The film was undoubtedly the most talked-about film of the decade, both for its spectacular, epic-style grandeur—the four-hour film was celebrated as the first to be shown in the White House—and for its virulent racism, which inspired censorship and protests in several major cities. Today, the racist logic that supports the film's celebration of the Ku Klux Klan is often attributed either to Griffith's southern upbringing or to the rabid bigotry of the film's source novel, Thomas Dixon's *The Clansman*. In fact, the film relies on an ideology that was widely embraced by northerners and southerners alike, one that was prominent in each of the major Griffith films in which Gish appeared during this decade.

The most definitive account of this political and popular ideology appears in Gail Bederman's *Manliness and Civilization*. Bederman argues that nineteenth-century discourse was dominated by an ideology of "millennial Darwinism," which adapted Darwin's theory of evolution to the Protestant belief that the eradication of sin would usher in a millennium of Christ's rule on earth, and the concomitant belief that European Americans were evolving toward an ideal civilization. Asians and Africans were considered to be primitive and barbaric peoples, evolutionary throwbacks, whereas European American civilization represented the most advanced stage of mankind. Moreover, sexual differentiation was taken to be a sign of advanced civilization. Civilized manliness—defined according to European and American gender norms—was characterized by self-control, firmness of character, and a willingness to protect the weak; womanliness was defined in terms of delicacy, spirituality, and domesticity. Within this logic, these gender norms signaled the racial superiority of European American nations, and manliness—defined as the white man's ability to control his passions by the strength of his character and will—authorized white male authority over women and nonwhite men.

However, Bederman argues, this ideal of manliness conflicted with a new valorization of masculinity in the early twentieth century. Changes in the economy meant that manly self-denial was no longer met with economic reward. Rather, labor in the new corporate economy threatened to lead to neurasthenia, which in men suggested a loss of vitality. Further, white male dominance appeared to be under threat, both from immigrant groups whose working-class existence appeared more virile than that of a predominantly Anglo-Saxon middle class and from women's increasing refusal to remain within the confines of the home. In response to these changes, white men began to embrace *masculinity* rather than valorizing *manliness*. The distinction between the two terms deserves emphasis. Whereas manliness was understood to be the province of white men alone, masculinity was intrinsic to all men by virtue of their sex, and it was associated with the primitive:

aggression, virility, and dominance. Thus white male gender identity came increasingly to be defined in opposition to white femininity, though it remained an explicitly racial concept.[3]

This ideology governs *The Birth of a Nation*. The film suggests that the Civil War was tragic because it pitted white men against white men, leading to the destruction of civilization rather than its advancement. The film also unfolds a historical lesson in which the era of Reconstruction was doomed to failure insofar as it extended civil rights, such as voting, to the primitive African American male who had not evolved sufficiently to appreciate and respect these rights. The film signposts black men's primitive nature in a variety of ways. Among them is his submission to black women; the film is spiced with comic interludes in which a black woman, a faithful servant of the Cameron family, physically dominates black men. Another sign of black men's racial inferiority within the film is his incapacity for self-control, which was understood to be the foundation of democracy. Hence, midway through the film, when the franchise is extended to black men, they stuff the ballot boxes so that the South Carolina House of Representatives is overrun by black politicians. Once in power, rather than fighting to impose order after the chaos of the war and ensure that the streets of Piedmont are safe for women and children, the black legislators instead pass a bill to permit interracial marriage; as they vote on the bill, the men lustfully eye the white women standing in the gallery. Moreover, when Silas Lynch, a mixed-race man, is elected lieutenant governor of the state, he plans on imposing a despotic rule and forcing a white woman (Lillian Gish) into the role of his queen.

According to the film's logic, black political empowerment poses a threat not only to American society but also to the very survival of the white race. And in response to this threat, the civilized white man must draw upon the primitive masculinity that he normally keeps in check through self-control. The white men of both North and South demonstrate their civilized manliness by caring for those understood as weaker. They treat women with delicacy and respect, and even in the battlefield they maintain a sense of fair play. In one sequence, for instance, southern colonel Ben Cameron interrupts the fighting so that he may minister to a northern man who lies dying in the field, and the men of North and South alike applaud his action. Throughout the initial sequences of the film, slavery is represented as a form of benevolent rule; the white men look on with amusement as black men dance and frolic during their dinner break. However, in the immediate postwar era, when law and order are threatened by black male rule, these white men—of North and South alike—discover that they must draw upon their primitive masculinity in order to salvage civilized society. Recalling the practices of their Scottish ancestors, they rally around the ancient symbol of the burning cross and form the Ku Klux Klan. As Klansmen, they adopt an alternate, masculine identity, merciless in their brutality against black men. Yet when their white robes are removed, their manliness is once again restored. In this sense, *The Birth of a Nation* directly addressed anxieties about white masculinity and the politicization of African Americans in the early twentieth century.

Lillian Gish's Elsie Stoneman plays a key role in this drama. She represents white womanhood, jeopardized by black male enfranchisement. More than her personal well-being is threatened when Lynch attempts to force her into marriage. Within the logic of millennial Darwinism, the future of the white race and, presumably, of civilization rests on her ability to bear the children of her chosen mate. As a civilized woman, she is naturally repulsed by the barbarism of Lynch and attracted to the manliness of Ben Cameron, for, according to the eugenicist logic of the time, a child of mixed race would be an aberration. Indeed, as a number of contemporary scholars have noted, the most villainous characters in the film are "mulatto." Elsie is driven not by sexual desire but by maternal instinct, an instinct that is essential to racial progress. Her nurturing of white animals repeatedly signals the purity of her desire. Elsie first appears in the film holding a white cat, which she coos over like a mother. Later, Ben Cameron gives her a gift of a white dove. Elsie kisses the dove's beak, and when Ben moves to kiss Elsie, she coyly scolds him, insisting that he kiss the dove instead.

The emotional highlight of the film comes with a dramatic race to the rescue, when Ben leads an army of Klansmen to rescue Elsie from the clutches of Silas Lynch. Afterward, Elsie and Ben help lead a triumphant parade through the town of Piedmont, where order has once again been restored. Their marriage promises the birth of a nation not just through the reconciliation of North and South, but also because the nation will remain white despite abolition; the threat of barbaric black rule has been overcome, and the promise of white civilization is assured. The film ends with a distilled image of the aspirations of millennial Darwinism. Elsie and Ben sit together on a bluff, imagining a future civilization inhabited only by white men and women, presumably the descendants of Ben and Elsie and the other white couples who have overcome the divisions of war and the threat of black enfranchisement. In their vision, we see Christ descend to earth, his coming ushered in by the evolution of an ideal, white civilization.

Gish consistently played a similar role in her films with Griffith, although their later collaborations would not argue for white supremacy in such an explicit manner. Indeed, offscreen as well as on, Gish's racial status was a key element of her stardom, signifying not only her beauty but also her breeding and purity, both sexual and racial. Beginning in 1914, publicity for Gish repeatedly described her as "the most beautiful blonde in the world," emphasizing in particular her blue eyes, pale skin, delicate features, and "profusion of long, shining hair, like golden silk" ("The Most Beautiful Blonde," *Montgomery Journal*, 9 January 1916). The emphasis on Gish's whiteness produced a proliferating set of terms, each a variation on what Richard Dyer pinpoints as the "aesthetic-moral equation of light, virtue, and femininity" ("The Colour" 4). Some commentators linked Gish's coloring to a genteel class identity: "Her skin is unusually white; her hair a soft, natural blonde, and her eyes a lovely blue-grey. She uses no rouge. She is all that is refined. A patrician from her head to her heels" (Martha Groves McKelvie, "The Lily of *Hearts of the World*," *Motion Picture*, August 1918, 120). For others, her appearance suggested an almost angelic delicacy: "Lillian Gish is so delicate and so pink and golden in her coloring that the word ethereal seems to fit her more nearly than any other term I have heard applied to her" (Louella O. Parsons, unidentified clipping, *Chicago Herald*, 10 July 1915). And over and over again, her coloring suggested purity: "Neat, blonde curls lined a pure little face, and big eyes, both blue and gray, looked at me. . . . The word that came to my mind as she faced me was just 'Purity.' . . . She reminds you of the lilies she so often carries. She is as clean and white and pure as the lily" (McKelvie 120). Indeed, Gish's name and appearance prompted writers and fans alike to associate her with a lily: "To us, all lilies symbolize purity, and while their white fragility is reminiscent of Lillian Gish, their true-in-heart meaning is even more so" (Apeda, "The Lily-Maid of the Cinema," *Motion Picture*, October 1919, 56).

Gish was the embodiment of the white feminine ideal—defined by delicacy, spirituality, and domesticity—upon which the future of the race purportedly depended. Not surprisingly, her films with Griffith invariably centered on her ability to reproduce, to give birth to a new generation of white children and fulfill her domestic role. Hence in *Intolerance* she plays the Eternal Mother, endlessly rocking the cradle of humanity. In *The Mothering Heart* (1913), the first film to showcase her acting talents, Gish plays a woman who desires only marriage and motherhood (Affron 67). She is introduced in the company of two puppies, one of which has its head stuck in a tin can. She gently removes the can and hugs the puppies to her chest, a gesture that signals her maternal, nurturing instinct. A number of scholars have pointed to the consistency with which Gish was filmed interacting with domestic animals: a duck in *Hearts of the World* (1918), for instance, or a cow in *True Heart Susie* (1919). She dotes on these animals as she would on a child, and this is the purpose of these scenes; they demonstrate a maternal drive that is absent of sexual desire. Indeed, in his homage to Lillian Gish, Edward Wagenknecht marvels that no other actress "could so beautifully have suggested the age-old miracle of the girl become mother" (*Lillian Gish* 18), as though her characters bypassed sexual desire and activities altogether.

However, the miraculous change Wagenknecht identified—from girl to mother—was under threat from changes associated with modern civilization. The nineteenth century had witnessed the gradual weakening of the ideology of separate spheres, whereby women's influence was limited to the home. In the wake of rapid urbanization, the cities appeared overrun with "women adrift"—working-class wage earners who were not tethered to husbands or fathers—as well as with New Women, members of the middle class who pursued college and careers rather than motherhood. As historian Wendy Kline amply demonstrates, the answer to these threats, as to the threats posed by immigration and an increasingly politicized African American public, seemed to lie in the eugenics movement. "By regulating the sexuality of working-class and immigrant women," she writes,

> eugenics would reform the sexual behavior of "women adrift" and limit the procreation of the less "civilized"—that is, nonwhite and working-class races. And by encouraging middle-class white women to return to full-time motherhood, eugenics would both prevent the New Woman from succeeding in her "vain attempts to fill men's places" and ensure that the white race once again would be healthy and prolific.   (Kline 14)

Thus eugenics promised to be a panacea for a variety of perceived threats to white, male hegemony and, by extension, the progress of civilization.[4]

The Birth of a Nation was not alone in positioning Gish as the imperiled ideal of white womanhood within the logic of millennial Darwinism. In film after film, changes associated with modernity threaten her ability to fulfill her role as the "eternal mother." No less than the future of white civilization is taken to be at stake in the hero's ability to make her his wife. While *The Birth of a Nation* overtly addresses white America's anxieties concerning miscegenation, stories in which Gish's characters are threatened by "women adrift" are far more common. In *The Mothering Heart*, a glamorous woman lures Gish's husband away from her, and the couple's infant dies. In *The Lily and the Rose* (1915), Gish plays a girl who has been raised by two spinster aunts and whose husband is seduced by an exotic dancer (Rozsika Dolly). In *Souls Triumphant* (1917), she is a curate's daughter whose husband is seduced by another woman, and their child's life is once again threatened. It is hard to miss the condemnation of the "vamp" figure in these films, of the ilk gloriously personified by Theda Bara in *A Fool There*

Was (1914) (see Studlar in this volume). Insofar as these films structure an opposition between idealized "mothering hearts" and the vamp-like "woman adrift," they preach a moral lesson regarding the dangers of choosing sexual passion over domesticity. The former contributes to degeneracy; the latter ensures that the white race will thrive.

True Heart Susie (1919) exemplifies this narrative. Gish plays Susie, a country girl in love with the boy next door, William Jenkins (Robert Harron). William doesn't have the money to attend college, but Susie is determined to marry an educated man, so she sells her beloved cow and scrimps and saves to pay his tuition anonymously. When William returns from college to assume the role of the town's minister, Susie hopes they will soon be married, but a "jazzy little milliner" from Chicago catches William's eye. Despite his assurances that "men flirt with that kind, but they marry the plain and simple ones," William is seduced by Bettina (Clarine Seymore) and marries her. William quickly recognizes his mistake. Unlike Susie, who is well adapted to domesticity, Bettina is a slovenly housewife and a poor cook. Rather than channeling her energies into nurturing those around her, she pursues the excitement of jazz music, fast cars, and flirtation. One night, she sneaks out of her home to attend a party and loses her key. She pleads with Susie to take her in for the night and to lie to William about where she has been. Susie reluctantly agrees, but Bettina becomes ill as a result of her night out and soon dies, leaving William free to marry Susie.

The threat of spinsterhood and barrenness haunt the narrative. The film is dedicated to unmarried women "and their pitiful hours of waiting for the love that never comes." On the night that William and Bettina become engaged, Susie sits between two spinsters, watching the happy young couple. In this way the film suggests that when men are "caught by the net of paint, powder, and suggestive clothes" of modern women, they leave barren the "true-hearted" women who seek not excitement but domesticity and are consequently more suited to raising future generations. Susie's "mothering heart" is signaled not only by her treatment of her farm animals, but also by her kindness toward Bettina; she nurses her rival through her illness, never betraying her anger to the girl.

Surprisingly, it is not the "jazzy" woman who represents the threat here, but the man who is seduced by her. In fact, the film exhibits a great deal of sympathy for Bettina, hinting that she merely seeks security through marriage, though she finds that she is unwilling to exchange the excitement of her former life for the dullness of her role as a minister's wife. In the words of one reviewer, she is an "unhappy butterfly, oppressed in her inappropriate, sunless home" (unidentified clipping, 1919). It is William

Lillian Gish (far right) in *True Heart Susie* (1919).

who is to blame for Susie's plight. He proves himself to be lacking in both virile masculinity and in manly self-control. The film begins with Susie and William as childhood sweethearts. But William does not have the courage to kiss Susie and consummate their relationship. As their lips are about to meet, he turns instead to carve their initials in a tree in what turns out to be an empty promise of eternal love. Ultimately, however, he succumbs to desire rather than exhibiting self-control when he chooses to marry the flirtatious Bettina instead of the true-hearted Susie.

While immigration, the increasing politicization of African Americans, and shifts in women's public behavior were felt by many as significant challenges to the future of civilized white society, an even greater obstacle emerged with the eruption of World War I. In the words of the *Los Angeles Times*, "Four years of war have accomplished as much as a century of time in obliterating the blonde" ("Good-bye, Golden Locks," 2 August 1919, 2:4). The war posed a threat not only through its brutality and destruction but also because it represented a clash between the civilized nations rather than a march of civilized advancement on more primitive peoples. Gish appeared in several war films—*Hearts of the World* (1918), *The Great Love* (1918), and *The Greatest Thing in Life* (1918)—that, along with her Liberty

Loan appeal, were designed to rouse Americans to arms. In each of these films, Gish represents white femininity imperiled by a corrupt and morally bankrupt white, European masculinity. As the films' titles suggest, the marriage of Gish's characters to the films' respective heroes suggests more than the couple's personal happiness. Their love represents hope for the future of civilization. In *Hearts of the World*, for instance, Gish plays an American girl living in the French countryside on the eve of war. When the boy next door sees her scolding a recalcitrant duck, he is immediately smitten; once again, Gish's nurturing of animals demonstrates that she is suited for marriage and motherhood. The boy and the girl are soon engaged, but their nuptials are interrupted by the war, and the girl puts aside "the wedding clothes she had sewed with white thread and whiter thoughts" (Julian Johnson, "Hearts of the World," *Photoplay*, June 1918, 111). The boy joins the army, and after her town is bombed the girl wanders the battlefield, clutching her wedding veil. Eventually, she stumbles upon the boy who appears to be dead. She lies next to him and, instead of a wedding night, they spend the night in a barren embrace. When she awakens the next morning, the girl finds that the boy is gone. Luckily, however, he survives the war and ultimately rescues the girl from a band of vicious Germans who hold the women and children of their town hostage.

Broken Blossoms (1919) arguably presents an even stronger indictment of war, though its narrative only refers obliquely to World War I. The film tells the story of the Yellow Man (Richard Barthelmess) who travels from China to London in order to "take the glorious message of peace to the barbarous Anglo Saxons, sons of turmoil and strife." But the Yellow Man does not have the strength of will to survive in the London slums; lacking the self-control that is a marker of civilized manliness, he soon slips into opium addiction. His misery is relieved only by the sight of Lucy (Gish), a child of London's Limehouse district. As the intertitles explain, "The Yellow Man watched Lucy often. The beauty which all Limehouse missed smote him to the heart." An illegitimate child raised by an abusive father, Lucy knows nothing but blows. Unlike Gish's other maternal heroines, Lucy's barrenness is prefigured by the fact that she has no kittens or puppies to mother but instead dotes on an inanimate doll, a gift from the Yellow Man, which she clutches to her chest even in death.

The family ideal that motivates the characters' actions in *Hearts of the World* is nowhere in evidence in *Broken Blossoms*. Indeed, when a neighbor warns Lucy never to marry, we are encouraged to share her view of marriage and motherhood as a cause for misery. The woman slaves for five unkempt children and an idle husband, evoking eugenicist fears about the proliferation of the fertile underclass. Moreover, in striking contrast to the adolescent girls Gish played in *A Romance of the Happy Valley* and *True Heart Susie*, girls who eventually put up their braids and lengthen their skirts as they prepare for marriage and motherhood, Lucy does not survive into adulthood. Instead she is beaten to death by her father after he finds her ensconced in the apartments of the Yellow Man.

Broken Blossoms presents a dystopic vision of modern life, of a society drunk on violence. Far from being condemned for his brutality, Burrows is celebrated by cheering crowds as he pounds his opponents in the ring, and his apartment is decorated with publicity photos of various pugilists. Allusions to the war imply a direct relation between the ravages of warfare and the brutish violence of the working classes teeming in the London slums. Significantly, Battling Burrows's boxing matches are performed for the benefit of the men working at a munitions factory, and when his friends rush to the police station to report that he has been shot and killed by the Yellow Man, they interrupt a policeman who is reading reports of the war in the newspaper; the officer comments that the situation is "better than last week—only 40,000 casualties." While the deaths of Lucy, Burrows, and the Yellow Man may pale in comparison to such statistics, their deaths suggest a far more insidious carnage, the inevitable outcome of a society fascinated by the spectacle of violence.

Despite his gentle pacifism, the Yellow Man does not offer a viable alternative to Burrows's brutal masculinity. Just as the mammy's masculinity in *The Birth of a Nation*—her ability to physically dominate black men—demonstrates the inferiority of the black race, so the Yellow Man's femininity implies that gender is not sufficiently differentiated in the Asian race. After Battling Burrows has beaten Lucy, the child wanders into the street and faints in the doorway of the Yellow Man's store. At first he thinks she is a vision produced by his opium-addled mind, but he eventually realizes that she is, indeed, real. He dresses her wounds, gathers the motherless child in his arms, and takes her to his apartment upstairs. There, he drapes her in silk robes and adorns her hair with ribbons. The nature of his adoration of Lucy is ambiguous. Are we to understand his interest in the child as platonic? Or does he feel sexual desire for the exquisite young girl enthroned on his bed? According to one critic, "He cares for the wounded child with the tenderness of a lover and the lack of desire for recompense of a mother" (Hazel Simpson Naylor, "Across the Silversheet," *Motion Picture*, August 1919, 66). In other words, his sexual desire does not signal masculine virility; rather, he assumes a feminine, maternal position in relation to the child. Indeed, his caresses resemble those that Lucy lavishes on her doll. While Lucy sleeps, the Yellow Man rubs her

Lillian Gish in *Broken Blossoms* (1919).

inanimate hand against his cheek in a manner that directly mirrors Lucy's rubbing her cheek against the hand of the doll he gave her.

Despite the Yellow Man's gentleness and restraint, his relationship with Lucy suggests perversion rather than manly self-control; in the words of one reviewer, his is "a love so pure as to be wholly unnatural and inconsistent" ("Broken Blossoms," *Variety*, 16 May 1919). Indeed, his gift of the doll stands as a substitute for the child the couple will never bear. Likewise, the ribbons with which he adorns Lucy's hair are akin to the ribbon her mother left for her, "for yer weddin,'" suggesting that theirs is a perverse sort of marriage. There are two moments in the film when it appears as though the Yellow Man will be overcome by sexual desire, as though he were about to kiss the child. First, when Lucy initially faints in his store, he leans toward her, drinking in her scent. Lucy draws back in confusion and he moves away. Later, when she lies upstairs in his bed, his face looms over her in a menacing close-up—a shot that is echoed later when Burrows looms over Lucy as she cowers in the Yellow Man's bed—and Lucy shrinks back in fear. One reviewer described this scene as one of the highlights of the film; Barthelmess "touched on one period of real greatness when he stood yearning over the couch of the sleeping child. All the starved longing of the world was in his glance" (Naylor 111). Rather than kissing the child's lips, however, the Yellow Man bends his head to kiss the sleeve of her dress, and the titles assure us, "His love remains a pure and holy thing—even his worst foe would say this." Ultimately his love is more spiritual, and feminine, than sexual.

In contrast to the Yellow Man's femininity, Battling Burrows embodies primitive masculinity, conspicuously lacking even a hint of civilized self-control. Indeed, Lucy's working-class father poses a far greater threat to white womanhood than the Chinese immigrant does. This irony is highlighted through Griffith's trademark cross-cutting. At the moment when Lucy seems most in danger from the Yellow Man, when he leans in as if to kiss her, the film cuts to Burrows's exhibition fight at the munitions factory. As in *The Birth of a Nation*, the fragile embodiment of white femininity is under sexual threat. However, the men who might ride to her rescue are preoccupied by Burrows's fight. Rather than recognizing that a white girl is in danger, they remain distracted by the violent entertainment. It is only after the danger has passed and the Yellow Man has overcome his desire that the crowd of men rushes to her rescue. However, these men are less interested in preserving her chastity than they are in the spectacle of more violence, egging Burrows on in his rage at discovering his daughter in the bed of a Chinese immigrant. A second sequence similarly intercuts between the endangered Lucy and her would-be rescuer. This time Lucy is threatened by her father. As she pleads for her life, he savagely beats her. The Yellow Man rushes to her rescue, the film cutting between his race to save her and Burrows's beating. However, whereas the Klan successfully saved Elsie from the clutches of Silas Lynch, the Yellow Man arrives too late to rescue Lucy.

In this vision of endangered white girlhood, neither the degenerate white man nor the effeminate Asian man can effect her rescue, though white men in the audience are invited to imagine themselves in the role of rescuer. The film offers one glimpse of hope in the figure of the virile American sailors we see in the film's opening sequence (Koshy 86). Unlike the Asian man, they are not weak and pacifist; they playfully fight among themselves. But neither are they bellicose like Battling Burrows; theirs is a good-natured scrap. Publicity for the film, too, offered an alternative vision of white male heroism. One publicity story describes cameraman Billy Bitzer's response to Burrows's beating of Lucy: "'Say, if that brute doesn't stop hurting that girl,' he remonstrated, 'I'm coming down there and beat him up!'" (Frederick James Smith, "The Lyric Lady," *Motion Picture Classic*, September 1919, 88). Thus readers were offered extradiegetic assurance that there are white men in America who are both virile and chivalric enough to protect white womanhood.

In *Broken Blossoms*, Lillian Gish enacts the role of a "white flower" that somehow blooms in the muck of London's slums. However, the film demonstrates that, without the self-control of civilized manliness and the protection of virile men, this flower will wither and die. No less than the future of civilization rests on her characters' ability to fulfill their maternal role; they must survive and raise future generations of equally white and virtuous children if the race is to thrive. While Gish's characters are as unchanging and dependable as time itself—as represented by Gish's role as the Eternal Mother, endlessly rocking the cradle in *Intolerance*—their progeny must rely on the manliness and masculinity of the civilized white man, whose virility and self-control are often put to the test. In these films Gish is the embodiment of an ideal of white womanhood: delicate, domestic, virtuous. And the physical qualities associated with her whiteness—her petite frame and features, her pale skin and light hair—reinforce this understanding of ideal femininity and link it directly to her body.

★★★★★ A Pale, Perfumeless Lily

Gish herself appears to have subscribed to this ideal of domestic femininity. In her letters to Becker, she describes the transformative effects of marriage on her former co-star, Mae Marsh: "Did you know Mae Marsh was married—to a very nice young man—it has changed her so much, she is so sweet and kind to everyone and she is going to have a little baby in time I think" (Gish, undated letter, 1919). In 1912, when Gish was performing in a Broadway play, Becker was newly married and pregnant with her first child. Gish's assessment of their respective lives clearly demonstrates that she understood and shared in the exaltation of motherhood that characterized her films: "Your little sister will be a real actress yet if you don't watch her. It is a wonderful art, Nell. But you, dear, think how much higher up you are than I—soon to have the most wonderful moment of your life. Think of it little woman, what you are soon to become. It is almost too sacred to write about" (Gish, 8 November 1912). For Gish, the "sacredness" of her friend's pending motherhood casts a pall on stage life. In one particularly poignant passage, Gish describes breaking into tears in response to one of Becker's letters: "I was reading in my dressing room and I happened to glance up at a mirror and there I sat all false with paint and cosmetics covering my face and it came to me what a distance it was from my life to yours" (Gish, undated letter, 1913). Gish assured Becker that she would not succumb to the artificiality of the stage: "I will come back to you as good and clean as I ever was. That life [of the theater] can be a small part of me—but I a part of it—never" (Gish, undated letter, 1912).

Clearly, Gish shared the belief that motherhood was sacred and that the life of an actress was potentially corrupting due to its artificiality. Ironically, she pursued an acting career because, as she explained to Becker, this was her only avenue to making a home for herself and her family. She and her mother and sister were poor, having been deserted by her alcoholic father. Again, writing to Becker, Gish explains, "I would like to make money enough to give D[orothy] a good education and build a house so we can have a home" (Gish, undated letter, 1912). For a young woman with a high school education, the alternatives to acting were hardly appealing. As a teenager, Gish had worked in a candy store, where she put in fourteen hour days behind a cash register, a stultifying existence judging by her letters. She was fortunate to land even a small role in a prestigious stage production under the direction of famed impresario David Belasco. However, the promise of a steady income and the possibility of living with her mother and sister trumped her artistic aspirations, and she broke her contract in order to join the Biograph Company in California: "As I am offered more money with the Biograph and the three of us can be together, I think it is better for me to play sick here and go out there" (Gish, undated letter, 1913).

Not surprisingly, these details were omitted from the many newspaper and magazine stories about Gish that were published during the teens. Rather than attributing Gish's turn to film acting to economic need, which might expose the inadequacies of a gender system predicated on women's economic dependence on men, publicity for Gish suggested that her peripatetic childhood and lack of formal education were the attributes of a glamorous childhood, not an impoverished one. Articles about Gish sidestep the fact that Lillian was often separated from her mother and sister while touring by suggesting that her labor was a sign of prestige and privilege: "Lillian . . . became a pupil in a Springfield dancing school. Almost immediately she was engaged as one of the fairy dancers with Sarah Bernhardt, then making one of her American tours, lasting two seasons" (unidentified clipping). The schools she attended were described variously as finishing schools or convents, and, according to her publicity, upon graduation she "started east to finish her dancing lessons in New York" rather than seek employment (unidentified clipping).

Notwithstanding such attempts to recuperate her biography, Gish's stardom destabilized the ideology of her films in subtle ways. It was and continues to be a convention of star publicity to expose the "reality" behind the stars' screen personae, to reveal to readers information that they could not derive through the stars' screen performances alone. As Richard deCordova argues, "With the emergence of the star [in 1913 and 1914], the question of the player's existence outside his or her work in film became the primary focus of discourse. The private lives of the players were constituted as a site of knowledge and truth" (98). If filmgoers perceived one Lillian Gish—the "old-fashioned bit of sampler embroidery"—readers of popular periodicals were privileged to know what she really thought of these roles: "I want to play real women—not impossible heroines or namby-pamby girls" (Julian Johnson, "The Shadow Stage," *Photoplay*, February 1919, 68; Julian Johnson, "The Real Lillian Gish," *Photoplay*, August 1918, 24). If Griffith's films centered on the preservation of white, maternal femininity against the threats of modern life, Gish's star image celebrated an image of modern womanhood that was not defined by its relation to home and family.

In contrast to the simplicity of the characters she portrayed on screen, Gish was described as sophisticated and ambitious. While her characters were often naïve and full of home-spun wisdom, Gish was fiercely intelligent, an "omnivorous reader," a "'lily maid of Astolat' who reasons like a modern college professor!" (Smith 16). Her characters often represented the ideal of country life, living by the philosophy that "New York is a terrible place, no farms or nothing," as Jennie declares in *A Romance of the Happy Valley*. In contradistinction, Gish was touted as "a smartly tailored New York girl type" who found the slow pace of California "deadening to ambition" (Smith 88). And her publicity often played on this contrast between her old-fashioned screen image and her offscreen status as the embodiment of modern womanhood: "Lillian Gish has always stood alone in the world of the cinema—a gentle figure of idylism [*sic*], a maid of poetic elusiveness. But she is infinitely more than all this, for she not only thinks intelligently, but her view is at once alert, advanced, and even radical" (Smith 16).

Often, publicity for Gish evoked the technology that defined the modern age, with Gish in the role of scientist or industrialist. Her characterizations of the "sweet, demure" creatures she played on the screen were inspired not by a feminine instinct for emotion but by intelligent analysis:

An electrician watching her work one day suddenly exclaimed, "That girl ain't an actress—she's a mechanic." He could give no explanation for his observation aside from a mumbled, "She knows her stuff." Examining Miss Gish's characterizations you find that she achieves greatness of effect through a single phase of emotion—namely hysteria. And she knows precisely the method of it. "It is expressed by the arm from the elbow to the fingers," she says scientifically, "and depends entirely on rhythm—the gradual quickening of movement up to the point desired."

(James R. Quirk, "What Does the Future
Hold for Lillian Gish?" *Photoplay* 1919)

Likewise, while she embodied domestic femininity on screen, Gish would never marry nor bear children. She explained to one interviewer why she intended to remain unmarried: "Marriage is a business. A woman cannot combine a career and marriage. . . . Marriage requires the same concentration, undivided energy, and skill that is demanded to successfully manufacture automobiles or steam yachts" (Smith 16). Gish's rhetoric—suggesting that a woman's role in marriage is the domestic equivalent of manufacturing modern machines—echoes the ideology of domestic femininity by suggesting an equivalence between women's role in the home and men's in the modern world of manufacturing, only to reject marriage in favor of a career.

To a certain degree, female stardom is by definition emblematic of modern womanhood simply by virtue of the stars' visibility. Gish was widely celebrated as "the most beautiful blonde in the world" and publicity capitalized on her status as an object for public consumption and a tool for advertising commodities, especially to women. Triangle, for instance, offered photographs and promotional tips designed to capitalize on her beauty. In promoting *A House Built upon Sand* (1916), in which Gish plays a society girl transplanted to a factory town where she recognizes the emptiness of her former life, Triangle proclaimed: "The first few reels comprise a real fashion show. Lillian Gish appears in some beautiful gowns and further adds to the ornamental value of the picture by giving a graceful exhibition dance" ("The House Built Upon Sand," *New York Telegraph*, 24 December 1916). Likewise, for *Diane of the Follies*, in which Gish played a frivolous showgirl, exhibitors were advised to trumpet the cost of the gowns she wore in the film. "There are some excellent photographs to be obtained of Miss Gish in many of the gowns worn in the picture. A lobby display made up from them would prove a strong magnet for women patrons" ("Flashes through Scenes of Interesting Tale," *The Triangle*, 2 September 1916). Far from positioning the fashionable, exhibitionist woman as a danger to the continuing progress of civilization, exhibitors appealed to women's presumed penchant for self-display, promoting fashion as a means for women to participate in modern life.

This is not to say that publicity for Gish entirely rejected the ideology of domestic womanhood that characterized her film roles. To the contrary, many stories about Gish attempted to resolve the tension between this vision of modern womanhood and the celebration of a more traditional femininity found in her films. Although Lillian Gish remained unmarried, interviews often positioned her within a family context, with Mrs. Gish in the role of the ideal mother. And Gish's work as a screen actress was reconfigured as woman's work, providing uplift on a grand scale. One interview with Mrs. Gish, for instance, quotes her explaining, "My girls believe in rather a close corporation so far as family life is concerned, but they do derive unlimited pleasure from the realization that they are helping to lighten the burdens of humanity by their artistry on the screen" (Billy Leyser, unidentified clipping). Although Gish did not enjoy the beneficent protection of a husband or father, magazine and newspaper stories produced the impression that D. W. Griffith had stepped into the role of paternal protector of his star.[5]

In this sense, Gish embodies the contradiction that underlies female stardom during this period. While mainstream American culture may have idealized female domesticity, women on the screen were by definition inhabiting a realm beyond the domestic sphere. Rather than representing heterosexual romance that would result in the perpetuation of the American family, they invited a different sort of love, a sterile adoration. James Branch Cabell captured the phenomenon in his controversial 1919 novel, *Jurgen*, which includes a character modeled on Gish. She is Queen Helen, a paragon of beauty who lives in the city of Pseudopolis and represents all women men have loved in vain. The novel's protagonist is overwhelmed by Helen's beauty: "Never had Jurgen imagined that any woman could be so beautiful nor so desirable as this woman, or that he could ever know such rapture" (228). However, Queen Helen remains as untouchable and remote as a film star, unaware of his admiration, or indeed his very existence.

This characterization of Gish as a sterile beauty was not limited to Cabell's novel. While most commentators associated Gish with the lily of her name, at least one journalist opined that "her exquisitely graceful personality reminds one of the wax-like gardenia" (Benjamin Zeidman, "The Lily of Denishawn," *Motion Picture*, October 1915). And while flowers might generally suggest fertility, Gish was a "pale, perfumeless lily" (Julian Johnson, "The Real Lillian Gish," *Photoplay*, August 1918, 24). Her pale coloring in this context connotes not racial purity, but the cool remoteness of a movie star. Likewise, in a letter to *Motion Picture* magazine, a fan fantasizes what he would do if he were "a young and handsome millionaire": "I'd get me a whole outfit and buy, bribe, bluff or marry Lillian and make her make pictures for me all the rest of her life, and they wouldn't be shown outside our home, 'eyether'" (E. A. Wamsley, letter, *Motion Picture*, January 1917, 166). The writer at once celebrates Gish's beauty and imaginatively repositions her within the home. Paradoxically, however, this wish-fulfilling fantasy shuns the image of traditional domesticity, replete with children, in favor of reproducing moving-picture images of Gish. However privatized the screenings, this fantasy retains and reflects the image of Gish as, precisely, a motion picture actress rather than the traditional embodiment of domestic femininity.

⭐⭐⭐⭐⭐ **Conclusion**

Gish's star persona was clearly at odds with the ideology promoted in her films. Ultimately, this worked to undermine the logic of millennial Darwinism. Gish was celebrated as a paragon of her race, "the most beautiful blonde in the world." However, while her films with Griffith demanded that idealized white womanhood be defined in relation to motherhood and domesticity, Gish herself demonstrated that the modern world offered new roles for women.

Further, the disparity between the meanings associated with Gish onscreen and off- helped to destabilize the relationship between image and reality that was the basis of eugenic thinking. In *The Birth of a Nation*, Ben Cameron falls in love with Gish's Elsie Stoneman long before he ever meets her. When he sees a photograph of Elsie, Ben is immediately smitten. He carries the photo with him to war, and there is never a moment of doubt that the real woman will fulfill the expectations produced by her image. In this way, the film suggests that there is a stable correlation between image and reality; her sweetness and virtue are visible, as apparent in the photograph as the color of her skin and hair. Likewise, in *Broken Blossoms*, the Yellow Man falls in love with Gish's Lucy when he sees her from afar; her delicate frame and pale skin signal that she is a gentle and fragile creature. Indeed, this trust in the correlation between physical attributes and moral character was one of the foundations upon which the ideology of racial progress rested: the visible characteristics associated with one's race signaled one's moral and intellectual stature.

Gish herself, however, was not what she appeared to be. As one commentator described her, "In reality Lillian, an ingénue in appearance, is a rather suave woman off the screen" (unidentified clipping, *Photoplay*, August 1918). Gish did not merely enact the roles she played on the screen; she embodied them. She was, after all, "clean, and white, and pure as a lily" (Martha Groves McKelvie, "The Lily of *Hearts of the World*," *Motion Picture*, August 1918, 120). The characteristics attributed to her race—her pale, almost translucent skin, her halo of golden hair, her delicate features—all contributed to her characterizations of fragile, pure, and innocent girls who long to transform themselves into mothers. However, this vision of whiteness was not what it appeared to be; her racial status was merely a mask that did not correlate to her personal qualities. Far from Griffith's cherished imago of the eternal mother, Lillian Gish—the star—was an ambitious and intelligent woman who sought fulfillment through the art of film acting.

Gish made only two more films with D. W. Griffith in the 1920s, *Way Down East* (1920) and *Orphans of the Storm* (1921), before she and the director with whom she was so strongly associated parted ways. Griffith would never again achieve the critical success that he had attained, in part, through the films he made with Gish. His narratives would come to seem increasingly old-fashioned. Gish, however, would enjoy a long and celebrated career, redefining herself on the screen through such roles as Mimi in *La Boheme* (1926) and Hester Prynne in *The Scarlet Letter* (1926). With these roles, and with directors such as Victor Sjöström and King Vidor, the contradictions between her on- and offscreen personae would become less pronounced and she would be remembered less for her representations of virtuous wives than for her dedication to the art of acting and to preserving the reputation of her former director.

NOTES

1. All correspondence between Lillian Gish and Nell Becker cited here and throughout the text can be found in Box 3 of the Lillian Gish Collection, Billy Rose Theatre Collection, New York Public Library.

2. Many newspaper and some trade sources cited in this chapter were accessed in the Robinson Locke Scrapbooks housed in the New York Public Library, Performing Arts section. Scrapbook cuttings excise page numbers and in some cases are unattributed and/or undated. Any archival citation missing page numbers, dates, or source may be assumed to be from the Robinson Locke Scrapbooks.

3. Bederman demonstrates how this ideology worked to support not only Euro-American male dominance in the writings of G. Stanley Hall and Theodore Roosevelt, but also the discourses that challenged white male dominance, such as Charlotte Perkins Gilman's arguments for (white) women's rights and Ida B. Wells's anti-lynching campaigns. I would argue that vestiges of this ideology persist in discourses about democracy, whether in the American drive to impose democracies overseas or in the debates over gay rights, which are often framed in terms of American society's evolution toward a complete democracy.

4. Griffith was well aware of the eugenics movement. The year before the release of *The Birth of a Nation*, he directed *The Escape* (1914), which opens with a prologue in which Dr. Daniel Carson Goodman traces the evolution of microscopic life forms. According to the *New York Times*, "*The Escape* treats of eugenics and sex questions and shows in an interestingly told story what . . . the producers believe to be the haphazard way in which human beings select their mates and contrasts it with the alleged care used in the same selection by the lower animals" ("Show D'Annunzio's Photo Play *Cabiria*," *New York Times*, 2 June 1914).

5. Later, rumors would emerge that Gish and Griffith had been romantically involved, but there was no hint of a romance between the two in their publicity during the 1910s.

4 ★★★★★★★★★★★

Sessue Hayakawa

The Mirror, the Racialized Body, and *Photogénie*

DAISUKE MIYAO

Many popular audiences of cinema remember Japanese actor Sessue Hayakawa (1886–1973) for his Oscar-nominated role as a frowning Japanese military officer in *The Bridge on the River Kwai* (1957). Yet Hayakawa was a movie star in the United States as early as 1915, and the only Asian matinee idol of the silent era (see Miyao). His astounding performance as a sexy villain in Cecil B. DeMille's *The Cheat* (1915) propelled him to superstardom during a time when the general public supported segregation and when mixed marriages were illegal in many states.

Sessue Hayakawa, circa 1918. From the author's collection.

In *The Cheat*, Hayakawa played the role of Hishuru Tori, a rich Japanese art dealer on Long Island, and famous stage actress Fannie Ward portrayed heroine Edith Hardy, a young married Caucasian woman. In a key scene, Edith faints upon hearing that her stock investment has failed. Under the moonlight, in front of a shoji screen shining white in the dark corridor of a Japanese-style house, Tori slowly leans toward her limp body, whose skin is strikingly alabaster, and steals a kiss. When Edith awakens, Tori offers her money in exchange for her body. She accepts. But when she tries to return his money after her husband's success in the stock market, Tori assaults her and brutally brands her naked shoulder with a hot iron bearing his trademark stamp. Edith fights back and shoots Tori in the shoulder. Ultimately, Edith's husband pleads guilty to the shooting in order to save her name and he is arrested on a charge of attempted murder. During the trial, Edith confesses the truth, reveals the brand on her shoulder, and an enraged courtroom audience attacks Tori.

The Cheat reveals an intriguing contradiction at the root of Hayakawa's stardom. On one hand, the violent reaction of the courtroom at the end of the film expresses white Americans' intolerance of the racial Other, and stresses the impossibility of fully assimilating the Japanese in American society. On the other hand, the affective charge of the scene in which Tori brands the white woman violently appealed to viewers and propelled Hayakawa to international fame. The powerful effect of the branding scene emanates from Hayakawa's face, revealed in a series of close-shots as Tori tears Edith's clothes, grabs her hair, and brutally throws her forward onto the desk. As he lowers the branding iron closer and closer to Edith's bare shoulder, pausing as the iron almost reaches her white flesh, the lighting from the brazier casts ominous shadows on his taut face, intensifying the tension of the scene. The branding itself is completed offscreen, but the smoke shimmers in front of Tori as he grimaces with a tightly closed mouth. The intensity registered by Hayakawa's face, its veritable assault on the viewer, was likened in its effect to that of a gun by French film critic Jean Epstein: "Hayakawa aims his incandescent mask like a revolver. Wrapped in darkness, ranged in the cell-like seats, directed toward the source of emotion by their softer side, the sensibilities of the entire auditorium converge, as if in a funnel, toward the film. Everything else is barred, excluded, no longer valid" (Epstein, "Magnification" 239–40).

The sensational appeal of Hayakawa's performance in *The Cheat* ignited his immediate ascent to stardom, launching a critical and popular acclaim that would grow throughout the remainder of the decade. Importantly, however, the recurrent motif in most of Hayakawa's star vehicles, the unbridgeable gap between two cultures or races, is often explained in a famous—and infamous—Orientalist line, "East is East, and West is West, and never the twain shall meet," from British author Rudyard Kipling's 1889 verse, "The Ballad of East and West." The line appears repeatedly as intertitles in Hayakawa's star vehicles, including *The Cheat*, and in reviews. *Each to His Kind* (1917), a Hayakawa star vehicle produced at Lasky, for instance, was described by the *New York Dramatic Mirror* as "a screen version of Kipling's assertion that 'East is East and West is West and never the twain shall meet'" ("*Each to His Kind*," 10 February 1917, 26). Although Hayakawa's fame enabled him to establish his own production company, Haworth Pictures Corporation, in March 1918, he pragmatically understood that in order to realize profits, it was necessary to maintain, or enhance, the star image that Lasky had constructed for middle-class American audiences. Hayakawa confessed later: "[At Haworth] I was not about to change away from the type of picture which had earned me my fame and following" (Hayakawa 143).

If the "type of picture" that defined Hayakawa's career suggests a stark distinction between "East" and "West," then the line that repeats "never the twain shall meet" can also be read as a warning to the viewer who is sensually attracted to Hayakawa's cinematic body. The point, quite simply, is that Hayakawa's screen presence, especially the close-ups of his face, had a profound phenomenological effect. Following the release of *The Cheat* at the Omnia Pathé Cinema in Paris in the summer of 1916, drama critic Louis Delluc wrote in *Le Film*:

> Of Hayakawa, one can say nothing: he is a phenomenon. Explanations here are out of place. . . . Once more I am not speaking of talent. I consider a certain kind of actor, especially him, as a natural force and his face as a poetic work whose reason for being does not concern me when my avidity for beauty finds there the expected chord or reflection. . . . It is not his cat-like, implacable cruelty, his mysterious brutality, his hatred of anyone who resists, or his contempt for anyone who submits; that is not what impresses us, and yet that is all we can talk about. . . . And especially his strangely drawn smile of childlike ferocity, not really the ferocity of a puma or jaguar, for then it would no longer be ferocity.   (Delluc 138–39)

In the most general and obvious way, Delluc's language is riddled with racism, locating Hayakawa's appearance as "cat-like" and "childlike," as well as "mysterious"—a "natural force." The primitivist associations with Hayakawa as an embodiment of the premodern East, however, are trumped by Delluc's overriding proclamation: that the actor's presence on the screen renders Western audiences inarticulate—incapable, that is, of civilized and communicative speech: "One can say nothing. . . . Explanations are here out of place." Taken together with Epstein's assessment of Hayakawa's face as an image that "excludes" all other meanings, it is clear that French intellectuals were "dumfounded" by Hayakawa's body on the screen (Hammond and Ford 330).

The French were not alone in their amazement. Throughout the latter half of the 1910s, Hayakawa's stardom was a site of continuous negotiation between what Vivian Sobchack calls "the carnal sensuality of the film experience" and what could be called the "classical" narrative strategies of meaningful codification (Sobchack 56). More specifically, Hayakawa's films labor to confine the signification of the Asian body through a series of assimilation narratives, through the motif of self-sacrifice, and through an increasingly sympathetic portrayal of the nonwhite character's racial difference. Such assimilation narratives often coincided with a nationwide Americanization Movement, organized by voluntary middle-class Americans, that sought to facilitate the social assimilation of new immigrants in the United States while maintaining a strict racial boundary to prohibit biological assimilation.

The tense line between social and biological assimilation define the narrative logic of Hayakawa's star vehicles in the late 1910s, especially *The Hidden Pearls* (1918) and *The Man Beneath* (1919), which this chapter scrutinizes. The recent availability of these prints, as well as other key titles such as *The Devil's Claim* (1920), provides a fresh historical lens for examining the complex, and often competing, meaning-making economies through which Hayakawa's body was simultaneously racialized and cast as an object of female and consumer desire at the height of his stardom. Hayakawa's capacity to transcend the existing vocabulary in film acting, such as restrained facial expressions and pantomimic gestures, undoubtedly participated in his capacity to perform racial identities while deviating significantly from any singularly determined ethnographic logic.

Moreover, it is crucial to recognize that Japanese media emphasized the physicality of Hayakawa's body as "cinematic" and tried to liberate it from the dominant "theatrical" tendency in Japanese filmmaking of the time. By reading "Japaneseness" into the Hollywood-made star image of Hayakawa, those who were engaged in the critical and practical discourses on films in Japan sought, for the first time, to formulate a specific identity of "Japanese cinema" understood as presentable and exportable to foreign markets.

☆★★★★ *The Hidden Pearls:* **The Americanized Body**

Not coincidentally, the Jesse L. Lasky Feature Play Company, which released *The Cheat*, attempted to assimilate their promising, but non-

American, new star by broadcasting the image of a physically and morally healthy all-American man. Around the time that *The Cheat* was released, the burgeoning U.S. film industry was attempting to acquire cultural legitimacy and thus appeal to middle-class audiences. Stars played a key role in this ideological project. In December 1918, *Motion Picture* magazine announced five winners of the "Motion Picture Hall of Fame" popularity contest—Douglas Fairbanks, Harold Lockwood, William S. Hart, Wallace Reid, and Francis X. Bushman—who collectively represented a "clean-living group of all-Americans" (Koszarski 299).

The popularity of these male stars with "all-American" images corre-sponded to a nationwide Americanization Movement organized by voluntary middle-class Americans. Sumiko Higashi argues that the legitimatization and institutionalization of cinema "meant the articulation of middle-class ideology in an era that stressed Americanization as a response to cultural diversity" (Higashi, *Cecil* 3). The ethnic reverberation set off in the United States by the outbreak of the European war in 1914 marked the opening of a far more intense phase of the Americanization movement (Gleason 40). In 1915, the National Americanization Committee was organized. On 4 July 1915, "Americanization Day" was celebrated by Chambers of Commerce and Industry, churches, organizations of mutual aid in immigrant communities, and so on in more than one hundred cities all over the United States. In 1916, Royal Dixon, an activist of the Americanization Movement, published a book entitled *Americanization,* insisting that immigrants forgo their respective cultural traditions and merge with the national community by identifying themselves with American principles and customs (Matsumoto 52–75).

As I have discussed elsewhere, Hayakawa's star image was meant to represent a successful assimilation narrative of Asian immigrants (Miyao 87–105). Perhaps the first article referring to Hayakawa's private life appeared in *Photoplay* in March 1916, suggestively titled "That Splash of Saffron: Sessue Hayakawa, a Cosmopolitan Actor, Who for Reasons of Nativity, Happens to Peer from Our White Screens with Tilted Eyes." Here, reporter Grace Kingsley exoticizes Hayakawa's national origin by referring to Japanese religion, but stresses his Americanized lifestyle:

> No, Sessue Hayakawa, the world's most noted Japanese photoplay actor, does not dwell in a papier-mâché house amid tea-cup scenery. He is working in pictures in Los Angeles, and he lives in a "regular" bungalow, furnished in mission oak, and dresses very modishly according to American standards. Even his gods are forsaken, for he owns an English bull-pup, named Shoki, which means "destruction," and is the name of a Japanese god.   (141)

The rhetorical strategy that Americanizes Hayakawa's Japanese identity and national origins by offering readers a glimpse of his very "regular" home and decidedly "American" taste in clothes repeats with relatively little variance in the flurry of reports to come. In each, Hayakawa's dog attains a peculiar totemic status. In a 1917 essay for *Picture Play Magazine*, for instance, reporter Walter Reed incorporates a photo of that same "regular" bungalow, in front of which stand Hayakawa and his wife, Tsuru Aoki, dressed in American clothes with a perky dog straining at the leash. Emphasizing that there is "still another nationality represented—by the English bulldog," Reed's investment in portraying Hayakawa's household as an illustrative example of refined cosmopolitanism, a kind of idealized melting-pot, thus manages to Americanize the dog as well ("The Tradition Wreckers," March 1917, 62). For reporter Pearl Gaddis, however, that bulldog was decidedly American to begin with, and hence emblematic of Hayakawa's willingness to fully identify with Anglo-American customs ("The Romance of Nippon Land," *Motion Picture Classic*, December 1916, 18–20).

Not surprisingly, the process whereby immigrants or racial others come to identify with Anglo-American customs dominates the plot of *The Hidden Pearls* (1918), Hayakawa's seventeenth film for the Lasky Company. Here, he plays the role of Maki, the prince of Uahiva, a Hawaiian tribe. Maki is raised and educated in America as Tom Garvin, the son of an American pearl trader, and understands himself to be wholly American. He loves Enid Benton, but her father tells Tom that he cannot marry Enid unless he acquires a fortune. Meanwhile, Tom's uncle reveals the secret treasure of the pearls that Uahiva holds, and Tom returns to his native island of Hawaii to obtain them. He receives a royal welcome from the natives and learns from Tahona, who loves him, where the pearls are hidden. He tries to escape with the pearls but is caught and branded for punishment. Tahona comes to his rescue, and Tom escapes to America with the treasure. But Tom's conscience bothers him. He cuts his arm, conceals the pearls under the skin, and returns again to Uahiva in time to save Tahona from being sacrificed for punishment.

The plot of *The Hidden Pearls*, in which the chief of a tribe sends his son to western society, appeared many times in "Indian films." Hayakawa himself played such roles several times in the films Thomas Ince produced at the New York Motion Picture Company before Hayakawa became a superstar at Lasky. According to the original script, Teariki, Maki's father, says, "When the traders learn of these wondrous pearls, they will come among us—with guns and Bibles," and there is a shot of "the girl and the little children—the innocents who inevitably suffer at the coming of the white man." In order to learn American ways and enlighten his people, Maki is sent to America to become an American; indeed, at the boy's birth his father declared, "My boy must grow up in the States—American." It is noteworthy that this element of the script echoes, almost verbatim, the story circulating in the press of Hayakawa's alleged reason for coming to the United States. As Pearl Gaddis explained in "Romance in Nippon Land" (*Motion Picture Classic*, December 1916, 18–20), Hayakawa's father recommended that his son should be Americanized in order to enlighten other Japanese people. He reportedly advised him: "Go to America, to an American college. Learn the American ways—the American plays—all that is best in American drama. Then bring it back to your countrymen." As we see below, various elements of Hayakawa's star image differ from the narrative structure of his films. For now, it is relatively easy to discern that the introduction to Hayakawa's character in *The Hidden Pearls* mirrors Lasky's strategy for Americanizing his star's image.

But Lasky's narrative strategy for *The Hidden Pearls* was also in accordance with the U.S. Americanization policy of Hawaii, which was annexed in 1898 and became a territory in 1900. Importantly, *The Hidden Pearls* presents Hawaii as a transitional zone between Japanese and American cultures. Even though Hayakawa plays a native Hawaiian, he symbolically represents the Japanese residing in Hawaii. As the actor explained in April 1918:

> Repression is characteristic of not only the Japanese, but of the entire Orient, and even extends its influence to the South Sea Islands and as far east as Hawaii. There are thousands of Japanese in this new colony of America and their influence has been strongly felt by the natives. In my most recent picture, "The Hidden Pearls," I take the part of a Hawaiian, and I tried to interpret it strictly along the lines of Oriental expression.
>
> (Harry Carr Easterfield, "The Japanese Point of View: And Incidentally a Chat with Hayakawa," *Motion Picture Magazine*, 15 April 1918, 119)

In reality, a great number of Japanese immigrants after 1865 started residing as migrant laborers in Hawaii, where they played a central role in developing the Hawaiian economy, especially in installing the sugar plantation system. Initially, American planters instituted a system of migrant labor that "was designed to control and exploit the productive labor of Asians and then to expel them when their utility had ended" (Okihiro xii). As workers resisted their exploitation and formed permanent communities of settlers, it was considered indispensable not only by the planters but also by U.S. foreign policy to Americanize the Asian laborers, and to transform "a sinister alien presence within the republic's gates—awaiting Japan's command to spring into action," into patriotic, Christian, and English-speaking Americans (Okihiro xiii).

The narrative of *The Hidden Pearls* emphatically stresses the Americanization of Hayakawa's Hawaiian character. The original script of the film overtly states: "Twenty years in the States changes little Maki into an American 'gentleman of leisure.'" The introductory close-up of Tom, in evening clothes, shows "very much the well turned out, athletic young American, with college antecedents and a sufficiency of money." Tom's Americanization is reinforced by his reaction to his childhood memories. When a shot of little Maki is inserted as Tom's subjective flashback, Tom "frowns slightly, shakes himself not pleased at the recurrence of memories of his childhood." The script pays particular attention to differentiating continental American space from the Hawaiian Islands in order to emphasize Maki's Americanized identity. The script notes:

> Make this interior in smashing contrast to the open space and simplicity of the islands—almost oppressive in its luxury. Everything in good form—he is not a vulgar nouveau riche, but a nouveau riche with the sense to trust to his interior decorator. The beauty and distinction of this set is useful not merely for contrast with the islands, but to emphasize Tom's assured and excellent social standing.

While Hawaiian people want the pearls returned because they are "taboo," Tom does not believe in such customs. Rather, his motivation to return them stems from a promise he made to a Hawaiian girl who loves him. If he goes back, he will surely be punished; if he does not return, the girl will be executed in his place. Here, the motif of chivalrous self-sacrifice makes Hayakawa's character the moral center of the film, within a notion of racial hierarchy. Since the role of Tahona, the Hawaiian girl, is played by a white actress, Tom's act could loosely be read as self-sacrifice for a white woman.

However, even in this narrative that emphasizes Tom's Americanization, Hayakawa's performance invites a tension between the literal inscription of race on the surface of the body—the "brand" itself (which was obviously a reinscription of the type of "branding" of the body in *The Cheat*)—and the character's interiority and identity. In the scene in which Tom decides to return to his native island, he stands in front of a mirror in a dark room. In a long shot, strong lights illuminate him from a frontal direction and frame Tom's body in sharp relief against the black background. He wears a dark nightgown, and his face and his naked chest are so white that they even appear to emit white light from inside. A long shot of a half-naked native Hawaiian woman, Tom's fiancée, in tears on the beach is inserted as his flashback. This heightened sense of his interiority is followed by a medium shot that frames only his reflection in the mirror. Within the mirror's frame, Tom gazes at himself without blinking. We see a black tattoo of a fish on the naked white chest of Tom's double in the mirror, a tattoo forced on him by the native people so that he would not forget his Hawaiian racial identity. The contrast between the whiteness of Tom's skin and the blackness of the tattoo is intensified by the so-called "Lasky lighting" techniques. Initially elaborated by Cecil B. DeMille and his cinematographer Alvin Wyckoff in *The Cheat*, such lighting techniques generate "confined and shallow areas of illumination, sharp-edged shadows and a palpable sense of the directionality of light," all of which enhance the dynamic visuality of Hayakawa's performance and appearance (Jacobs, "Belasco" 408).

This luminosity of Tom's body comes close to what Thomas Elsaesser astutely observes in his examination of the UFA studio's lighting styles in Weimar Germany. Elsaesser claims:

> Lighting turns the image into an object endowed with a special luminosity (being lit and at the same time radiating light) which is to say, light appears as both cause and effect, active and passive. In short it suggests "authenticity" and "presence," while remaining "hidden" and "ineffable." The object, and the human actor as object become irreducibly immanent, more-than-real in their "there-ness" and "now-ness," but by a process that confers this presence on them from off-frame, off-scene . . . the luminous becomes ominous becomes numinous. . . . The special kind of luminosity that comes from objects being lit and at the same time radiating light, brings forth the illusion of a special kind of "essence."   (Elsaesser 44, 251)

The whitening of Tom's appearance in this scene enhances his psychological struggle, the dramatic battle between his internalized sense of self and the way his body is marked as different. The "essence" of Tom's self remains "hidden" but the special luminosity confirms its "presence."

But the question remains: what *is* the "essence" of Tom's self in the narrative of *The Hidden Pearls*? Is it his Americanized, white identity enhanced by the Lasky lighting? Or is it the "primitive" Hawaiian racial identity indicated by the tattoo, starkly visible on his white chest? Tom's luminous half-naked body signifies Tom's Americanization that morally condones such a primitive custom as tattooing; it also simultaneously reminds the viewers of his racial otherness *and* evokes primal desire for that other. Thus, the special luminosity and the split of self-image in the mirror conspicuously enhances Tom's identity crisis, the struggle to balance his Americanized self and his status as a native Hawaiian. The scene also provokes the viewers' moral struggle, an internal battle between the fear of miscegenation and sensual (visual) attraction to prohibited pleasure.

Later in the narrative, a very similar setting of a dark room with a strong spotlight from above is restaged. This time, the half-naked Tom sticks a knife in his left arm. A close-up reveals red/black blood seeping over his white skin, as if an inner darkness symbolically "covers" an Americanized/white surface. Moreover, Tom has cut open the skin of his forearm with a knife to conceal the pearls, the religious/essential treasure of his native race. "Hidden pearls" thus suggestively signifies Tom's true self, hidden under the Americanized white skin. Importantly, there is no mirror in this scene. As a result, there is no visual splitting of the bodily image but rather a singular image of self, one determined by "blood." Indeed, by the end of the film, Tom chooses his native Hawaiian identity and accepts his inability to fully assimilate in the States, forgoing his love for Enid in favor of saving Tahoma.

In a series of newspaper articles titled "Are the Japanese assimilable?" Sidney Gulick, a former missionary in Japan and a pro-Japanese professor, insisted that there were two types of assimilation, "biological" and "social." He wrote: "Biological assimilation may touch upon the issue of miscegenation, but social assimilation is surely possible because it can be achieved by education and surrounding conditions. The Japanese can learn our language, way of thinking, and democracy" ("Nihonjin wa dôka shiuruya (1) [Are the Japanese assimilable?]," *Rafu Shimpo* 3581, 8 August 1915, 2). It is hardly coincidental that Martha Grover McKelvie, writing for *Photoplay*, called *The Hidden Pearls* "a picture of educational value" ("Playing with Fire in Hawaii," November 1919, 46). What *The Hidden Pearls* teaches is, once again, that the race barrier in American society must be maintained. By maintaining it, as one reviewer for *Motion Picture News* noted, Hayakawa's character becomes safely identifiable: "The author [Beulah Marie Dix] has furnished—one important element which is necessary for Mr. Hayakawa to reach the hearts of his audience, and that is sympathy" (23 February 1918, 1181).

Notwithstanding the safely sympathetic distance that *The Hidden Pearls* affords middle-class Anglo-American audiences, Hayakawa's performance and physical presence also generates alternative "affective experiences" (Shaviro viii). Indeed, the excessive spectacle of Hayakawa's onscreen body, and blood, produces treacherous ecstasy—a crucial element in his star image to which we now turn.

✰✰✰✰✰ *The Man Beneath*: The Racialized Body

The motif of the mirror becomes a crucial onscreen entity for Hayakawa's films in the latter years of the decade. As noted in the previous discussion of the mirror scene in *The Hidden Pearls*, the mirror is a device that tactfully balances/divides the direct physicality of Hayakawa's body and the racial and sexual ideology that body signifies. In an expansive survey of cinematic styles developing in a wide variety of countries in the 1910s, Kristin Thompson points out that the mirror is used for expressive cinematic effects but not necessarily for narrative legibility. Thompson claims: "Mirrors, with their reversal of relations among objects, provided an obvious way of undercutting spectators' understanding of scenes" ("International" 261). In Hayakawa's films, by contrast, the expressivity of the mirror as a prop bears a key narrational function: it displays the nonwhite protagonist's encounter with and reconfirmation of his racial otherness that prohibits him from coupling with white women. These mirrors also serve a particular ideological purpose that reminds the spectator of the racial order. Ironically, however, the same mirrors and close-ups that reflect and reframe Hayakawa's body engender sensuous effects for the spectator that could be subversive to the same order. In other words, on one hand, in the mirror, Hayakawa's Asian heroes quite literally "reflect" on their racial identity. On the other hand, reframed in the mirror, the close-up of Hayakawa's body, especially his face, generates "affective experiences" for the spectator (Shaviro viii). *The Man Beneath* (1919), a star vehicle Hayakawa made at Haworth and a story of "the tragic situation created by a race barrier blocking the gates of love," according to Margaret I. MacDonald of *Moving Picture World* ("The Man Beneath," 5 July 1919, 111), exemplifies this intricate doubling effect.

In a telling scene midway through *The Man Beneath*, Hayakawa's Dr. Ashuter, a young and successful Hindu scientist working at a university in Scotland, looks intensely into a mirror in his dark room. He has just received a letter from Kate, a white woman he loves. Ashuter has confessed his love to her on a beautifully moonlit terrace at a party honoring Ashuter's achievements. Kate regards Ashuter as a great scientist, but she refuses his love because of their racial differences. She writes to Ashuter, "Racial differences and racial hatred exist, in both the East and the West. A love that goes against social beliefs is egotistical and brings unhappiness to those who break this law. It also brings disaster and tragedy to innocent offspring."

In medium close-ups, Ashuter reads Kate's letter of rejection without a blink. When the camera reframes to a medium shot, he finally closes his eyes. In the long shot that follows, Kate appears at the dark corner of the room in double exposure. As Ashuter tries to come close to her, the image disappears. With a melodramatic gesture of depression (he extends his arm to the air and then lowers it to his head), Ashuter walks to another room with a mirror. A

The mirror reveals Dr. Ashuter's (Hayakawa's) expression in a key scene from *The Man Beneath* (1919).

close-up of a photo of Kate in Ashuter's hands is followed by a close-up of Ashuter looking at it. A long shot from his back reveals two images of Ashuter holding the photo: one in the room and one in the mirror. The different positions of the two images are important, since the mirrored image of Ashuter reveals his expressions even as his back is turned to the camera. Discussing Victor Sjöström's 1913 film *Ingeborg Holm*, Kristin Thompson writes, "Logically, it would seem that hiding a central character's facial expressions would detract from narrative clarity. Yet, by putting Ingeborg's back to us, Sjöström displays an awareness that a de-emphasis on her facial expression could actually enhance our sense of her anguish and the poignancy of the moment" ("International" 256). By showing both Ashuter's facial expression and his back, this scene in *The Man Beneath* achieves both "narrative clarity" and "enhancement" of our sense of Ashuter's "anguish and the poignancy of the moment." The darkened background vividly heightens the illuminated reflection of his figure in the frame within the frame. In a close-up, with his eyes wide open, Ashuter's double in the mirror recklessly grips the flesh of his right cheek with his left hand. He grabs the skin so strongly that bloody spots appear on his face when he releases the skin from his hand. Then Ashuter's double desperately but implicitly curses his nonwhite skin color. In

In a close-up from *The Man Beneath* (1919), Hayakawa's Dr. Ashuter grips the flesh of his cheek while looking in the mirror and curses his nonwhite skin color.

intertitles, he says, "O! God of my fathers! Take pity on your son. See, this blood that runs is red   red. . . ." Significantly, it is Ashuter's double that performs these violent physical and verbal actions. The inclusion of part of the mirror's frame in the shot reminds us that we are watching Ashuter's reflection, rather than the man himself. When we see both images of Ashuter in the mirror in a long shot again, he is a gentleman as he always has been and always will be. He closes his eyes for the first time in this room and turns his head up as if he has surrendered to the logic of the letter, accepting the racial differences between himself and his beloved Kate.

By reflecting Ashuter's hidden self ("the man beneath"), the mirror reminds the nonwhite hero of his racial status and urges him to figuratively sacrifice himself for the heroine. And as I have noted, the motif of self-sacrifice was crucial to the creation of Hayakawa's star image (Miyao 106–16). Robert Sklar claims that noble sacrifice of oneself for womanhood or honor was a major character trait of the romantic hero of the genteel tradition, which was "so ubiquitous a part of American culture as it was like air" for about half a century until World War I (Sklar 20). Insofar as Hayakawa's romantic heroes of the genteel tradition sacrifice themselves and sometimes even die for the good of white American women, their actions alleviate anxieties related to miscegenation. Thus, the motif of self-sacrifice could place Hayakawa's nonwhite characters at the moral center of the narrative while preventing their full assimilation into American society and prohibiting them from interracial marriages. While Tori in *The Cheat* is capable of social assimilation but remains morally inassimilable, the motif of self-sacrifice renders Hayakawa's later characters near heroic examples of a rigorously achieved moral refinement .

Stretching beyond even Tom's sacrificial act of returning to Hawaii in *The Hidden Pearls*, Hayakawa's character in *The Man Beneath* quite literally rescues and restores the sanctity of a white family. When Bassett, Ashuter's college friend, comes to seek his help when being pursued by the murderous secret society Black Hand, Ashuter protects him with his secret scientific formula. Ashuter thus makes up for the mistake that the naïve white American man made in the past. Considering the linkage in the popular discourse of the time between Black Hand and Italian immigrants (as detailed by Giorgio Bertellini in his chapter on George Beban in this volume), Ashuter eliminates the unwelcome non-Caucasian alien to protect the white American couple. He provides an opportunity for Bassett to change into an ideal husband of a white American family. Safely bringing Bassett back to Mary, his fiancée and Kate's younger sister, Ashuter bids another farewell to Kate, kissing her right hand as always, while Bassett and Mary kiss each other on the lips. As a result, Ashuter earns the sympathy of other characters as well as the (white) viewers of the film.

Thus, sympathy is primarily generated through the manner in which the film articulates the protagonist's struggle with, and acceptance of, his racial difference. In this sense, in addition to being the narrational device, the mirror and the close-ups of Hayakawa's face in it have a peculiar ideological function. The presentation of Hayakawa's Asian body in close-ups in *The Man Beneath* differs from the exhibition of exotic others in world fairs that Alison Griffiths describes as "an index of biologically determined racial identity" or "an ethnographic sign" (Griffiths 68, 184). To the spectator of *The Man Beneath*, Ashuter's recognition of his skin color and its difference from Kate's is not a literal but a symbolic one. While Hayakawa's face is recognizably Asian, the use of white makeup in *The Man Beneath* renders his appearance extremely pale onscreen. In turn, the blood on his face looks as "red" as that of any white actors, thus narrowing the visible difference between Ashuter's skin color and that of the white characters.

Alternately, we might say Ashuter's racial identity, which is "split" in the mirror, turns into an "act," one that generates a virtual racial object. As Andrew Parker and Eve Kosofsky Sedgwick claim, "performativity" is an act of constructing "identities . . . through complex citational process" (Parker and Sedgwick 2). Objectified in the mirror, Ashuter's face reminds him that racial differences exist as social beliefs. In other words, the mirror visualizes the division between Ashuter as a social being and Ashuter as the man *beneath* the social being. The social, that is, racialized, being is a "performative" one, but eventually the virtual object inside the mirror comes to control the emotion and behavior of the self who is performing. Because of the mirror Ashuter comes to recognize, or reconfirm, the ideology of race and the unsurpassable power relations between white and nonwhite, subject and object, performing and performed. He needs to perform for social beliefs; the virtual object forces him to control/hide his inner feelings toward the white woman he loves. Here, the mirror affects Ashuter's behavior in "positive" ways for a society dominated by the Caucasian race. The hero played by Hayakawa does not cheat any longer but consciously maintains the unconquerable barrier of different races.

★★★★★ The Man in the Mirror: *Photogénie* and Carnal Sensuality

The violent action in the close-up of Hayakawa's face in the mirror, or the intense materiality of Hayakawa's fragmented body that urgently involves racial politics, also has strongly sensual effects on the spectator that could subvert the ideological point of the scene. As Miriam Hansen persuasively argues, women's increased significance as consumers for the film industry often proved contradictory to the systematic imposition, on the level of film style, representation, and address, of masculine forms of subjectivity, and of a patriarchal choreography of vision. The Valentino cult typifies this ambivalence. Hansen argues that Rudolph Valentino's film vehicles "offer women an institutional opportunity to violate the taboo on female scopophilia" (Hansen 277, 282). Gaylyn Studlar also points out that visual objectification of the male in film and its surrounding discourses, especially when Valentino became a star with his image of a "woman-made man" or a "creation of, for, and by women," gained enormous public attention as the act of women looking at men became symbolic of the tumultuous changes believed to be taking place in the system governing American sexual relations (Studlar, "Perils" 288–89).

To a certain extent, Hayakawa also was represented as a fascinating consumable ethnic other for white female spectators and was conspicuously positioned as an object for female audiences in his publicity. For instance, a one-page ad for *The Brand of Lopez* (April 1920), another of his star vehicles, foregrounds a framed photo of Hayakawa in a western suit with a bull-fighter cap while a drawn image of a white woman looks up in admiration at the photo. Similarly on the screen, the narrative of Hayakawa's films overtly comments on the practice of objectifying the male star for female consumption. On the surface, for instance, *The Devil's Claim* (1920), another Haworth production, has the structure of an adventure comedy: shootings, kidnaps, fistfights, and escapes. However, the film displays a commodified male star "in ways associated with women's interest in objectifying men" (Studlar, *Masquerade* 101). Hayakawa plays Akbar Khan, a Greenwich Village novelist of Indian extraction. Akbar and his novels are so popular among female readers that his previous girlfriend, a young Persian girl, Indora (Colleen Moore), tries to murder him out of jealousy. In this opening scene, Akbar is clearly captured by Indora's gaze via continuous use of the point-of-view structure. Long shots and medium shots of Akbar strolling on a New York street at night and checking out his newly published book, *Karma*, at a street vender are constantly followed by close-ups and medium close-ups of Moore with a pistol in her right hand. Akbar is an object to shoot. Eventually, in a long shot with a deep space composition, Indora fires her gun at Akbar while his back is turned.

Witnessing the whole event and impressed by Indora's devotion to her emotion, Virginia, another female reader of Akbar's novels, conspires a plot in order to bring Akbar back to Indora. At an exotic café in "New York's Latin Quarter," Virginia pretends to be a fugitive from a secret society and lures Akbar into the tale of devil worship. Akbar sees Virginia at the café as his point of view. When he catches sight of her, in close-ups, he opens his eyes wide without blinking and moves his eyes fervently, probably out of desire. In reality, though, he is the one who is already gazed at, objectified, and captured in the plot schemed by the female characters. In fact, Indora stands outside the café and sees Akbar listening to Virginia's story in her point of view. Clearly, Akbar is an object of Indora's gaze. Inspired by Virginia's story, Akbar starts writing his new serial novel for the *Metropolitan* magazine, *Mark of Satan*. With its story-within-a-story structure, Hayakawa plays the second role in the film, Hassan, a Persian adventurer. Akbar thus commodifies himself—turning the events of his life into a novel to be consumed. Moreover, now that Hayakawa plays both Akbar and Hassan, his body is doubly commodified for the spectator: for the onscreen readers of *Mark of Satan* and simultaneously for the viewer of *The Devil's Claim*.

It could be said that Hayakawa's star image was doubly commodified, insofar as he came to embody a refined, even idealized, consumer lifestyle, as well as an object of desire for female viewers. The photos attached to a 1917 article in *Picture-Play Magazine*, for instance, emphasize Hayakawa's personal life in a home surrounded with exotic but refined objects. In these photos, Hayakawa and his wife Tsuru Aoki wear western clothes and dance a western-style dance in front of elegant Japanese-style furniture; Hayakawa reads English literature surrounded by gorgeous Japanese objets d'art; Hayakawa and Aoki have tea with dainty porcelain tea cups seated at a dining table; and, as noted above, the Hayakawas appear in western clothes in front of an American-style bungalow with their "English" bulldog (Warren Reed, "The Tradition Wreckers: Two People Who Became Famous, Though Few People without Almond Eyes Can Pronounce Their Names," March 1917, 62–65) Typifying Hayakawa's offscreen performance of race, these photos and accompanying text may mirror the onscreen roles that Americanize Hayakawa's characters, but they deviate from the mutually reinforcing tropes of sympathy and sacrifice dominating his film vehicles. To be more exact, Hayakawa's Japanese traits in fan magazine discourse symbolize his refined taste in an American home, a product of his own choice. It is a visual display of consumer culture that encourages middle-class readers to imitate his actions through the purchase of furniture of Japanese taste (Miyao 140–41).

Ultimately, however, the affective appeal of Hayakawa's cinematic body was limited neither to the female gaze nor to an idealized codification of consumer culture. *Wid's Films and Film Folk Independent Criticisms of Features*, for instance, claimed of *The Cheat*: "His [Hayakawa's] careful timing of his slow movements and the wonderful control he has over his facial muscles, makes his work grip you in a truly effective manner" ("Feature Films as Wid Sees Them," 16 December 1915, n.p.). It is noteworthy that in *The Devil's Claim* there is a scene on a New York subway train where a middle-aged Caucasian man reads Akbar's story in the *Metropolitan* magazine. In a manner similar to female readers of the magazine, including a middle-class woman on a living room sofa and sales girls in a department store, he is so riveted by the story, which features numerous close-ups of Hayakawa's face, that he misses his stop at 125th Street and realizes that he is already in Yonkers.

The uniqueness of Hayakawa's body, especially his face, transcended the existing vocabulary in film acting, such as restrained facial expressions suited for close-ups and pantomimic gestures, and redefined them with inscrutable facial expressions and an economy of gesture (Miyao 195–201). An article in *Current Opinion* in 1918 quotes Cecil B. DeMille's comment on Hayakawa's performance in *The Cheat* and enhances the novelty of Hayakawa's acting styles. DeMille quips: "I don't understand it [Hayakawa's acting style]; it is new and strange, but it is the greatest thing I ever saw" ("Is the Higher Art of the Movies to Come from Japan?" January 1918, 30).[1]

Hayakawa recalled in an interview in 1963, "My facial expression was highly valued as expressionless expression" (Yoshiyuki 48). Yet Hayakawa's face, such as the one framed in the mirror in *The Man Beneath*, is not simply expressionless, in spite of his own comment. Here, the close-up of his face in the mirror freezes an action in intense ambiguity, or in ambiguous intensity. The moment of restraint, or repression of emotions or motivations, is simultaneously that of being exaggerated. Hayakawa's face certainly registers his intense emotions—anguish, suffering, irritation, desperation, and so on—no matter how "expressionless" it looks. This is clearly an emotional intensity that the prop of the mirror exploits. Caught in the mirror in close-ups—especially in those shots that hold as his eyes stare wide, often without blinking—Hayakawa's physical/physiological motility may appear subtly understated but is surely exaggerated cinematically. In *The Hidden Pearls*, for instance, the action is noticeably restrained: Tom/Hayakawa stands perfectly still. But the enhanced luminosity of his body, reflected in the mirror in the dark room, achieves ambiguous intensity in meanings.

Jean Epstein called the close-ups of Hayakawa's face on the screen "*photogénie*, cadenced movement" ("Senses" 243). Louis Delluc argued that "*photogénie*" changes "real" into something else without eliminating the "realness," and makes people, through the camera/screen, "see ordinary things as they had never been before" (Abel, "Photogénie" 110). Five decades after Delluc called Hayakawa "a phenomenon" and connected his "beauty" to "a natural force," André Bazin revived the notion of "*photogénie*" by repeating the same words that Delluc used: "Photography affects us like a phenomenon in nature, like a flower or a snowflake whose vegetable or earthly origins are an inseparable part of their beauty" (Bazin 13). Via viewing Hayakawa's body, French film theorists developed the "utopian vision of an originary, phenomenological plentitude of perception, preserved and extended by the cinematic apparatus" (Shaviro 18).

With the intense ambiguity or ambiguous intensity in the action of violence displayed onscreen, Hayakawa's image had "radical potential to subvert social hierarchies" of race and sex and "decompose relations of power" (Shaviro 65). It is true that the close-up of Hayakawa's face in the mirror in *The Man Beneath* and the luminous body of Hayakawa in the mirror in *The Hidden Pearls* change the "real" body of the actor into something else: a racialized object. But at the same time, even if the view of the two identical bodies within the frame provides the viewer a pseudo-objective perspective, the spectator of *The Man Beneath* and *The Hidden Pearls* is "caught up in an almost involuntary mimicry of the emotion or sensation of the body on the screen" (Williams, "Film Bodies" 704). Viewed in this light, we

might understand Hayakawa's immense appeal as a type of mimetic relationship, the likes of which Jennifer Bean elaborates in the context of early
fandom by elaborating Walter Benjamin's notion of the "mimetic faculty."
As she writes, "Mimesis stresses the reflexive, rather than reflection; it
brings the subject into intimate contact with the object, or other, in a tac-
tile, performative, and sensuous form of perception, the result of which is
an experience that transcends the traditional subject-object dichotomy"
(Bean, "Technologies" 46).

To speak of a mimetic response to Hayakawa's screen body means to
speak of a carnal or sensuous experience that is neither joyous, nor
thrilling, but rather measured by a reflexive relationship to the utter deso-
lation and intensified agony of what it means to be human. "The beauty of
Sessue Hayakawa is painful," wrote Louis Delluc. "Few things in the cinema
reveal to us, as the lights and silence of this mask do, that there really are
alone beings. I well believe that all lonely people, and they are numerous,
will discover their own recourseless despair in the intimate melancholy of
this savage Hayakawa" (Delluc 138–39). In *The Man Beneath*, the left hand
of Ashuter/Hayakawa grips his own facial skin as well as ours. In *The Hidden Pearls*, when the right hand of Tom/Hayakawa cuts open his flesh, the
blood is simply, "universally," red. Like Delluc, we gaze at Hayakawa's cinematic body and feel the "pain."

★★★★★ Conclusion

Walter Benn Michaels claims, "Nativism in the period just
after World War I involved not only a reassertion of the distinction between
American and un-American but a crucial redefinition of the terms in which
it might be made. America would mean something different in 1925 from
what it had meant at, say, the turn of the century; indeed, the very idea of
national identity would be altered" (Michaels 2). According to Michaels,
there was a distinctive nature to nativism in the 1920s. In what he calls
"nativist modernism," the possibility of Americanization for immigrants
was denied, and the ultimate difference between "American" and "un-
American" was emphasized. In "Progressive racism" before World War I,
Michaels argues, "projects of 'Americanization'" always existed behind the
racist discourse. The "inferiority of 'alien' races" was emphasized, but eventually new immigrants were considered to be able to assimilate to American
society as Americans. However, in "nativist modernism," Michaels claims,
immigrants' ultimate "difference" was emphasized, and "'American' desig-
nates not a set of social and economic conditions but an identity that exists

prior to and independent of those conditions" (Michaels 8–9). In fact, Frances Kellor, who had been a central figure of the Americanization movement, claimed in 1921 that American people began to think it was wrong to consider that all foreigners were future American citizens and that political, economic, and educational opportunities should be equally provided (70, 72).

In the 1922 Ozawa case at the U.S. Supreme Court, Japanese bodies were clearly distinguished from American. Ozawa Takao originally filed an application for U.S. citizenship on 14 October 1914, after twenty years of studying in an American university and working in an American company. After his application was denied, Ozawa challenged the rejection in the Federal District Court for the Territory of Hawaii in 1914, but the court ruled that Ozawa was not eligible for naturalized citizenship (Daniels 151). In 1922 Ozawa informed the Supreme Court that "at heart" he was "a true American." Ozawa insisted that he did not have any connection with the Japanese government or with any Japanese churches, schools, or organizations. His family belonged to an American church and his children attended an American school. He spoke English at home so that his children could not speak Japanese. He even chose for a wife a woman educated in American schools instead of one educated in Japan. However, Ozawa lost his petition, because physically his body was "clearly" "not Caucasian" (Takaki 208).

Under these conditions, the numbers of fiction films displaying Japanese bodies decreased by the early 1920s. In 1921, the Japanese film magazine *Katsudô Shashin Zasshi* reported, "There is no film about Japan this year [in the United States], even though there were many last year. There are films about China, instead" (Aoyama Yukio, "Beikoku katsudô shashin no miyako yori (13) [From the capital of American motion picture]," February 1921, 79). Hayakawa's stardom in the United States also came to a turning point by 1921. His popularity was clearly declining. According to a poll of film stars conducted by *Motion Picture Magazine*, Hayakawa was ranked number 44 in December 1918, but in December 1920 his rank dropped to number 124 ("The Motion Picture Hall of Fame," December 1918, 12; "Popular Contest Closes," December 1920, 94). Hayakawa left Hollywood in 1922.

Across the Pacific, Hayakawa's body played a key role in the Japanese reception of his stardom. While the Hollywood studios that created Hayakawa's stardom tried to confine (but not eliminate) "the carnal sensuality of the film experience" (Sobchack 56) that his screen presence could provoke, Japanese media emphasized Hayakawa's sheer physicality. In so doing, the Japanese media underscored, even liberated, the materiality of Hayakawa's body that his film narratives sought to codify and control; they also laboriously reinscribed that body's meanings in the racial politics of Japan.

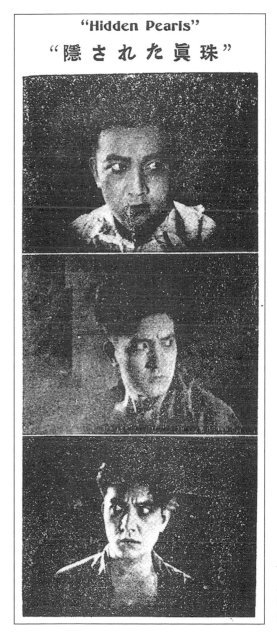

"Hidden Pearls"

"隠された眞珠"

The Japanese film journal
Kinema Junpo highlights
Hayakawa's expressive capacities
in its April 1920 issue.

Initially, Japanese media followed the politics of race in Hollywood cinema, but in a negative tone. They criticized Hayakawa for appearing in such films as *The Cheat* that would "insult" Japan and enhance anti-Japanese sentiment in the United States, and they regarded him as a "traitor" to the "Japanese race" (*Katsudô Gahô*, January 1919, 14). Yet, after Hayakawa established his status as a U.S. matinee idol, the negative tone that regarded

Hayakawa as a national/racial shame almost completely disappeared. Instead, Japanese media started publicizing Hayakawa's cinematic achievement. In fact, there were teleological discourses on cinema in the period that tried to distinguish and elevate cinema from other theatrical forms of entertainment and spectacle, including kabuki, which were often connected to lower class and juvenile spectators in Japan.

In particular, Hayakawa's body was regarded as "beyond the average Japanese people" and praised as more "cinematic" than those of other Japanese actors (Kaeriyama 2–5). Hayakawa was reportedly taller than most Japanese actors, much closer to American actors in stature. Other reports claimed that Hayakawa was not only practicing facial expressions, but also training his body with a rigorous daily schedule similar to other American film actors.[2] As I have argued elsewhere, in early-twentieth-century Japan, a "Caucasian complex" was observable in the discourse of physical appearances. Japanese bodies were considered to be "shameful" compared with well-built and well-balanced western bodies (Deguchi 104–23). The terms *nikutai-bi* (the beauty of the body) and *hyôjô-bi* (the beauty of expressions) gained wide currency as vogue words at that time. Under such conditions, Hayakawa's biological body was highly valued because it gave hope to Japanese people to become physically equal to the perceived beauty of western bodies. Hayakawa's body was regarded as one that could even overcome Darwinism, or the presumption of naturally determined western racial and social hegemony. Conceived as the ideal physical embodiment of a western style of modernization, Hayakawa's body was thus, finally and ironically, deprived of its materiality and confined in the discourse of race in Japan.

NOTES

I would like to dedicate this chapter to the Nederlands Filmmuseum, the George East-man House, and the Museum of Modern Art for their magnificent efforts in film preservation. The prints of *The Man Beneath* (NF), *Hidden Pearls* (GEH), and *The Devil's Claim* (GEH) were restored and became available for viewing only after I completed my book manuscript, *Sessue Hayakawa: Silent Cinema and Transnational Stardom*. The Museum of Modern Art included *Hidden Pearls* and *The Devil's Claim* in its retrospective of Hayakawa films in September 2007. *The Man Beneath* was screened at the 27th Giornate del Cinema Muto in October 2008, together with *His Birthright* (1918) and *The Courageous Coward* (1919), two more Hayakawa films restored and preserved at NF. I would like to acknowledge Elif Rongen-Kaynakci (NF) and Charles Silver (MoMA) for their generous support. Lastly, I thank Jennifer M. Bean for inviting me to write about Hayakawa one more time.

1. The subtitle of this entry is *Current Opinion* is particularly telling: "Japanese Actors, Obtaining Remarkable Emotional Effects Without Moving a Face Muscle, Astound Our Masters of the Craft."

2. See Mori, "Eiga Haiyû no hanashi" 72–73, and Mori, *Hayakawa Sesshû* 37–38.

5 ☆☆☆☆☆☆☆☆☆☆☆

Theda Bara

Orientalism, Sexual Anarchy, and the Jewish Star

GAYLYN STUDLAR

In referring to unmarried females in the period of transition to twentieth-century modernity, Elaine Showalter says: "Sexual anarchy began with the odd woman" (Showalter 19). I would like to direct her statement to the exploration of Theda Bara, one of the earliest and, by some accounts, oddest manifestations of female stardom to emerge from American film culture in the 1910s. Bara, like her Victorian predecessors in odd femininity, undermined gender and sexual norms, but through more spectacular means—by being inextricably linked to film's predatory "vampire" or "vamp," an unmarried woman who became the screen embodiment of seductive feminine evil.

Theda Bara, "The Queen of Vampires." Undated photo.

Although she most famously came to represent the vampire on screen, Bara did not originate the type. William Selig's film company released *The Vampire* in 1910, and Kalem followed with another female vampire film in 1913 (Staiger, *Bad Women* 151–52; Koszarski 274). However, the motion picture appeal of the vamp was not decisively established until Bara's first major film appearance in Fox Film Corporation's *A Fool There Was* (1915). Variously referred to in fan magazines, newspaper articles, and studio-originated publicity as "The Arch-Torpedo of Domesticity," "The Queen of Vampires," "The Wickedest Woman in the World," "Purgatory's Ivory Angel," "The Ishmaelite of Domesticity," "The Devil's Handmaiden," and the "Priestess of Sin," the actress known to the public as "Theda Bara" enjoyed a brief reign—from 1915 to 1919—as one of the top box-office attractions of the early years of the star system, and her success inspired numerous imitators and rivals.[1]

Fox shaped the script of *A Fool There Was* from the Porter Emerson Browne play (1906) and novel (1909), both sharing the same title as the film; all were loosely based on Rudyard Kipling's well-known poem "The Vampire" (1897). The latter was written to accompany a Philip Burne-Jones's painting of the same name that depicted a woman with long, dark hair poised menacingly over a young man who appears almost lifeless on the bed. A small mark on the man's chest suggests that the female vampire hovering over him in her sleeveless negligee has used him to satisfy a supernatural lust for blood. The vampire's face registers a slight smile, suggesting her sadistic enjoyment of an obviously sexualized triumph over masculinity.[2]

The iconography of Burne-Jones's 1897 painting would be reproduced in the selling of Porter Emerson Browne's novel and would also become a foundation of the visual characterization of Theda Bara's first vampire role. In spite of this shared iconography, Bara's "vamp" was not a supernatural, bloodsucking creature of the kind who took hold of late nineteenth-century imaginations and was given expression in Burne-Jones's painting as well as in other cultural texts such as Bram Stoker's *Dracula*. Because this highly sensual and manipulative woman was often identified in her film representations as foreign (non-U.S.) and exhibited elements associated with the exotic Middle or Far East, this trend in movie seductresses of the late 1910s was widely referred to as the "Cobra and Incense" period.

In Fox's film adaptation of *A Fool There Was*, directed by Frank Powell, Bara plays an unnamed adventuress of unknown origins; she victimizes a string of men who masochistically succumb to her sexual allure, an allure that transgresses the ideals of Anglo-Saxon white womanhood. The character is literally a dark seductress, haughty and imperious, inured to the suffering of her male victims—or their families. Boarding an ocean liner for

Europe, she appears as a spectacle designed to attract the male gaze. While other women are attired in conservative gabardine and sturdy tweed traveling attire meant to cover and protect, she is overdressed in satin and fur, velvet, and tight hobble skirts, the latter emphasizing her sensual walk and her shape. In a close-up of her looking out of a porthole at her sexual prey, the vamp's kohl-ringed eyes are emphasized, suggesting the power of a gaze that exercises hypnotic power over men. In private, she lets down long black hair to recall both Burne-Jones's vampire painting and the Victorian obsession with luxuriant hair as a register of female sexual power (see Gitter). While the vampire is pursuing a wealthy American envoy to Europe, one of her hapless lovers commits suicide in front of her. Unmoved by this tragedy, she proceeds to lure the married envoy into illicit sex and a life of alcoholic dissipation. The vampire alienates him from his wife and young child; he is stripped of his diplomatic post and shunned by respectable society. In the last scene of the film, he is on the verge of death. Remorseless, the vampire poses triumphantly, scattering rose petals on the prone body of "the fool."

Bara's performance in *A Fool There Was* made her a star—a rather surprising occurrence considering the actress's lack of previous film experience or theatrical success. In 1914, director Frank Powell recommended that Fox hire Bara, then an unknown New York–based stage actress who called herself "Theodosia De Coppet," to play the vampire in his film. De Coppet, almost thirty years old, had never been able to advance her career beyond Yiddish theater and minor roles in legitimate New York City stage productions or in touring companies (Hamilton 18–20; Genini 7–8). Whether Powell first saw her when she was an extra on a Pathé film, *The Stain* (1914), or whether he discovered her at a casting call is uncertain. In any event, he saw something promising in the actress, and on his advice Fox committed De Coppet to a contract and the primary female role in Powell's film (Genini 15; Hamilton 18).

Fox hired De Coppet in what appears to have been the financially strapped studio's strategy to avoid paying the kind of salary many established screen personalities were demanding (Sinclair 56–57). Not long after, W. Stephen Bush, writing in *Moving Picture World*, railed against the "evil" of "gouging stars" who demanded "fabulous and ridiculous salaries" merely because they thought they had "a name" ("Gouging Stars," 5 August 1916, 100). The strategy of casting an unknown paid off: *A Fool There Was* created a sensation at the box office. With the nine other feature films Fox rushed Bara into that year, it was instrumental in making the actress that rare film industry commodity—an overnight star. As one fan magazine writer proclaimed in *Photoplay* a few months after the release of Bara's debut film, "I know of no actress who has become so widely known in such a short space of time" (Wallace Franklin, "Purgatory's Ivory Angel," September 1915, 69). Fox continued to energetically exploit Bara's vampire image in all but a half dozen of the thirty-eight other star vehicles the studio produced for her over the next five years.

As a result, "To Thedabara" became American colloquial for the particular form of seduction associated with the "beautifully wicked" woman (Mary B. Mullett, "Queen of Vampires," *Motion Picture Magazine*, September 1920, 34). Becoming a star who changed the English language added to the virtual inseparability of Bara's name from the figure of the vamp. As early as 1916, a theater magazine was prescient in articulating the running theme of all later commentary on Bara's stardom when it predicted, "If she ever escapes the cloth of red with which she has been shrouded, she will be little less than superhuman. . . . Just as actresses of the legitimate stage are always remembered by the roles they have played so Theda Bara is marked for life by the films as a sorceress and a vampire" ("The Vampire of the Screen," *Green Book*, February 1916, 263). In 1919, Fox decided the vamp phenomenon had run its course. They declined to renew Bara's contract. Her attempts in the 1920s to orchestrate a successful film comeback failed to reignite her earlier box office appeal.

Unfortunately, Bara's films are almost all missing today, most having disappeared, disintegrated, or been destroyed in the Fox archive fire of 1937. The only Bara feature film made during the height of her fame that is widely available in a complete print is *A Fool There Was*. Without firsthand knowledge of Bara's films, there is much regarding her appeal to audiences, her performance style, and her stardom that we will never know. However, we do know, through newspaper, fan magazine, and industry trade paper sources, that Bara's films often ignited censorship by city and state boards and controversy.[3] Ronald Genini claims that Bara's portrayal of an Irish heroine in *Kathleen Mavoureen* (1919) incited rioting by Irish American societies offended that "an Irish heroine was being played by a Jewish actress" (50).

These riots relate to the last crucial element of "oddness" in Bara's stardom—her Jewishness. Born in Cincinnati, Ohio, she was the daughter of Jewish immigrants from central and eastern Europe. In an era that glorified Anglo-Saxon whiteness through female film actresses such as Lillian Gish, Mary Pickford, Pearl White, Mae Marsh, and even Gloria Swanson, Bara, as a Jewish star, transgressed normative requirements of female stardom in terms of ethnic, religious, and even (as perceived by some Americans) "racial" difference. While the film industry depended upon the talents of many Jews in important creative and financial positions, it appears to have operated on the assumption that gentile-dominated audiences wanted to see actors they could easily presume were also gentiles.

Did the revelation of Bara's Jewish immigrant background contribute, not only to Hibernian Society riots, but, as Maria Elana Buszek implies, to Bara's marked decline in popularity in 1919? Buszek argues that this decline in the star's box office clout reflected Anglo-Saxon America's racism directed against "the wave of new immigrants from Southern and Eastern Europe" (163). Yet attributing the decline in Bara's stardom to pure and simple antisemitism raises the question of how Bara could have become a star just four years earlier. While any star's fall from popularity is likely to be a complex phenomenon, it is worth exploring the question of how Bara's Jewishness was negotiated by star discourse in relation to her star appeal. This also means exploring how the vamp may have functioned as an image of racialized femininity, the sexually seductive Jewess associated with the East. Discussing this *fin de siècle* stereotype in a German cultural context, Sander L. Gilman argues that actress Sarah Bernhardt and the fictional Salome—two important referents for Bara's stardom, as I show here—were primary cultural embodiments of a broadly circulating stereotype that represented more than just feminine corruption; as a Jewess identified with both modernity and the more primitive East, this seductress was regarded in Germany as a source of contagion who spread death amongst non-Jewish males (Gilman 77–85).

In spite of the loss of her films and the briefness of her popularity, Bara has achieved iconic status for almost one hundred years as one of the most recognizable of motion pictures' inscriptions of seductive feminine evil. While her films obviously have not played a role in the perpetuation of her image, a number of production stills and publicity portraits have. Our contemporary vision of Bara is shaped chiefly through these images and through those of other women who imitated her signature characteristics: a predatory pose from atop a divan or bed, scanty Orientalist costume, and heavy-lidded, kohl-ringed eyes, the latter often aimed at the camera with startling directness. Even the screen epitome of 1950s blond sexuality, Marilyn Monroe, reproduced this iconic Bara look for Richard Avedon's camera in a photo feature on sex goddesses for *Life* in 1958 (December 22, n.p.).

Beyond these individual images, star discourse as represented by fan magazines, newspapers, advertising, general interest magazine commentary, and other ephemera such as sheet music and commodity tie-ins, while not substituting for Bara's missing films, can move us in the direction of understanding her stardom, how it was constructed by the studio with the cooperation—and sometimes complicating participation—of the actress.

Star discourse can also help us understand how that star construction negotiated the tensions between American culture and Bara's differences to
secure her popularity with audiences as a Jewish woman playing a dangerous Orientalized vampire. The myriad sources that make up this discourse
also suggest how the industry sought to stabilize sometimes contradictory
meanings that were generated by the actress's performances, onscreen and
off, as "Theda Bara."

☆☆★★★ Figuring the Orient into the Odd Woman

The implications of Bara's stardom run deeper than her connection to a screen fad emphasizing an extremely stylized vision of feminine evil that is easily dismissed as a misogynistic projection of male
fantasies and fears. Instead, as Antonia Lant has pointed out, there is "a
complex intersection between definitions of the vamp . . . and Orientalist
discourse" (Lant, "Curse" 90–91). Even though early cinema learned to borrow from almost every mode of popular entertainment and trend in art
appearing during its time, Orientalism was a particularly powerful attraction, especially in the United States (see Edwards). Across high and low culture, in many venues, including consumer advertising, dance, the
decorative arts, fashion, movie palace architecture, literature, theater, and
vaudeville, the Orient was figured through narrative tropes and visual conventions based on a tradition that had been thoroughly codified by Victorian culture. In this tradition, "The East" was offered as fascinating in its
exotic picturesque qualities. Like the vamp, it was also regarded in the
Western imagination as "Other," decadent and immoral, aligned with primitive, even perverse, sexuality, and with extremes of power (as in the sultan and slave girl). Those extremes were enhanced by the mystery of the
seraglio, where, it was imagined, surrender to unspeakable sexual impulses
went unchecked by Anglo-Saxon, Christian morality.

While the sultan and the dancing harem girl were conventional Oriental figures who became ubiquitous in advertising of the turn of the century
(particularly favored in cigarette advertising), another, more radical figure—that of the imperious Orientalized woman—also came to be central to
some cultural discourses that proved particularly popular with women as,
indeed, Bara's stardom was. In opera, ballet, painting, film, and theater, bib-
lically and mythically inspired women (such as Cleopatra, Judith, Lilith,
Medea, Medusa, Phaedra, Salome, Thaïs, the Empress Theodora, Turandot,
and "The Sphinx") often occupied center stage, capturing the public's imagination and creating controversy around performances of femininity that

transgressed existing norms of female sexual propriety and the gendered alignment of power.

One example of this controversy-generating transgression in female performance occurred with Sarah Bernhardt's portrayal of a French version of Cleopatre in the 1880s and 1890s. Anticipating Theda Bara's association both with Orientalist-grounded feminine evil and female sexuality enacted beyond the pale of existing social norms, Bernhardt's U.S. appearance evoked this comment from the *New York Times*: "Good folk regarded her art as something forbidden, an alien evil. Young people did not tell their parents when they went to see her. . . . That scene in which the Serpent of Old Nile drew her coils round the throne of Marc Anthony, circling ever nearer with the venom of her wiles, was a revelation of things scarcely to be whispered" (Ockman and Silver 36). Bernhardt's performances, like Bara's, violated the dearly held Victorian belief that women were primarily spiritual rather than sexual or physical beings.

Earning her the disparaging nickname of "Sarah Barnum," Bernhardt was a relentless promoter of her star image. In her exhibitionism, she prefigured studio promotion of Bara, but Bernhardt also anticipated Bara's trading on public fascination with the Orient and its implications for femininity. Both women relied on Orientalist tropes to complicate woman's presumed role in passively satisfying a voyeuristic male gaze. Stage director Félix Duquesnel never forgot his first glimpse of Bernhardt, whom his maid mistook for a "Chinese lady" because of the actress's embroidered Chinese-style tunic and stylized coolie hat (Gold and Fizdale 67). Orientalized style in Bernhardt's personal dress and her apartment décor was used to support her onstage spectacle of an Orient already feminized—as well as sexualized—throughout Victorian culture (Shohat 23–25). *The Times* of London reveals the perception that Bernhardt was inseparable from popular notions of the Orient in its pejorative as well as intriguing connotations of Otherness: "The actress [created] a new type—the embodiment of Oriental exoticism: the strange, chimaeric idol-woman: something not in nature, a nightmarish exaggeration, the supreme of artifice" (Ockman and Silver 136). Not only did Bernhardt capitalize on these associations in her staging of her roles as Phaedra, Medée, Cleopatre, and the Byzantine empress Theodora, but she was forever linked in the public's mind with a role written for her but which she never publicly performed, the title role of Oscar Wilde's 1892 play, *Salomé* (Ockman and Silver 71, 175). The central character of Wilde's play, the Judean princess who dances so that she might kiss the dead lips of John the Baptist, was considered so daring that even Bernhardt abandoned plans to star in its production (Glenn 98; Taranow 201–02).

Carol Ockman has credited Bernhardt with establishing "the template for show business icons as we know them" and launching "the vogue for fashionable vamps" (Ockman and Silver 71). The construction of Bara's star persona certainly attempted to affiliate her with the thespian accomplishments as well as the eccentric Orientalized femininity of Bernhardt without linking her to Bernhardt's well-known Jewishness. Fox publicity men Al Selig and Johnny Goldfrap imaginatively played off some elements of Bernhardt's biography in their invention of Bara's. In addition, Bara's public identity, even after her years at Fox, was carefully staged as that of a grand diva in the Bernhardtian mold—the self-possessed, independent woman with a claim to Old World, thespian credentials. Like Bernhardt, she was credited with having an unusual talent for self-promotion. One frequent commentator wrote: "Theda, you're a wise little girl; when it comes to providing what newspapers and magazines know as 'copy,' you are in a class by yourself" (Archie Bell, "Theda the Vampire," *Cleveland Leader*, 24 October 1915, n.p.). However, we should not forget that in addition to prefiguring elements in the star construction of Bara, Bernhardt was around long enough to actually compete with the screen star: the last of Bernhardt's many "farewell" tours of America occurred in 1916–1918, when she performed *Antony and Cleopatra* (in French) to U.S. vaudeville audiences at the same time that Bara's much anticipated epic, *Cleopatra* (1917), was in release.

In advancing her thespian credentials as an actress and not just as a movie star, Bara proclaimed that she had been educated by Bernhardt "when I played in Paris," but this claim, like so many of her recollections of her life before the movies, was pure fabrication, even if it was consistent in the attempt to associate the film star with artistically elevated, if eccentric (and foreign) femininity (*Motion Picture Classic*, October 1916, 25). A similar strategy is evidenced in Bara's claim to have been taught to walk in a "serpentine" fashion for her performance in *The Clemenceau Case* (1915) by her "warm friend" Isadora Duncan (Hamilton 42). "Serpentine," a term often used to describe Bernhardt, carried associations aligned with the Orient, as well as with feminine evil. Bara was claimed to possess a muscular resemblance to the snake ("The Vampire of the Screen," *Green Book*, February 1916, 264), and Archie Bell declared that a voice specialist "would find the coils of the python or ancient oriental poison" in the silent film star's voice ("Theda Bara—The Vampire Woman," *Theatre*, November 1915, 246). We should not forget too that Duncan, like Bernhardt, was a woman whose sexual nonconformity as well as her public performances were the subjects of great controversy.

The Soul of Buddha (1918)—Bara representing the mystery and sensuality of the Orientalized woman.

What do Bara's connections to Orientalism mean for historical and theoretical considerations of women's spectatorship? While it has often been assumed that she appealed primarily to men (a dangerous fascination satirized in limericks, satirical stories, songs, and poems that sprang up almost immediately after her first film successes and lasted longer than her stardom),[4] Bara often had more to say about her appeal to women who, she claimed, were "her greatest fans" (May 106). Certainly Hollywood Orientalism of this period was constructed to appeal strongly to women, trading on female fantasies in relation to the indulgence of both consumer and sexual desires beyond the established boundaries of proper social norms. In so doing, Hollywood traded on what historian Holly Edwards calls a "new phase of American Orientalism" at the turn of the century, one marked by "the evolving therapeutic role" in which "the Orient provided metaphors and models for greater sensuality and liberated passions, relaxing enforcement of strict propriety" (Edwards 45). In a 1917 issue of *Motion Picture Magazine*, Roberta Courtlandt quoted a Columbia University instructor who made a similar claim, noting: "'Most girls are good, but good girls do not want to see other good girls on the screen. . . . Through the medium of

"Theda Bara" was an anagram for "Arab death" (Sinclair 57; P. A. Parsons, "Here Comes the Latest Thing in Vampire Ladies! 'Ware, Theda!" *Motion Picture Classic*, February 1917, 33–34). In short, Theda Bara was presented as a diva, an "artiste," in the sensationally exotic tradition of Bernhardt and, indeed, she came to be called "The Divine Bara." Years later, William Fox claimed that the actress herself had come up with the idea of being born in the Sahara Desert as a more interesting alternative to admitting she grew up in Cincinnati, as Theodosia Goodman, one of three children of a lower-middle-class Jewish family. Bara's father, a tailor, had emigrated from Russia, and her mother had family ties in France and Switzerland (Sinclair 57; Genini 16; Hamilton 19–20). Fox thus replaced Bara's Jewish immigrant parents with adventuresome European artists (a painter and an actress) while allowing her Egyptian birthplace to provide a touch of the exotic without giving up the actress's claim to whiteness.

Nevertheless, some potentially problematic confusion arose about Bara's racial identity. William Fox remembers that they decided she would be their first Arab star (Sinclair 56–57), but Fox's publicity machine soon made it clear that the studio's exciting new acquisition was not an Arab in spite of her anagrammatic name and birthplace. Fox's clarification (or restatement) likely was motivated by the fact that many (if not most) white Americans (like Brits) considered Arabs and Egyptians to be black. This is illustrated by one of the central conceits driving the taboo-challenging E. M. Hull novel, *The Sheik* (1919). The novel's English heroine travels in the Sahara where she is kidnapped and raped by a "black" (as she refers to Sheik Ahmed Ben Hassan). Lady Diana falls in love with the sheik, but in order for them to be happily united in the end without violating Anglo-American racial hierarchies, he—whether in the novel or played by Rudolph Valentino in the film released in 1921—must be revealed at the last moment to be of Spanish and British blood rather than Arab. The delicious, taboo-breaking thrill of "interracial" romance can still be vicariously enjoyed for, as Richard Koszarski asks of Valentino's *The Sheik*, "who in the audience remembered or cared that Sheik Ahmed Ben Hassan had been a European all along?" (Koszarski 301).

Bara's alignment with the Orient, onscreen and off, anticipated Valentino's star persona in permitting viewers to enjoy a taboo-defying slippage between whiteness and an ethnic or racial Otherness. Bara's "dark" Otherness, like that of Hull's "black" sheik, was linked to a dangerous and fascinating sexuality. Fox hired illustrator Charles Dana Gibson to wax ecstatic over Bara in a press release: "In her dark eyes lurks the lure of the Vamp; in her every sinuous movement there is a pantherish suggestion that is wonderfully evil" (Golden 57). Bara was quoted as declaring: "You say I have the most wicked face of any woman. You say my hair is like the serpent locks of Medusa, that my eyes have the cruel cunning of Borgia, that my mouth is the mouth of the sinister scheming Delilah, that my hands are like the talons of a Circe or the blood-bathing Elizabeth Bathory. And then you ask me of my soul—you wish to know if it is reflected in my face" (Hamilton 29).

How bad could Bara be? As noted, by the time she came to the screen, the American film industry was in transition in how it used screen actors' identity as a marketing tool. By 1915, the industry was well beyond its earlier strategy of advertising screen actors as "picture personalities" whose "existence outside of films emerge merely as an extension of an existence already laid out within films" (deCordova 88). Instead of seamlessly reproducing the onscreen personality of the actor's roles in his or her offscreen identity, publicity was being leveraged in more complex ways to construct a coherent extrafilmic identity for the actor that would not contradict the tenor of his or her screen casting. As a result, the star's offscreen identity might share something with the screen persona, but its measured distanciation from the screen persona would make the "star" a more marketable and versatile commodity.

In *Theatre* in 1918, Mildred Cram's "Popularity and the Press Agent" uses Theda Bara as her prime film-based example of the power of the press agent. Interestingly, she laces both within an Orientalist discourse: "In ancient Greece, in Troy, Carthage and Sicily, the P. A. was an oral liar. He sat in sunny market-places with his back against a wall and talked and talked and talked . . . he sang of a certain Helen . . . the delectable vampire of antiquity. What would happen to-day, I wonder, if some inspired P. A. should stand with his back against the *Times* building, singing, tenderly, of Theda Bara?" (May 1918, 363). Cram's article acknowledges the press agents' duping of the public. Fan magazines sometimes also sometimes referred to the gullibility of the public, but as frequently acknowledged the gap between the star's offscreen identity and his/her onscreen image, in both the tone and substance of their articles. Letters from readers were often published that substantiate the public's awareness of the role of studio publicity departments and press agents in creating outright fictions regarding actors' backgrounds, suppressing facts that might conflict with their players' screen image (such as being married or divorced), and organizing events or incidents that would lead to free press coverage (see Studlar, "Perils of Pleasure" 273–75).

While the vamp as an onscreen harbinger of sexual anarchy had to be publicized and exploited by Bara's offscreen persona, the latter had to be brought into compliance with the film industry's anti-theatrical model of respectable film stardom. Bara could be bizarre. She could be exotically eccentric. But central to her construction as a film star was the imperative that her offscreen identity could not follow the model of Sarah Bernhardt in one important direction—she could not follow Bernhardt down the treacherous path of sexual nonconformity. This strategy was advanced consistently in written texts such as "The Divine Theda," where the author claims that ancient Egyptian inscriptions prophesy Bara's appearance as a woman "who shall seem a snake to most men. . . . Yet . . . she shall be good and virtuous" (Roberta Courtlandt, "The Divine Theda," *Motion Picture Magazine*, April 1917, 59).

Photographs, however, were not as consistently on message. Like those for other stars, they often emphasized Bara's resemblance to her screen characters and sometimes suggested a different identity altogether. In a 1915 portrait of the star in *Motion Picture Magazine*'s "Gallery of Picture Players," Bara is shown attired in an elaborately embroidered Chinese robe covering her almost completely (November 1915, 14). In spite of the Orientalist theme, the actress's rather passive expression as well as the modesty of her costuming contribute to making the photo a somewhat anomalous visualization of Bara in relation to what would become the dominant tropes of her femininity.

In contrast, many publicity images regularly featured Bara in revealing Orientalist costumes (usually from her films) or shoulder-baring dresses. Characteristically, a studio portrait featured in a 1916 *Motion Picture Classic* article shows Bara dressed in black and appearing in profile. One of her hands is placed underneath her chin; her fingers point away from her face in an approximate imitation of Ruth St. Denis's signature pose from her famous dance, "The Cobras" ("Theda, Misunderstood Vampire," October 1916, 27). Often quite sensationally, photos aligned Bara with symbols of death and darkness, as in the shot that serves to introduce the same article (25). In this photo, she is shown straddling a skeleton, with her hair flowing over the remains, thus creating a sexually suggestive "hair tent" recalling Burne-Jones's vampire painting. This image, one of several that exist of Bara posed with a skeleton, might have been influenced by a 1914 Orientalist painting entitled *Sphinx* produced by American artist William Sergeant Kendall (Dykstra 263). First used in conjunction with the selling of *A Fool There Was*, Bara's image is accompanied here by a caption that evokes the ending of the film: "The vampire mourns over the remains of one of her former victims." It also may have conjured up memories of the cabinet card featuring Sarah Bernhardt sleeping in a coffin and the legend that the stage actress kept the skeletal remains of a young man who died for love of her

Publicity for *A Fool There Was* (1914) shows Bara straddling a skeleton, with her hair flowing over the remains. Courtesy of the Academy of Motion Picture Arts and Sciences.

in her apartment. In a similar vein, a publicity shot for *Cleopatra* shows Bara, dressed in street wear, staring down onto an Egyptian mummy casket, with reflections off the glass museum case superimposing the face of Bara onto that of the mummy.

At the same time that photos like these linked Bara to her films and their representation of the dark woman as a harbinger of desire inseparable from death, some fan articles worked against the grain of the disturbing connotations of these photographs to suggest that the actress was completely different from her screen image as a destructive vamp. Roberta Courtlandt does this first through the title of one of her articles, "Theda, Misunderstood Vampire," but also in its subtitle, which asserts that Bara's "greatest wish" is "to play the part of a sweet, essentially feminine woman" (*Motion Picture Classic*, October 1916, 26). To support the appropriateness of this wish, Bara is depicted on a subsequent page in a flower-print diaphanous frock and a beribboned hat. This image is said to show how she "appears off the screen," but it actually depicts Bara in costume for one of her rare nonvamp roles as the sacrificing mother in *East Lynne* (1916).

"Theda, Misunderstood Vampire" is typical of fan magazine star discourse and its approach to Bara. It works to distance the actor from her screen image, but also binds Bara to the vamp's image of deadly sexual allure. Courtlandt affirms that distance as well as the inevitable binding by observing that "a picture vampire gives up much in order not to step out of her character" (26). That Bara has a natural connection to her casting as a vamp, in spite of trying to play "her character" offscreen, is advanced in Courtlandt's recounting of a story from the actress's schoolgirl days. Other children "were afraid" of Bara as a reaction to her "big and black and strange-looking" eyes and the "sometimes weird fancies that possessed her" (25). The mistaken belief that she is dangerous haunts her adulthood as well: Bara reveals her womanly sensitivity by bemoaning the fact that "people hate me so" because "they refuse to believe that I, in real life, am not as I am in my screen life" (26). The article concludes that the actress is not a vamp, but "just a warmly human woman, with a woman's loves, desires and ambition" (28). Thus, while proving that Bara has a natural affinity for playing strange women, readers can be comforted by Courtlandt's first-hand knowledge that the star does not possess the same dangerous and deviant nature as her screen characterizations. Similarly, in "A Peep into Their Boudoirs" (*Motion Picture Classic*, May 1917, 19–20), Bara is revealed as living in a house that is not a vampish den of iniquity, but "a treasure-house of splendid, old-fashioned Chippendale and Sheraton bits," that reveals her tasteful (and expensive) penchant for antiques that turns her home into a model for consumerism (another favorite theme of fan magazines). Bara is shown posing in the mirror of her expensive vanity, with reporter Carol Lee extending to her readers the all-important gesture of reassurance: "Miss Bara isn't a bit like the cruel, designing creature that scenario writers would have you believe" (20).

While fan magazines sometimes assumed an ironic and undermining tone toward star construction, this seems especially evident in their response to the movie industry's textual conflation of the modern sexualized woman with the oriental archetype of the vamp. Specialists in vamping in the 1910s—including but by no means limited to Bara, Valeska Suratt, Louise Glaum, Virginia Pearson, and Mutual's Bara-look-alike, Margarita Fischer—might assume aspects of the stereotypical screen vamp in interviews and photos in order to call attention to and fulfill their obligation to "sell" their screen roles. As a result, fan magazines might inscribe an actress as eccentric or odd, confused about her identity, or even a poseur taken in by the industry's pressure to create a sensational masquerade for her fans' consumption, but she could not be promiscuous and predatory.

Star discourse might align the offscreen style and sexual allure of the star with the stereotypical screen vamp, but inevitably attention is drawn also to the exaggerated nature of the latter. In 1916, Bara's rival in vamp-dom at Fox, Valeska Suratt, became the subject of a fan magazine tongue-in-check description of her bedroom: "Black and white, please know, is typical of screen vampires. . . . Why this should be so must ever remain a mystery. . . . Returning to Miss Suratt's gorgeous den of iniquity—it is here she plans the devastation of men's lives and the wrecking of their homes—we find a splendid example of the effectiveness of black and white for boudoir use" ("A Peep into Their Boudoirs," 19). Suratt's over-the-top attempt to express her screen personality in her private life through the stereotyped vamp style is rendered ridiculous.

While Valeska Suratt could not be taken seriously for trying (over-strenuously) to be like her screen characters, Bara's attempt to escape vamp roles and show that change through her lifestyle is rendered equally excessive and silly in Alma Whitaker's tongue-in-cheek article for the *Los Angeles Times* in 1918 ("New Theda Bara Is Born of Exclusive Society Setting," 28 July 1918, 2:1–2). Whitaker explores Bara's private life in relation to the announcement that the actress "will vamp no more" (see also Grace Kingsley, "Theda Bara, Expert on Tears, Makes Smiles," *Los Angeles Times*, 7 July 1918, 3:1). Whitaker relates that Theda and her sister Lori are ensconced in a Los Angeles mansion once owned by socialite Mrs. Randolph Huntington Miner, with Bara's life consisting of reading *Little Women* and "feeding the little chick-a-biddies in the backyard." Whitaker teases: "I ask you, could she continue to play Cleopatra in two breast plates and a wisp of chiffon for the sensation of the rabble after that?" (2:1–2).

In general, an overtly skeptical attitude in star discourse toward the off-screen identity of actresses who played orientalized vamps—chief among them Bara—appears to reflect an understanding that these actresses were called upon to encourage the public's desire to consume their taboo-violating screen roles. Yet within the framework of the industry's demand that its players be respectable, a star like Bara—and her numerous rivals in vamp-dom—needed also to be distinguished from vampire screen roles in ways that actors who played more sympathetic and less sexually transgressive roles might not require. Star discourse's disavowing "I know but neverthe-less" strategy thus served to reaffirm the tendency to play hide and seek with the "truth" of the star's personality, sometimes aligning a female star like Bara with power, independence, and nonconformity, but only in the star's expressed thoughts, in her personal style, or her professional choices—never in her private sexual behavior. Thus, whether feeding "little chick-a-biddies" in the backyard or even in a reverie calling up her past lives in Spain, Egypt, or points further east, Theda Bara remained as sexually "pure" offscreen as Mary Pickford was on.

☆★★★★★ "I'm Bad," or How a Nice Jewish Girl Becomes a Star

In 1909, songstress Fanny Brice performed the Jewish comedy song "Sadie Salome, Go Home!" in burlesque. Written by Irving Berlin and Edgar Leslie, the song was the centerpiece of Brice's parody of a well-known phenomenon among women: young single females—including Jewish ones (like Brice herself)—became "stage-struck" and left home to try show business (see "The Stage Struck Girl," *Theatre*, November 1917, 249–50). In her burlesque routine featuring the song, Brice sang about Sadie, a girl of the Jewish immigrant class who decides to become an "actress lady" by dancing the role of the Judean princess, Salome. Sadie's boyfriend, Mose, reacts with alarm: "Don't do that dance, I tell you Sadie. That's not a bus'ness for a lad-y! . . . Oy, Oy, Oy, Oy—Where is your clothes? Oy! Such a sad disgrace. No one looks in your face."[5]

Brice's parodic performance depended not only on her audience's knowledge of stage struck girls, but upon public awareness of the wave of "Salomania" that had recently rolled across the Atlantic from Britain to the United States (see Glenn 119; Showalter 160–62). This controversial fad took the form of women who performed Salome's "dance of the seven veils" in many amateur and professional venues—at all-female house parties, dance schools, or on the stage (see Kendall 10–12; Showalter 161–62; Studlar, "Out-Salome-ing" 106). Via "Salomania," Salome, the Judean princess, became the center of attention in the United States. One New York newspaper commentator suggested that Salome's appeal was simple: "She is bad and that is a great element in her attraction" (Glenn 96). Although Sarah Bernhardt (another Jewish "Sadie") rejected the role of Salome, in her wake Mary Garden, Maud Allan, and Gertrude Hoffman went on to enact Salome to great audience demand in (respectively) opera, legitimate theater, and vaudeville. The Ballets Russes took the "Dance of the Seven Veils" and transferred it to their version of *Cleopatra* for Ida Rubenstein to perform (Showalter 160). In 1908, New York's Metropolitan Opera promised an equally high-brow *Salome* (in the form of Richard Strauss's opera), which censors banned. Nevertheless, a trove of performing women, including Brice, pitched their portrayals of Salome—in varying degrees of mirth or melodrama—at American audiences. These included La Sylphe, Olive Fremstadt, Julia Marlowe, Eva Tanguay, Laura Guerite, Lotta Faust, and Aida Overton Walker, the first African American Salome ("All Sorts and Kinds of Salomes," *Theatre*, April 1909, 130).

Fox claimed Theda Bara was an exotic artiste born out of the meeting of Europe and the Middle East, but she was actually another "Sadie

Salome," the stage-struck daughter of Jewish immigrants who had settled in Cincinnati (Genini 6). And, like Sadie of the song, Theodosia left home to become a sinful Salome. As one of those many Sadies who, in seeking stardom, offered exhibitionist display of their bodies as Salome, Bara had absorbed a phenomenon that Susan Glenn argues had become thoroughly Americanized. Not only did American women do what Bernhardt (twenty years before) had not dared, these stage-struck girls, many from immigrant backgrounds, had taken up "the godless sex-crazed ways of American mainstream popular culture, including its Salome dancing" (Glenn 120). Arguably, Bara would become the most famous Salome of the 1910s. Inarguably, because of the "miracle of the movies," her performance of Oscar Wilde's dancing Jewish princess was seen by more of the American public than any other incarnation of the role.

Salome may have been "bad," but Bara denied that the character as she portrayed her was a "vamp" ("Theda Bara Sees Salome as Pale-Green Flower," *Los Angeles Times*, 17 February 1918, 3:1). By 1918, Bara's typical interview strategy was to deny the obvious redundancy of roles that much of the public regarded as mere vamps. In keeping with her attempt to artistically elevate her acting, "La Bara" represented her Salome as serious rather than sensational: "As Salome I tried to absorb the poetic impulse of Oscar Wilde. I tried to interpret the extraordinary, the hopeless moral disintegration of a woman's soul with sincere artistic effort" (Glenn 123). In spite of such pronouncements, Bara would be on the receiving end of many cries from city and state censorship boards who asked, like Sadie Salome's Mose, "Where is your clothes?" Bara claimed to be uninterested in censors (like those in St. Louis) who were appalled by her characters' daring costuming: "I never think of the flesh when I am working on a role such as Salome," she sniffed (Hamilton 54).

Did Bara or her studio try to repress her Jewish background? How did the star's Jewish origins figure in star discourse focused on Bara and in the trajectory of her brief career? Bara's true birth name, with its implication that she was a "Sadie" from the mundane Midwest, appeared in print no more than a few months after the debut of *A Fool There Was*. These revelations directly contradicted her studio-generated biography, and the publication of her actual birth name may have allowed some viewers to infer the actress's Jewish origins.

In general, fan discourse left space for contradictions and discrepancies in the revelation of the "authentic" truth of the star's identity, but pressure was put on Theda Bara's star construction by the need to negotiate the contradictions created by the circulation of biographies that so radically contradicted

Theda Bara as the Queen of the Nile in the kind of costume that enraged censors but made the actress a box office bonanza.

each other. Bara's two biographies began to emerge almost simultaneously with her first screen success. In *Photoplay* of September 1915, Wallace Franklin offered up the contradictions in Bara's star construction in typical fan magazine style with a tongue-in-cheek satire on the excesses of Fox's publicity department make-believe combined with his farcical imitation of likely fan reaction to the news of Bara's plain American upbringing: "I wish to believe, I am going to believe, I do believe that Allah is Allah, and that Bara is Bara; that the ivory angel of purgatory is an Eastern star, born under the shadow of the sphinx" ("Purgatory's Ivory Angel," 69). He goes on to assert that he has chosen to disbelieve "those stupid people who insist that Theda Bara's right name is Theodosia Goodman and that she is, by, of and from Cincinnati" (70).

Also demonstrating how a problem or truth "gap" in star construction could be placed in the category of Hollywood humbug, Archie Bell, writing in *Theatre* ("Theda Bara—the Vampire Woman," November 1915, 246, 254), concluded that Bara, with her claim that she has been reincarnated many times over and her habit of placing two Amen-Ra clay statuettes beside her "vampire lunch" plate of raw beef and lettuce, displayed behavior so very, very strange that the actress could never have been born Theodosia Goodman of Cincinnati, Ohio: "No, it is impossible. Theda Bara must have been born on Saturn, Mars . . . or perhaps on Venus." Bell's acknowledgment of Bara's impossibly wacky, over-the-top Hollywood excess, however, did not absolve the actress of the burden of accounting for how she could be born in both Cincinnati and the Sahara, nor did it help the actress cultivate public confidence in the authenticity of her star persona, a quality often cited as favorably differentiating film stars like Mary Pickford from stage actors like Bernhardt (Gordon Gassaway, "Personality—Plus," *Motion Picture Classic*, September 1915, 55–57).

Bara and the studio kept up the pretense of her birth "in the shadow of the Sphinx" throughout 1916 and into 1917. During this time period, Bara's identity is put into question time and time again, and she seems to have tired of being asked about her origins. In February 1916, she answered a reporter's questions about her real name and background by testily responding: "And what, pray, has that to do with my art? What does it matter who I am or whence I came?" In November 1917, the *New York Times* revealed that members of Bara's immediate family were all legally changing their names from Goodman to Bara. By 1918, Bara's sister, Lori Bara, formerly known as Esther Goodman, was appearing frequently in stories focused on Theda's home life.[6] Certainly a family name change was not an unprecedented gesture among stage and screen folk: stage actress Gladys Smith's family changed their name to "Pickford" when Gladys attained success as "Mary Pickford." However, the Goodman to Bara name change of Theda's immediate family may also have been an attempt to repress public perception that her parents were Jewish émigrés. This is in keeping, it might be argued, with the repression of Douglas Fairbanks's Jewish father, Charles Ullman, in his superstar son's biography. Still, there seems to have been no direct reference to Bara's Jewish origins in star discourse before 1918, and the star stepped into film as a cultural platform in which many Jewish performers became important cultural icons.

Bara became an object of satire almost from the beginning of her appearance in film, but none of these mild satirical jabs (at least in fan magazines) appear to have referred to her Jewishness, only to the excesses of the screen vamp. However, in 1916, Fanny Brice made Bara the object of a devastatingly satiric imitation of the movie star in "I'm Bad" for the Ziegfield Follies. In the same year, another Jewish comedy song appeared, obviously derived from Berlin's "Sadie" song. Its overdetermined references to Jewishness (Salome/Sadie/Bara/Brice) were also present in Brice's performance of "I'm Bad." "Since Sarah Saw Theda Bara," by Alex Gerber and Harry Jentes, now made Bara the new Salome to be imitated by Jewish ghetto girls like "Sadie Cohn": "Oi, how she rolls her eyes, Oi, she can hypnotize. With a wink she'll fascinate, And she wiggles like a snake. . . . Since Sarah saw Theda Bara, She's a wer-ra wer-ra dangerous girl" (Gerber and Jentes, "Since Sarah Saw Theda Bara," Leo Feist Inc., 1916).

In 1918, an openly hostile account of Bara, her dual biographies, and her constructed and exotic persona as a cover for her Jewishness appeared in *Photoplay*. The author, Delight Evans, draws pointed attention to the actress's "rather painful [French] accent" and evasive answers: "She is a consummate actress; but it is such a pity that she must make up for the role. She had a part to play that afternoon; and she played it much more cleverly than she played 'Cleopatra.' The only thing her p.a. doesn't tell about her is the truth." Part of that truth as reported by Evans is one man's account of knowing Bara when she played "second parts" "in a little Jewish Theatre on the East Side" ("Does Theda Bara Believe Her Own Press Agent?" May 1918, 62–63, 107). A 1920 article in *Picture Play* on the Orientalized dancer/film actor Doraldina suggests the humbug of the film industry in general and of Theda Bara more specifically. The author, Herbert Howe, notes, "There are moments when my faith in the wickedness of Salome and Cleopatra is sorely tried. It is my experience in motion pictures which has caused me to disbelieve everything that is written." His primary example of this experience is "the expose of Theda Bara, with proof positive . . . [that she] is a dutiful daughter of Ma and Pa Goodman and a regular attendant at the synagogue" ("Outstripping Salome," November 1920, 44). By 1921, Bara's mother was authoring an article in *Motion Picture Classic* accompanied by pictures of Theda, mother Pauline, and sister Lori (Pauline L. Bara, "My Theda Bara," Part 2, January 1921, 19–20, 79). However, this was after Bara's contract with Fox was abrogated, and she was looking for reentry into the movie industry.

Buszek argues that Bara's ethnic difference, her "darkness," and her Jewishness made her subject to "the larger American panic" over immigration (160–63). But how can such a simplistic reflection theory of society/mass media account for why Bara could attain such overwhelming popularity in 1915 and be a "has been" in mid-1919? Is there actual evidence that views on this matter changed so quickly during U.S. involvement in the war (1917–1919)? Had Bara become so unpopular so quickly because of her Jewishness—in spite of her much-lauded public efforts for the war effort and her articulate, heart-felt assertions of American patriotism at war-bond rallies and visits to army hospitals (see "Southern California Goes Over Top on Liberty Day," *Los Angeles Times*, 27 April 1918, 2:1; Genini 71–73)?

☆☆☆☆★ Conclusion

Bara's very rapid falling out of favor as a star is obviously a complicated phenomenon, made even more challenging as a research subject because of the loss of most of her films. Unlike Pickford, Fairbanks, or Chaplin, she never gained control of her career or her films. She was at the mercy of Fox in determining the quality of her productions, which was often, according to reviews, not very good. Fox oversaturated the public with her vamp films and, like rival studios, featured other players (like Suratt) in similar vehicles . Thus, Bara became subject to fluctuation in production trends that, in this circumstance, may have been exaggerated by virtue of the great number of vamp-centered films made within a short time span. Also, the vamp type was a figure of feminine seduction so exotic and extreme and so "touchy" and troublesome in its sexual implications to Americans that it easily became a target for anxiety-deflecting ridicule.

Yet when Bara ventured into roles beyond the stereotyped vamp character, audience response was mixed at best, and she herself acknowledged this in interviews. By 1918, the *New York Times* suggested of "the old-time vamp": "a surfeited public emphatically says it has had enough of her" (Antony Anderson, "Drama," 4 December 1918, 2:3). In the same year, it was obvious that Bara was tired of playing Fox's game, and by 1919, with the vamp phenomenon having reached its maximum return, Fox was unwilling to pay the actress almost $5,000 a week for what promised to be less box-office return on their dollar.

Would things have been different had Fox offered Bara better vehicles all along? Had she been a more accomplished actress? Had she not been called on to negotiate the daring and extravagant spectacle of the vamp figure? Would her fate have been different had she, like Pickford, been able to

But while Farrar obviously represents a classic instance of the star-making strategy of borrowing fame garnered from elsewhere, this chapter argues that the specific contours of Farrar's personality and training made her far more valuable to the film industry than her opera prestige alone would suggest. Her importance resided in her ability to unite two apparently incompatible aims: she permitted film to make a claim for the upper-middle-class carriage trade at the same moment that she helped to domesticate a cadre of risqué "brothel play" roles.

Farrar was perhaps the most popular American-born opera star of the first quarter of the twentieth century. After beginning her career in 1901 in Germany, where she trained with Lilli Lehmann (Farrar 34) and was rumored to be a possible marriage prospect for the son of Kaiser Wilhelm II, she returned to the United States in 1906, where in 1907 she performed as the first American Cio-Cio-San in Giacomo Puccini's *Madama Butterfly*, opposite Enrico Caruso. She continued her career largely at the Metropolitan Opera under the general direction of Giulio Gatti-Casazza, performing frequently with Caruso in operas such as *Carmen*. Farrar developed a fervent following, with troops of primarily female "Gerry-flappers" (including Dorothy Gish) worshiping at her shrine (Wagenknecht, "Geraldine" 24). Indeed, during her final performance at the Metropolitan Opera in 1922, the "Gerry-flappers" unfurled a banner reading "None But You" (Brenda Ueland, "Geraldine Ferrar and Her Father," *Liberty*, 25 April 1925, 23), and Tim Page noted that "Farrar was mobbed by thousands of admirers who escorted her open car up Broadway" after her last matinee ("The Opera's First Superstar," *New York Times*, 28 February 1982, D19). Cecil B. DeMille attempted to explain the swarms of admirers by describing the Farrar personality as "not synthetic. It was magic" (DeMille 140). When she signed her first film contract in 1915 with Lasky, her participation in filmmaking was considered quite a coup; Lasky, Morris Gest, and Samuel Goldwyn all emphasize their personal roles in garnering her services, suggesting how important her stardom seemed to each of them (Gest, "Winning Farrar," *Photoplay*, July 1915, 115; Lasky 116; Goldwyn 83). Indeed, William C. de Mille describes her at the time of her first contract as a star so important that she was Famous Players's best hedge against the drawing power of Mary Pickford, who had been signed by Adolph Zukor (de Mille 147).

Clearly, then, Farrar's film career, involving only fourteen films and four directors, marks a moment when the film industry successfully used class to appeal to the mass. Both Lasky and Goldwyn claim in their autobiographies that Farrar's presence before the camera represented a bid for high culture's long-delayed approval of cinema (Lasky 116; Goldwyn 83), a view ratified by

Sumiko Higashi, who sees Farrar's contract as the sign of a more aggressive and programmatic attempt to extend the mass of filmgoers upward (*Cecil* 1). But more than obvious lion-hunting explains Farrar's value to her producers: she was not only already famous but associated with particular kinds of realist dramas that her two studios (Paramount and later Goldwyn) desired to replicate onscreen. If Farrar's movies attracted highbrow audiences, they also made it possible for producers to introduce less genteel stories and more daring performances than would have been acceptable had they been undertaken by someone without Farrar's associations with European high culture and Yankee rectitude. Specifically, stories of "the woman who pays," the reformed or unreformed woman of ill-fame, would not have been as acceptable onscreen had they not been enacted by an opera star whose reputation as a performer was associated with a notable gift in classical music.

These roles, which represent a significant portion of major nineteenth-century repertoire for sopranos, consorted both with Farrar's taste and with her operatic résumé. Katie Johnson notes that a "consistent feature of both highbrow and lowbrow entertainments [was] . . . the repeated obsession with the prostitute figure" (2), adducing as evidence fifty stage plays involving such characters produced in New York between 1898 and 1922 (1), rising to a peak during the panics about young urban women being sold into white slavery during the early 1910s. While narratives of this sort had been present in film as well, they were often presented clinically, buttressed by claims that they were forces for social hygiene rather than entertainments, and/or featured competent but asexual heroines whose aim it was to contain sexuality rather than to celebrate it. Farrar's reputation, fan following, respectable background, and association with serious music made it possible to claim for art her performances as a sexually liberated woman, thus cementing the respectability of quasi-operatic and sexually suggestive plots for a status-conscious and socially vulnerable industry. That Farrar was simultaneously, as an actress, part of what Johnson calls the "display economy" essential to narratives of the fallen woman of the early twentieth century (22) and a woman who earned her living through the mastery of a demanding training explains the dual nature of her appeal. As a performer impersonating the seduced or the seductress on stage, Farrar flirted with the déclassé; but as a competent, admired singer she held the déclassé at arm's length. Her offstage reputation for hard work, probity, and devotion to her parents also made any imputation of personal irregularity unthinkable. Clearly, Farrar possessed a shrewd understanding of her gifts as a performer and of the state of two performance traditions, one well established and the other just developing.

Farrar was an alert businesswoman in addition to being an insightful and articulate performer, and her decision to sign with Lasky indicates that the gratifications of Farrar-on-film were not exclusively on the studio's side. The offer to appear in motion pictures (which might even have originated with Farrar, as Goldwyn's account implies [Goldwyn 83]) came at the moment when the opera houses of Europe were closed to her as a result of World War I. When Farrar returned to the Metropolitan in triumph, signaling the Americanization of European high art, she doubtless intended to devote a significant part of her time to American audiences. Had the war not intervened, however, she would have expected to accept engagements in Europe that did not conflict with the Met season. Notably, her work in cinema was contained entirely in five summers, whether in Fort Lee or California, when her services as singer would otherwise not have been much in demand. For a woman who could foresee her eventual retirement from the opera stage (as Farrar mandated for herself at age forty), motion picture work offered a hedge against lost income and an opportunity to accumulate capital.

In a bid for recognition of the gentility and wealth of film producers, much was made of the size of Farrar's contracts in the press, with *Photoplay* and the *New York Times* reporting Jesse Lasky's offer of two dollars per minute of sunlight for the summer engagement (Gest, "Winning Farrar," *Photoplay*, July 1915, 117; "Miss Farrar in Movies," *New York Times*, 28 April 1915). Farrar received other emoluments, such as the use of a private rail car out to California, a furnished house, servants, and a private dressing room/bungalow equipped with grand piano (de Mille 140). Her salary for film work ultimately compared favorably with her compensation for singing. Farrar's 1918 contract with the Metropolitan Opera offered her $1,500 a performance for a season of forty-five performances (FP, box 12, folder 15),[1] an improvement upon her 1915 contract with Lasky, which provided $20,000 for eight weeks work (according to William de Mille [148], although the editor's note in Gest's account calculated her salary at $75,000 for the summer [115])—but her 1917 contract with Goldwyn offered her $150,000 for four months' work in each of her final two years, 1918 and 1919 (GP, File 4770, 12 July 1917 memo regarding contract). Farrar's penultimate contract with Goldwyn contained the provision that she would receive the larger of 10 percent of the gross or $300,000 for the two years' work, a stipulation that sales figures never triggered (FP, box 12, folder 11), but there was no doubt that Farrar was earning one of the largest salaries granted a "part-time" movie star. Her multiple sources of income meant that when her popularity waned and Goldwyn sought to suspend her contract for a time, she could afford simply to tear up the agreement, an act of generosity so unprecedented in Goldwyn's experience that he marvels at it in his autobiography (Goldwyn 154–56).

Film also had the potential of multiplying the effects, in terms of both money and fan following, of recording contracts that Farrar had already negotiated. Like Caruso, Farrar performed early for Victor Records (beginning in 1907), evidently commencing her recording career in Germany a year or two prior. Film similarly held out the promise of preserving another aspect of her persona, as a 1915 plug in *Woman's Home Companion* attested. In it, Farrar acknowledges the importance of the phonograph in popularizing her work but notes that "to you in the thousands of small towns and to many of you in the big cities I am but the voice, an elusive being—no visible personality. It is because I want to come closer to you in reality that I have taken up that other imperishable record—the motion picture. I want to record my work as an actress in 'Madame Butterfly,' 'The Goose Girl,' 'Carmen,' as well as my singing. I want to give you these records now, while youth smiles upon me" (Helen Duey, "The Newest Motion Picture Star," August 1915, 16). Farrar's recordings may also have helped the domestication process, making her seem a more familiar figure, as someone associated with the home phonograph. Her film performances, as she suggests, are likewise an amplification of an already extant persona and not a creation *de novo*.

Farrar's correspondence shows her to be alert to the status problems in opera, and, in another instance of mutual colonization between Farrar and her producers, she may have hoped to win opera fans through cinema performances. Her opera career commenced as the less disciplined, more demonstrative audience for such entertainments, as detailed by Lawrence Levine in *Highbrow/Lowbrow*, was subdued into well-behaved bourgeois worshippers at the shrine of culture. Farrar's return to New York occurred at just the moment that Gatti-Casazza noted that American audiences were so disciplined that they might be insufficiently critical of poor work (Levine 194). The price of the disciplined audience was the loss of some of its members to more popular entertainments, and Farrar appears to have come down on the side of maintaining concessions to popular taste even within "highbrow" forms. In an undated reply to a letter from stage actress Minnie Maddern Fiske, who was apparently contemplating the writing of an opera libretto, Farrar writes that "a good imitation of our popular repertoire is not to be despised. If there is a melody or motif for mechanical reproduction, so much the better for operatic success. We are using double bills often—and the change is very appreciable to offset the heavy repertoire of great length and stereotyped opera form" (FP, box 9, folder 12). As this letter suggests, both the film industry and contemporary opera (represented presumably by figures such as Ruggero Leoncavallo as well as Puccini) experienced a hunger for texts that were at once popular and critically well regarded.

It may be worth briefly comparing Farrar's screen career to those of her contemporaries Caruso and the Scottish-born Mary Garden, who moved to films more slowly and whose performances on celluloid never received much praise beyond their novelty value, limiting them both to just two films each. Farrar was able to turn her operatic background to greater advantage (*Carmen* alone gave rise to numerous filmic spinoffs, as I argue below), whereas Caruso and Garden floundered when they attempted to parlay stardom in opera into stardom on the screen. Caruso, for example, played a Caruso-like opera singer in *My Cousin* (1918), which did so badly at the box office that his second feature, *A Splendid Romance* (1919), which also had a musical background, was never released; Garden made the unpopular *Thaïs* (1917) for Goldwyn, another courtesan role chosen presumably because of her strong association with it on the stage. Garden's second film, *The Splendid Sinner* (1918), in which she plays the erstwhile mistress of a German spy, similarly exploited a somewhat risqué past—although evidently not very successfully, inasmuch as *Variety* commented that "some people will say that this picture did not get over because it did not have the usual happy ending. To the majority of the audiences the fact that Mary Garden as the heroine was shot at sunrise will be an extremely happy ending" (5 April 1918, n.p.). Notably, only one of Farrar's film roles, her *Carmen* (1915), was an adaptation of an opera, although several of her films were set in the world of opera or involved the travails of a struggling young performer.

★★★★★ Farrar and Role Construction

The length of Farrar's screen career relative to Caruso's and Garden's can be explained in part by her good fortune in being associated with David Belasco and the de Milles,[2] who made her the recipient of stories that suited her performance style. Not only was Belasco a close connection of the De Mille theatrical dynasty, having worked with Henry De Mille and William C. de Mille and Cecil B. DeMille, but he also helped as both playwright and impresario to mediate between the worlds of opera and the stage. His work (often with collaborators) was the source of two Puccini adaptations, *Madama Butterfly* and *La Fanciulla del West*, and he also adapted Pierre Berton and Charles Simon's *Zaza* in 1898, which two years later became the opera by Leoncavallo, with which Farrar was to finish her career at the Met. Gest, one of the figures who claimed to have captured Farrar for cinema, was Belasco's son-in-law, reinforcing the importance of the connections among Belasco, the de Milles, and, of course, Lasky. This shared connection with Belasco suggests that Farrar was to some degree already well integrated, certainly on a personal level but also in terms of taste, with the figures who were experimenting in film with realist texts involving, to paraphrase Victorien Sardou, the "tortured woman." Indeed, Belasco has very strong associations with the brothel play; beyond *Butterfly* and *Zaza*, there are his productions of *The Easiest Way* and *Lulu Belle*. Farrar's opera repertoire had already exposed her to the kind of drama that appealed to the tastes and business strategies of the film producers of the mid-1910s, and her understanding of herself as performer mandated, as we shall see, a desire for more Belasco-like texts.

Indeed, developing the right texts for Farrar initially proved to be a family affair for the de Milles and their immediate circle, likewise steeped in Belasco. Cecil directed all six of Farrar's Paramount pictures, and William wrote or co-wrote the scenarios for the first three: *Maria Rosa* (1916), the former Sarah Bernhardt vehicle that also starred Farrar's husband Lou Tellegen during its American run; *Carmen*, which obliged William to return to the Prosper Mérimée novella for reasons of copyright; and *Temptation* (1915), a project shared by William with Hector Turnbull, scenarist of *The Cheat* (1915). Now apparently lost, *Temptation* shares *The Cheat*'s interest in a woman who is obliged to "pay" for services rendered, bringing it in line with the plots of a number of Belasco texts. The screenplay reveals *Temptation* to be the story of a young woman who is brought to the verge of prostituting herself to a malignant impresario who demands her sexual favors to forward her opera career and the career of her fiancé, a violinist and composer played by Pedro de Cordoba. The final scene spares the heroine the agony of surrendering herself to her pursuer through a convenient murder performed by her discarded rival, but not until she presents herself to pay her "debt." Stills indicate the film's interest in orientalist detail, including costumes associated with a production of *Butterfly*, the appearance of Sessue Hayakawa in a minor role, and the deployment as decoration of the brazier so prominently featured in *The Cheat* as the means of heating the iron chop by which the heroine is branded in that film, suggesting an attempt to integrate Farrar into a narrative that shared some of that film's preoccupations (they were released within two weeks of each other in December 1915). While *The Cheat* now looms large in any account of the important films of 1915, Higashi observes that *Carmen* received bigger notices among domestic critics (*Cecil* 111).

Farrar and DeMille on the set of *Temptation* (1915). Courtesy of the Academy of Motion Picture Arts and Sciences.

The war itself was the inspiration for her fourth film, *Joan the Woman* (1917), in which Farrar played Joan of Arc in a patriotic narrative of the rescue of France framed by the experiences of a young British soldier (Wallace Reid), who must die in the trenches to atone for the sins of an ancestor responsible for Joan's martyrdom. *Joan* marks the second phase of Farrar's association with Paramount, the final three screenplays for which were supplied by Jeanie MacPherson, who also performed as a cigarette girl in *Carmen*. The remaining two MacPherson scenarios include *The Devil Stone* (1917) and *The Woman God Forgot* (1917). Beatrice De Mille (mother of Cecil and William) supplied the story idea for *The Devil Stone*, which survives in a partial print at the Library of Congress and describes the travails of a Breton woman in thrall to a malignant jewel that appears also to dominate earlier incarnations of the heroine and which causes her to kill her first American husband. *The Woman God Forgot* is a tale about the fall of the Aztec Empire in which Tecza, daughter of Montezuma, works against her father for love of a Spanish soldier again played by Reid. The latter film, now apparently lost, clearly hoped to capitalize on DeMille's post-*Joan* confidence with large casts and historical detail. Stills from the film suggest that it looks forward in some degree to DeMille's racier films of the early 1920s (there was a sequence in which Farrar's attendants rose clothed from a bath while birds were released upward [Farrar 177]); at the very least, *Woman* clearly involved Farrar in the most risqué costuming of her film career.

If one were to characterize these films generally, one could say that they manifest three distinct strategies for packaging Farrar, the first two of which persisted into her association with Goldwyn from 1917 to 1919. The three strategies are, first, stories based on her association with a particular opera text (*Carmen* and its lesser avatar *Maria Rosa*, set in a similarly hot-blooded and violent peasant milieu); second, stories based on Farrar's connection with the social world of opera (*Temptation*); and, finally, stories that combine the topical with the historical epic or offer the epic alone. The first two strategies indicate a certain initial caution in the development of Farrar's screen persona, a judgment borne out by an examination of the planned opening credits for *Carmen* and *Maria Rosa*, which display photographs of Farrar's performances in a series of operas (see screenplays in SC). Similarly, the sharing of visual details between *The Cheat* and *Temptation* suggests that DeMille was feeling his way in the deployment of Farrar in

Farrar on set and in costume for *The Woman God Forgot* (1917). Courtesy of the Academy of Motion Picture Arts and Sciences.

narratives not immediately associated with roles for which she was already famous but that nonetheless mobilize the figure of the "woman who pays," beloved of both Belasco and Turnbull.

MacPherson's participation in role construction moved Farrar's persona in a different direction, partly in response to the ongoing war, but also, perhaps, in response to the competition presented by *The Birth of a Nation* (1915). *Joan the Woman*, for example, appears to be an opportunistic compound of interest in the topical (the war) and the conviction that Farrar was a substantial enough performer to carry the weight of an epic. *The Woman God Forgot* drops the topical element but turns the plot of *Joan the Woman* inside out: in *Joan*, the heroine refuses a sexual connection to serve her God and country; in *Woman*, she chooses love over service to her father and her Mexican deities, to the ruin of both. Not enough of *The Devil Stone* has survived to permit much analysis, except to note that it shares, like *Joan* and *Woman*, an interest in exotic locales and eras not contemporary with its making, including a part for Farrar as a barbaric Nordic queen in addition to a role as a modern American wife (who was raised as a simple Breton peasant!). Nonetheless, of these three narrative modes, *Carmen* represents both Farrar's best film and most important generic model.

☆☆★★★ The *Carmen* Prototype

Carmen elicited from Farrar an extraordinarily physical performance, involving dancing, biting, scaling a wall, and a knockdown fight with a fellow cigarette girl. While her other surviving performances do not have this kinetic component to the same degree, *Carmen* appears to be a significant template, inasmuch as films showcasing tigerish Spanish or part-Spanish women featured not only at the outset of Farrar's career but also in her engagements with the Goldwyn Company, which began when she did not renew her contract with Lasky after the summer of 1917 owing to difficulties created by her husband Tellegen at Paramount. Farrar's heroines for Goldwyn include Pancha O'Brien in *The Hell Cat* (1918), who is part Spanish; *The Stronger Vow* (1919), set in Spain; and *The Woman and the Puppet* (1920), which shares the Pierre Louÿs novel with Josef von Sternberg's *The Devil Is a Woman* (1935), describing the fortunes of Concha Perez. Despite Farrar's mounting frustration with weak scripts at Goldwyn, these efforts to leverage her association with one Spanish heroine into success with several others were clearly attempts to recapture the good box office of *Carmen*. Indeed, Farrar noted the similarity in one case, claiming in an interview about *The Hell Cat* that Pancha O'Brien is "more like Carmen than any other part I have ever played. She has the same quick temper and imperious nature" (Weitzel 39). The selection of these roles also attempted to play to Farrar's command of the psychology of the rebellious, unfeminine, and highly sexual heroine of that opera.

Because *Carmen* is a major structuring element in Farrar's film career, it is worth pausing to examine in more detail what that role might mean historically. In her account of nineteenth-century female performance in opera, Susan Rutherford suggests that sexual "knowingness," described as a woman's consciousness of her power to seduce and her eagerness to use it, was read as particularly licentious (268). *Carmen*, which premiered in 1875, shocked contemporaries because it appeared to require this attribute if the star, playing a worker in a cigarette factory who seduces a soldier, were to act the part in keeping with the new vogue for realism, which often meant, for example, studying the clothing of actual cigarette girls. Rutherford notes that realism in female performance was often read as sexual rebellion, and it maintained its power to alarm even sophisticated viewers to the end of the nineteenth century, when George Bernard Shaw reported himself shocked by Emma Calvé (one of Farrar's heroines and models). Her Carmen was "a superstitious, pleasure-loving good-for-nothing, caught by the outside of anything glittering, with no power but the power of seduction, which she exercises without sense or decency" (Rutherford 269). While Farrar might have disputed Shaw's notion of Carmen as wanton, she endorsed the view of the character as deliberate seductress. Writing at some length on "the psychology of Carmen" for *The Bookman*, she argued that Carmen's "beauty, her position, her race compelled her to be what she was. Admiration she demanded and obtained as freely as the flower demands and absorbs the sunshine that gives it life. The mere indifference of José aroused her—truly womanly—sense of injustice and pique. Homage was her birthright. And she proposed to have it—obtain it as she might" (Farrar, "The Psychology of Carmen" [as recorded by Frederic Dean], *The Bookman* 42.4, 1915, 413).

Twenty-one years after Calvé's 1894 performance, this interpretation of Carmen's character must have been prevalent, inasmuch as Theda Bara, partisan of the vamp-as-feminist school of performance in films such as *A Fool There Was* (1915), was simultaneously appearing in a version of *Carmen* as Farrar's film was distributed. Nevertheless, Farrar facilitated making the seduction trope respectable in its translation from opera stage—where, after initial reactions of horror, it had been made safe for consumption by cultivated women—to the screen, where it still had the capacity to alarm in 1915. The *New York Times*, for example, commented of Farrar's performance that "her playing is able. Also it is bold, bald, and in dubious taste," and the review noted that Bara's *Carmen* had "none of the elements which make the Lasky 'Carmen' remarkable, and none, it should be added, of the elements which make the latter picture objectionable" ("Geraldine Farrar: Seen But Not Heard," *New York Times*, 1 November 1915). It is notable that Bara, who was presented offscreen as an exotic and mysterious heartbreaker vamping in the cause of feminism (Koszarski 274–76), found herself in a film that could afford fewer risks with the presentation of Carmen than did Farrar, whose offscreen persona was that of the middle-class American girl who made good in a difficult art. Even so, as this criticism of Farrar's performance implies, a too-knowing presentation of the seductress could still cause discomfort. Farrar's autobiography observes that *Zaza* disturbed and excited Metropolitan audiences as late as the early 1920s (151), suggesting that, even in opera, scenes of seduction had not been entirely domesticated. As further evidence of the contemporary perception of sensuality in Farrar's performances, Gertrude Atherton's 1923 novel *Black Oxen* includes a description of Farrar's Butterfly: "Farrar, almost supine in the arms of the seducer, was singing with the voluptuous abandon that makes this scene the most explicit in modern opera" (111). Nonetheless, Farrar's prestige was such that, as Lasky observed to Farrar when he signed her, "whatever you do, your public will accept it as right" (Lasky 116). For at least one upper-class young woman, Farrar's pictures were the first she was permitted to see, solely because her family had known Farrar at Lake George (Nash 186n36).

⭐⭐⭐⭐⭐ Farrar's Performance Style

Farrar understood herself to be as much actress as singer on the opera stage, as demonstrated by her relish for the psychological dimensions of the heroines of the realist plays that were coming to dominate both the legitimate theater and the opera. She was, moreover, an intuitive performer who counseled the aspirant to opera to "sing, not from the outside, in; but from the inside, out" (Rutherford 272). Edward Wagenknecht reports that Farrar had "often spoken slightingly of her voice. At the height of her operatic career, she referred to her 'mediocre instrument,' and described herself as 'an actress who happens to be appearing in grand opera'" ("Geraldine Farrar" 26). Paying lip service only to the idea of what constituted opera performance at the time, William de Mille observed that "on the operatic stage, 'Jerry' was known as a fine actress, which meant that she had more than two facial expressions, that she never tripped over her own feet and that her gestures were not semaphorical" (148). In setting the acting competence bar comically low, de Mille organizes a continuum from opera to cinema, or what he calls "the most distant and artificial form of acting known to modern man to the closest and most naturalistic method which had yet been evolved," that certainly overstates what Farrar learned in California (148).

Where Farrar learned her filmic performance style speaks to several key issues, namely the questions of priority in invention between opera and cinema and Farrar's autonomy as a performer. The origins of the performance in *Carmen* in particular would also seem to bear on the question of what a good opera performer could offer film in terms of expertise with the highly sexualized roles derived from brothel plays or, indeed, *Carmen*. Did this kinetic approach originate on the stage with Farrar, did she learn it in Hollywood directly from William de Mille or Cecil B. DeMille, or did she take the greater freedom of a new location and a new medium to experiment with characterizations that the conventions of the opera stage had not previously permitted? Because only *Carmen*, *Joan the Woman*, and *The Devil Stone* remain as evidence, this question can be answered only indirectly, but it is striking that Farrar's performance in *Carmen* is authoritative, interesting, and far less dated than her performances in *Joan* and *The Devil Stone*; indeed, if one arranges these performances chronologically, her work becomes successively less compelling with more time spent in Hollywood, although one may make allowances for differences among genres and scenarists.

Despite the evidence of the films, a famous piece of Farrar lore credits her experience on the set of *Carmen* in the summer of 1915 with causing her to rethink the role when she next performed it on stage. She notoriously "introduced 'a lively wrestling bout in which she threw her opponent easily and had all but succeeded in plucking out handfuls of her hair when the rude soldiers intervened,' [and] according to gossip, slapped Caruso's face and clung to him so violently that he was obliged to pinion her in order to be able to sing, and half threw her to the floor when he had finished," causing Caruso to hiss in annoyance, "Do you think this is an opera house, or a cinema?" ("Music or Movies?" *The Independent*, 28 February 1916, 294). Farrar's own autobiography would appear to endorse this account: "Caruso is said to have given me a sharp reprimand about such tiger-like tactics in my scenes with him, with special emphasis on the unfortunate importation of movie technique!" going on to add, "I . . . know he never sang better in his life—nor did I—and we shall let it go at that" (170). In a sensitive and informed consideration of the release of the Kino videotape of *Carmen* in 1994, Peter G. Davis also argues for Farrar's film experience as having revivified her stage Carmen, offering in evidence the contemporary reviews of her opera performances that would seem to suggest a stark before and after ("Cruella Seville," *New York Magazine*, 21 November 1994, 81). Nonetheless, the question is more complex than this story of film teaching opera new tricks would suggest.

Beyond the well-established phenomenon of *Carmen* as a laboratory for realist experimentation on the part of the soprano (who was often, as Farrar claims to have been, responsible for the design of her costumes and makeup, a role that no longer belongs to the performer either in opera or on film and that clearly goes some distance toward shaping an interpretation of the drama), there is the question of just how much direction Farrar received from DeMille. Her autobiography suggests that his function was primarily to license an interpretation that she already harbored but had not been permitted to realize on stage. For her first essay in front of the camera (*Maria Rosa*), she recalls that DeMille

> outlined briefly the scenes, their intended length, the climax—and with the minimum expenditure of precious energy in preliminaries, set his camera at all angles to catch the first enthusiasm of a scene, which spontaneous impulse was always my best interpretation. We were not cautioned to beware of undue emotion, disarranged locks, torn clothing, etc. We were allowed free action as we felt it; so we acted our parts as if we were engaged in a theatre performance. . . . At any rate, Mr. DeMille understood my enthusiasm and left me free to express natural impulses wherever my feeling prompted them.
>
> (168–69)

This account implies that Farrar received comparatively little overt instruction about the role per se and perceived film acting to be a release from the many strictures, both vocal and physical, that she had experienced on the stage.

Perhaps unexpectedly, DeMille's autobiography ratifies Farrar's recollection of autonomy; he observes that "I tried to help her bring out her own best performance, rather than force upon her arbitrarily my concept of her role" (143). When one considers that Farrar was by far the most experienced with the text of *Carmen* of any member of the cast or crew, it seems still less likely that her interpretation was not dominant, a view shared by Carl Van Vechten:

> It has seemed strange to me that the professional reviewers should have attributed the added notes of realism in Miss Farrar's second edition of Carmen to her appearances in the moving-picture drama. The tendencies displayed in her second year in the part were in no wise, to my mind, a result of the cinema. In fact, the New York critics should have remembered that when Miss Farrar made her début at the Metropolitan Opera House in the

Farrar at her dressing table. Courtesy of the Academy of Motion Picture Arts and Sciences.

rôle of Juliette, they had rebuked her for these very qualities. . . . No, Miss Farrar is overzealous with her public. She once told me that at every performance she cut herself open with a knife and gave herself to the audience.
("Interpreters: Geraldine Farrar," *The Bellman*, 24 March 1917, 324)

In the same piece Van Vechten speculates that, for better or worse, Farrar was often the inventor of prominent stage business, extending to aspects of make-up and costumes (322, 324), granting her an authority that she certainly wanted for herself. Writing in *Vanity Fair* ("The Art of Acting in the Movies," November 1918, 90), Farrar nods at the notion of the director as a type of Svengali, commenting that the director "must so enthuse, and hypnotize his players, that he will bring them to the creative pitch required for effective and telling acting." Yet she claims even this function for herself in the end, going on to note that "if a motion picture star has this self-starting dynamo, or power of self-hypnosis within her, so that she need not rely on the director for her artistic stimulus, so much the better for her and for all concerned."

In contrast to her presentation of herself offstage as businesslike, down to earth, and dedicated to her art, Farrar actively sought out the roles that would give scope to her conception of her stage persona as passionate and even sensual. While Wagenknecht sees Farrar's stage persona divided into two character types, the spiritual (the Goose Girl in *Die Koenigskinder* or Elisabeth in *Tannhäuser*, for example) and the earthy (Carmen or Zaza) ("Geraldine Farrar"), it is clear that for film, at least, Farrar wanted vehicles that spoke to the earthy side. When Goldwyn offered her society dramas without spice, she protested. In a letter written during the filming of *The Hell Cat* in summer 1918, Farrar expressed her serious dissatisfaction with Goldwyn's taste in scenarios:

> Do you realize how badly you need to give me the right kind of story? I wish I could impress it upon you how vital such a subject is for my screen appearances. . . . Please get me material in modern dress that has *guts* in it, like "Tosca," "Fedora," "Resurrection" and "The Pirate Woman." Don't bother to consider the race track story because I fear . . . that the advertisement of the Saratoga race track as the biggest asset of the feature . . . is not the material for me. I think this story much better for the ingénue type of woman.
>
> (FP, box 9, folder 26)

That Farrar was actively looking on her own for sources to be adapted into screenplays with "guts" may possibly be surmised from an undated letter from Belasco to Farrar responding to her request for performance copies of *The Girl of the Golden West*, *Adrea*, *The Darling of the Gods*, and *Madama Butterfly* (BP, box 1, folder 48). The presence of two titles that were already well established in the opera canon suggests that this request was almost certainly for the purposes of adapting one as a screenplay or perhaps attempting to provide a model to Farrar's Goldwyn scenarists.

The failure to find good scripts at Goldwyn was probably one of the contributing factors to the waning of Farrar's box office draw, but another was certainly the distraction caused by her marriage to Tellegen in 1916 and its prolonged breakup until the divorce decree was granted in 1923. Tellegen apparently attempted to upstage Farrar when they appeared together in films, and he ultimately became *persona non grata* both in Hollywood and in New York before his suicide in 1934. Belasco, for example, delicately wrote to Farrar in 1919 claiming that he would like to supply a part to Tellegen, "but when I got the translation in cold type, I found it was fundamentally a woman's play and that all other parts were bound to be subservient" (FP, box 8, folder 5). Farrar's position as half of a star couple consequently did her career more harm than good, leading not only to her departure from Famous Players–Lasky but also creating friction with Goldwyn, particularly on the matter of the billing of Tellegen (Goldwyn 150–53), who starred opposite Farrar but made only a fraction of her salary ($600 per week to her $18,750 [GP, file 5042, 24 July 1919 memo of contract]).

When film historians look at cinema's associations with high culture in the first and second decades of the twentieth century, they have typically viewed them as the means by which canny producers leveraged snippets of "genteel" culture in order to garner more of the middle class for cinema audiences and to elevate the cultural prestige of film generally. Those desires are certainly visible in the decision to hire Farrar. At the same time, however, I want to suggest that the "genteel" culture imported into film might not have been quite so genteel as it is usually regarded; indeed, I have argued that Farrar's association with racier roles on the stage made her the ideal stalking horse for their respectable importation into cinema. In seeing Farrar as to some considerable degree desiring to command the roles associated with her, it is perhaps more possible to see the texts associated with Farrar as continuous with the texts of the 1920s, such as *The Sheik*, that have received feminist readings from scholars such as Gaylyn Studlar. Farrar's autonomy as a star, commanding a prestige that owed nothing to the film industry, rigorously trained in an art that, again, owed nothing to the film industry, gave her an authority that was positively masculine. Goldwyn noted that

> Miss Farrar is, like Mary Pickford, a captain of industry. She has the same masculine grasp of business, the same masculine approach to work. The difference between them is construed not alone by the immeasurably greater cultural equipment of Miss Farrar but by many temperamental divergences. Whereas Mary Pickford's manner and voice are always marked by the feminine, almost child-like appeal to which I have referred, the prima donna's speech has a man's directness of import. She picks her words for strength, as might a Jack London sea-captain or an Elizabethan soldier.   (85–86)

That Farrar combined this masculine presentation of the offstage self with her self-confessed delight in playing the range of sexually vulnerable and sexually powerful figures that embraces Cio-Cio-San and Carmen suggests that we need to sift the stereotypes both of the early female star and early roles for women with more nuance.

Genteel is not always milk-and-water, and the film industry's apparently radical mores in the 1920s may owe more to nineteenth-century high culture than at first it might appear. Farrar stands as an important, if forgotten, foil to stars such as Pickford, on the one hand, who combined offscreen business sense with onscreen childlike innocence, and Bara, on the other, a fellow "feministe" in seduction parts without Farrar's wholesome offscreen reputation. Farrar consequently emerges as a female star who combined authority and femininity in a compelling and idiosyncratic fashion, as her legions of female fans demonstrated. Indeed, the physical dimensions of her performances in *Carmen* and *Joan the Woman*, which spoke very much to an embodied heroine who could dance, ride, and fight, paved the way for the more masculine, yet sexual, heroines of the 1920s such as Clara Bow.

NOTES

I would like to acknowledge gracious support for travel to archives from the Melbern G. Glasscock Center for the Humanities and Texas A&M University. Barbara Hall of the Margaret Herrick Library, Academy of Motion Picture Arts and Sciences, was extremely helpful in arranging for access to screenplays, stills, and papers from special collections for this project. I would also like to thank the librarians at the Library of Congress and the Billy Rose Theatre Collection of the New York Public Library for assistance with those collections, and Peter Bentley for permission to quote from Farrar's papers.

1. For the purposes of space, the following acronyms are used for citing special collection sources: BP, Belasco Papers, Billy Rose Theatre Collection, New York Public Library; FP, Farrar Papers, Library of Congress; GP, Goldwyn Papers, Margaret Herrick Library, Beverly Hills, California; SC, Special Collections, Margaret Herrick Library.

2. The original spelling of the family name, retained by William and his daughter Agnes, was de Mille. Henry and his wife, Beatrice, preferred "De Mille," while Cecil fluctuated among three variants but generally used "DeMille" for professional purposes.

7 ★★★★★★★★★★★

George Beban
Character of the Picturesque

GIORGIO BERTELLINI

George Beban was arguably the only Anglo American film star of his time never to have played the role of an Anglo American character. Beginning in 1915, his feature-length cinematic impersonations of charming but ill-fated Italian immigrants catapulted him to stardom. Yet both the form and significance of his characterizations may be perplexing unless placed within the wider context of how American culture as a whole aestheticized racial diversity. Furthermore, without Beban's popular and sympathetic characterizations, one of the next decade's superstars, Rudolph Valentino, might never have emerged.

George Beban, undated photo. From the author's collection.

Born in San Francisco in 1873 of an Italophilic father, Rocco Beban, who had migrated from southern Dalmatia, and an Irish mother, Johanna Dugan, George Beban started his stage career at the age of eight with the Reed and Emerson Minstrel shows. In the 1890s, after years of close contact with the New York scene of American and foreign stage companies, he made a name for himself in the vaudeville circuits as a comedian. By 1908, he was regularly cast as a French count in George M. Cohan vaudeville productions (Odell 419; Brownlow 319). Initially uninterested in moving pictures, his aspiration was to embark on serious, dramatic stage performances. He was unable to find suitable material and persuade stage impresarios, however, and in 1909 he co-wrote the short play *The Sign of the Rose: A Play in One Act* with a successful Broadway playwright, Charles Turner Dazey. It was the heartbreaking story of an honest Italian immigrant who endures first the loss of his daughter in an automobile accident and subsequently an unjust criminal indictment. In the early 1910s, Beban staged the play and impersonated the role of the main character throughout American stage circuits and even in England. In 1914, the play became the basis for a nine-reel film, variously titled *The Sign of the Rose* or *The Alien*, produced and directed under the supervision of Thomas H. Ince for the New York Motion Picture Corporation and released in 1915. Together with *The Italian*, also released in 1915, the adaptation launched Beban's film career and made him a household name. Until his accidental death in 1928 as a result of injuries sustained after being thrown from a horse, Beban acted in eighteen films, wrote either the story or the script for eleven of them, and directed three—all were mostly about Italians and, to a smaller extent, French characters.

Unlike many of the stars discussed in this anthology, such as Mary Pickford and Douglas Fairbanks, George Beban has not enjoyed a sustained global and perpetual fame. Over the decades, his name, face, and characters have not been instantly and widely recognized. The archival record, in and of itself a symptom rather than a cause of enduring oblivion, is not in his favor either: only one film, *The Italian* (1915), is widely available for study or public viewing. In order to rediscover and appreciate the fabric of Beban's once extensive and intense popularity, this chapter draws a broad aesthetic trajectory. Since most of his films are either set in New York or resonate with iconic New York settings and characters, the rich palimpsest of sociological studies and multimedia representations of the city's modern development and diverse populations acquires central critical relevance. This once familiar cultural universe played a central role in how Beban constructed and developed his characters—narratively, visually, and ideologically—and how contemporary American audiences made sense of them.

Directly and indirectly, Beban adopted the familiar lessons of social pro-
gressives concerned about immigrants' living conditions and the agenda of
tourism promoters boasting of the city's attractive monuments and exotic
immigrant quarters. His characters also embodied the lowbrow appeal of
vaudeville traditions and the middlebrow one of Italian opera and stage
performers. Still, while differing from the sensationalist film productions
about Italian American criminals, Beban's films were not just entertaining
renderings of Italians' folkloric life, performed through highly melodramatic and, at times, even populist tones. Instead, they also resonated with
the recent, modernist, and all American incarnations of the Picturesque—
an established European painterly tradition that American visual culture
had used for decades to represent its once pristine natural sceneries and,
more recently, its fast-growing urban settlements. The same fascination for
the aesthetically pleasing coexistence of modern urban sights with
unspoiled natural sceneries that informed the design and experience of
Central Park also sustained the representational appeal of uncouth immigrants' colorful city quarters. Between the second half of the nineteenth
century and the early twentieth, this well-codified convergence of ethnog-
raphy and aesthetics imbued a vast array of American cultural productions,
from literature and stage plays to photography and moving pictures.

In this sense, and unlike the global appeal of many contemporaneous
stars, Beban was first and foremost an American star on American soil. His
characterizations were attractive to native Anglo-Saxon audiences and
foreign immigrants, not just Italian newcomers, because both old and new
Americans were familiar with the history and the dramaturgies of
transoceanic adaptation. Further, the heightened and stylized realism of his
Old World impersonations touched both artistic and sentimental cords. In
1915, the *Fort Wayne Journal-Gazette* (Indiana) praised one of his films as "a
work of art from the beginning to the ending" (16 November 1915, 10).
"Never in the history of the photodrama," boasted the *Fresno Morning Republican*, "has any singlehanded portrayal ever even remotely touched the
appealing and heartrending performance of Beban" (26 September 1915,
19). More specifically, his characterizations were described as "picturesque
and pathetic," as two midwestern dailies put it in April 1916 with regards to
his role in Maurice Tourneur's *The Pawn of Fate* (1916) (*Waterloo Times-Tribune*,
2 April 1916, 14; *Sheboygan Press*, 15 April 1916, n.p). Two months later, the
Nevada State Journal resorted to the same trope when advertising the film as
a "picturesque story of deep pathos and compelling human interest" (11
June 1916, 4). As artistic and universal as his picturesqueness was, however, Beban could not maintain the same high degree of popular appeal

over the following years. By the early to mid-1920s, a decade that displayed what Lea Jacobs has called "the decline of sentiment," Beban's quaint, sentimental, and by then quite repetitive performances seemed outmoded and old-fashioned.

☆☆★★★ Sympathy for the Picturesque

Over the course of the second half of the nineteenth century, New York had come to personify both the most dynamic manifestations and the most detrimental excesses of capitalist modernity. As converging social and economic forces propelled the elevation of daring skyscrapers upward, mass circulation and mobility demanded the extension of complex rail transportation systems and the completion of impressive interborough subway lines. Meanwhile, plebeian multitudes of poor American workers and foreigners of different races, religions, and cultures crammed the lower, darker, "pathological" organs of the city—the dreary quarters of shady alleys, filthy boarding houses, opium dens, and all-night dives of the "Lower" East Side, of Hell's Kitchen, and of East Harlem.

The sensationalist coverage of newspapers, magazines, and novels identified the "invading" multitudes of millions of immigrants from Europe and Asia as the cause for New York's (and urban America's) social disorder. Politicians' speeches, newspaper editorials, and cartoons expressed fierce opposition to the unrestricted arrival of strangers crossing once foreboding oceans and displaying a disturbing degree of diversity in dress, customs, and religion that far surpassed that of earlier immigrants. Furthermore, immigrants' deplorable living conditions and visible squalor, stemming from labor exploitation and prohibitive rents, became a common subject of interest for a range of urban, "ethnographic" discourses. Urban life and racial characters were favorite subjects for mainstream (and sensationalist) journalism: reformers' writings; pioneering social and pictorialist photography (from Jacob A. Riis and Lewis W. Hine to Alfred Stieglitz); the Ashcan school of painting; the new "realist" literature of William Dean Howells, Theodore Dreiser, and Henry James; and the so-called tenement melodramas of Abraham Cahan, Fanny Hurst, and Israel Zangwill as well as countless vaudeville scenarios. This ethnographic interest often oscillated between two extremes, one of social dystopia and one of aesthetic appreciation.

Hailing their creed as a pillar of the American social order, apprehensive moral crusaders and reformers translated the sensationalist literary and journalistic exposés through the scripts of the new social sciences—Social Darwinism and eugenics. Through their reports, they broadcast a depressing view of New York "as solely the site of urban problems" (Blake 19). With regard to immigrants' role in the city's much-publicized predicament, the reformers blamed either the immigrants themselves or the environment in which they happened to live, particularly the corrupt political leadership of Tammany Hall. Over time this dualism deeply affected American media's racialized dramaturgy. If the first position augmented narrative determinism, the second allowed for a range of tales of immigrants' endeavors to adapt and adjust to America's physical, social, and moral environment. Beban, as we shall see, belongs to this second strain of dramaturgic options.

While reformers voiced concerns, tourist operators, real estate developers, and business groups established an influential constituency that had a vested interest in broadcasting positive and appealing images of the city. They endeavored not only to represent New York's diversity and uniqueness from the rest of the United States, but also its quintessential American character. Rather than promoting a "topography of social problems located in isolated urban pockets," these commercially oriented proponents stressed the city's "topography of 'sights,'" which included monumental skyscrapers, new shopping districts, Central Park, *and* immigrant quarters (Blake 50). "In no place on this continent," boasted the tourist guidebook *The Hints for Strangers, Shoppers, and Sight See-ers in the Metropolis* (1891), "can a visitor view such a kaleidoscopic scene as is continually presented by the crowds upon our streets" (Blake 71). Through postcards, stereographic views, and photographic albums, American tourism patterned a respectable sightseeing experience of Chinatown and the "Ghetto," which would anticipate, inform, and later parallel film spectators' voyeuristic access to immigrants' ill-fated quarters and lives. This process was defined by the familiar and transnational aesthetic of the picturesque, which in New York acquired ostensibly American features.

Today the term "picturesque," mainly used as an adjective and generally signifying a quaint, scenic landscape (or a curious, striking individual), masks rather than reveals its rich formal and ideological history. Emerging in the seventeenth century as a painterly style, but soon also encompassing practices of garden-making, landscape design, and theater scenery, the picturesque was associated with the representation of "a landscape that to the experienced viewer seemed either to have been composed after a painting or was designed to be the subject of one" (Hunt 6). Its new effects of irregularity, variety, and roughness of design strikingly contrasted with the harmonic symmetry traditionally sought out by pictorial representations. The picturesque achieved broader international popularity in the eighteenth century, when it developed into the dominant pictorial style that northern

European elites adopted to transfix their cultural experience of Mediterranean regions—Italy, in particular, but also Europe's many marginal provinces—into imaginative and comforting views of distant landscapes and exotic characters. In widely circulating paintings, prints, and illustrations about Italy, for instance, the violent wilderness of volcanoes became a charming spectacle of primeval force; a ruin-dotted countryside appeared as a mythical and pastoral heaven; and notoriously vicious bandits, or *banditti*, as they were known, came into view as romantic and colorful outlaws. Picturesque representations' formal and thematic cast, centered on the liminality of natural landscapes with urban views and historical ruins, visualized places and characters perceived to be distant in both space and time, and became influential and pervasive on both sides of the Atlantic. Eventually, the picturesque traveled to the United States, where it became "the first American aesthetic" (Conron xvii). Projected onto the country's unspoiled prairies and its soon-to-be tamed wilderness, beginning with the Hudson River Valley and then the Wild West, the picturesque style codified and popularized a set of alluring and reassuring national scenes of immaculate landscapes, traversed by explorers and, soon, the railway, amidst peaceful natives. Picturesque renderings of Niagara Falls, Grand Canyon, and Yosemite became staple images in the catalogs of traveling lecturers and tourist promoters who, along with the ubiquitous slogan "See America first!," made consumption of the domesticated American landscape the ritual of American citizenship. In between Wild West reenactments and such filmed travelogues as *Picturesque Yosemite* (1902) and *Picturesque Colorado* (1911), American filmmakers recognized the paradigmatic setting of romantic national narratives in the western landscape of pristine forests and wild but tameable Indians, as in D. W. Griffith's *Ramona* (1910) and Thomas Ince's *The Invaders* (1912).

In late-nineteenth-century America, the rise of urban culture enabled another formulation of the picturesque. At its center was New York City, which, as the most visible social and economic *locus* of American progress, industrialization, and social interest, prompted impressive aesthetic effects. The city's unique aesthetic aura rested on two defining features: its earthbound low-end tenements and its skyward high-rise buildings, and their aesthetic and ideological relationship. If mass migrations and immigrant quarters were readily recognized as emblems of America's multinational fabric, then a unique architectural structure—the high office building—identified the city's skyline as "American." Although in theory high office buildings could not appear more distant from the natural wonders of the American West, they were nonetheless absorbed into the picturesque aesthetic. In his work for *Scribner's Monthly* and *Century*, the renowned illustrator Joseph Pennell, who also illustrated the volumes of the Italian journeys of William Dean Howells and Henry James, aligned the city's skyscrapers with the mighty canyons of the Far West, one of the most emblematic symbols of the American natural landscape. His extension of the picturesque framework was not a solitary enterprise.

Beginning in the late nineteenth century, bohemian critics, newspaper illustrators, Ashcan school painters, photographers, and early filmmakers highlighted the city's visual appeal by fostering a notion of "urban picturesqueness." In their works the picturesque meant much more than a pleasing compositional organization. Following and extending the work of Alfred Stieglitz, Edward J. Steichen, and Alvin Langdon Coburn, who had all photographed the city amidst winter fog, through tree branches, or on windy days, New York–based American cinema devoted a number of films to the city's architectural monuments (the Statue of Liberty, the Flatiron Building, and the Brooklyn Bridge), to spectacular squares (Union and Herald Squares), and to hectic traffic. The stylistic recurrences involved in such urban travelogues as *The Blizzard* (AM&B, 1899), *At the Foot of the Flatiron* (AM&B, 1903), and *New York City "Ghetto" Fish Market* (Edison, 1903), or fiction films such as *In Little Italy* (Biograph, 1909) and *A Child of the Ghetto* (Biograph, 1910), are revealing. These films display the protocol of the picturesque mode at work: the literal or metaphoric insertion of the spectacle of nature into the city's rational landscape, from the "natural island" of Central Park to the uncultured migrants barely surviving in the tenement-house districts.

Overall, the picturesque presented two overlapping, yet also distinct, modes of signification. Whether evoked in the impressionistic style of paintings, etchings, and films or echoed in critics' writings, on the one hand picturesqueness was repeatedly understood as expressing pictorial suggestiveness through endless contrasts. "The essence of picturesqueness is variety," wrote art critic Mariana Griswold Van Rensselaer in an 1892 essay symptomatically entitled "Picturesque New York" (*Century Magazine*, December 1892, 164). "Variety" referred to the striking juxtaposition of the frenzied vertical development of new office buildings and the folkloric and horizontal scenes of immigrants' life. Yet, on the other hand, such urban variety also had an unmistakable ethnographic quality. "We cannot appreciate the picturesqueness which New York wears to both mind and eye," Van Rensselaer added in the same essay, "unless we go immediately from the stately commercialism of its down-town streets to the adjacent tenement-house districts" (172). What appeared particularly striking was the colorful diversity of the immigrant population, both destitute and restless, whom art critic John C. Van Dyke described as showing, with reference to a familiar picturesque subject, "as little repose in its streets as in the lava stream of a volcano" (*The New New York*, 11). It was within this ideological and aesthetic condescension that the illustrator William Allen Rogers conceived his popular drawings of immigrants' daily plight, caught against the towering backdrop of the city's skyscrapers, and that made him "*Harper's* specialist on the picturesqueness of poverty" (Hales 185). Writing about the "Hebrew quarter," cultural critic Allan Sidney (a pseudonym for Carl Sadakichi Hartmann) championed this aestheticization of destitution in even more explicit terms. The ghetto's "very dinginess and squalor . . . ," he noted, "is the great harmonizer in the pictorial arts, the wizard who can render every scene and object—even the humblest one—picturesque" ("Picturesque New York in Four Papers: The Esthetic Side of Jewtown," *Camera Notes* vol. 6, 1903, 145). That immigrants' squalid living conditions were described in purely visual terms reveals a conservative political stance: social inequalities are reduced to decorative elements and thus expunged from any politics of social change.

In the 1890s, just before the inception of American cinema, Jacob A. Riis and William Dean Howells propelled the notion of the picturesque into the mainstream of American visual and literary culture. By looking at, and writing about, New York ghettoes as a foreign country populated by exotic subjects, Riis and Howells endeavored to soothe the perception of immigrants as frightening foreigners and thus transmuted the distressing topic of immigrants' lives into a subject of romantic cultural interest. The appreciation of racial diversity for entertainment purposes was also a staple of the New York–based American vaudeville. Vaudeville instituted a "national currency" of heavily stereotyped characters that included beer-guzzling Germans, dimwitted yet amusing African Americans, gesticulating Jews, pigtailed and wily John Chinamen, inebriated and carefree Irish Pats and Bridgets, and emotional and aggressive Italians. A whole corpus of manuals of jokes and songs were published in the late 1800s. In them, the character of the "Eyetalian wid big whiskers" speaks an almost incomprehensible vernacular, is both naïve and cunning, and is always quick with insults and his stiletto (*Italian Dialect Joke Book* [Baltimore: I. & M. Ottenheiimer, 1909], 74).

The emergence of an "urban picturesque" speaks not of the oft-cited shocks of modernity, but of minor jolts, expected surprises filtered through a reassuring touristic paradigm that aestheticized and depoliticized immigrants' destitution and alleged racial inadequacy as a pleasurable exoticism. As an aesthetic and sociological currency, the "urban picturesque" helped to make sense of and manage the diversity of urban immigrants and, in the process, in Carrie Tirado Bramen's words, "helped to equate ethnic variety and urbanism with modern Americanism" (Bramen 446). The New York–based American cinema readily embraced this aesthetic possibility as a unique commercial opportunity. While striving for national representativeness against competing foreign films, the U.S. film industry emplotted the drama of the city's immigrants—which constituted its most numerous and regular audience—into respectable, and distinctively *American*, narratives.

☆☆★★★ Italians in American Cinema

Italian immigrants' widely emphasized Neapolitan, Sicilian, and Calabrian origins divorced them from Italy's traditional association with glorious antiquity and artistic excellence. Their southern background, instead, contributed to a racial typecasting predicated upon alleged terms of incongruous physicality, violent and hyperemotional regimes, and thus the tenuous state of a spurious citizenship. A frequently recurring measure of racial underscoring was the law, with its sets of rules and regulations defining a social contract that Italians were depicted as *naturally* breaching. At times benevolently rendered in folkloric and picturesque terms, this "racial dissonance" signified Italian immigrants' racial unsuitability and "unfitness" for American citizenship.

Particularly newsworthy was Italians' allegedly "normal" affiliation with criminal organizations, usually identified as Black Hand societies (that is, Mafia and Camorra), regularly presented in vaudeville sketches, newspaper articles, and cartoons. Beginning with the mass production of fiction films in 1905–1906 and duplicating the yellow press sensationalist reports about kidnappings and other brutalities taking place in Little Italy, early American cinema magnified (and fictionalized) what many Americans imagined about the inner circuits of the metropolis but which they were too afraid to explore. Beginning in 1906, with the trend-setting film *The Black Hand*, cinema identified Italian characters (more than Chinese and Jewish ones) with the criminal outgrowth of seedy urban ghettoes located just a few blocks away from ordinary city life.

To be sure, gangster films did not cast *all* Italians as Mafia criminals. Often the story line divided immigrant characters into two clear-cut groups, or created a space of moral indecision within a single character. The distinction between "good" and "bad" Italians was a profitable narrative compromise. Embodying the Italian community's racial difference in the figure of the Latin criminal, these films reaffirmed mainstream middle-class cultural prejudices and granted cinema the high moral ground of documenting and denouncing real delinquency. Simultaneously, by exhibiting Italian characters' honesty and frequent victimization and integrity, they pleased the self-contention of Italian and, generally, immigrant spectators. Films could do so by exhibiting characters whose outfit, customs, and literacy signified their abandonment of past traditions and embracing of American ideals of justice and ways of life. The emergence of films devoted to the real figure of Lieutenant Joseph Petrosino, head of the New York City police force's anti-Mafia squad, from *The Detectives of the Italian Bureau* (Kalem, 1909) to *The Adventure of Lieutenant Petrosino* (Feature Photoplay Co., 1912), provided a model for the reformed Italian. Petrosino's actual and fictional figure counterbalanced the recurring figure of the gangster and hoodlum, whose defiant dwelling in the city's narrow and dark alleys communicated a linguistic and cultural isolation and an abiding racial disjunction *within* mainstream "white" society.[1]

These films' narrative and ideological framework relied on the idea that for Italians assimilation was a challenging, but not impossible, process of moral domestication and adjustment. Although allegations of natural criminal inclinations remained a constant narrative subplot, other films of the period found different ways to accentuate Italians' racial and cultural diversity. In a combination of ethnographic realism and curiosity, for instance, they emphasized Italians' widely admired artistic talents or intense family bonds. Other films emphasized such estranging traits of pathological jealousy and impetuous anger, as in Griffith's *The Italian Blood* (Biograph, 1911), the story of how an Italian wife tries to revive her husband's love through artifices of jealousy only to risk losing her own children. In other instances, Italians' temper, passions, and inclinations for *vendetta* were ambiguously justified in the face of dreadful adversities and coupled with their allegedly intense attachment to family bonds. In *The Wop* (IMP, 1913), a widowed father named Luigi, after being unfairly jailed, seeks a violent revenge. Only the sight of his own daughter stops his fury. Overall, the emphasis on Italians' disproportionate reactions and emotional outbursts was commonly rendered by the acting style of Anglo American actors playing Italian characters—as would be the case for George Beban. Within the melodramatic genre, a favorite in American cinema, the difference between operatic stock figures and psychologized individuals marked a crucial separation, charged with racialized connotations. Melodrama exhibited the divergence between clear-cut narratives whose racialized characters' "realistic" behavior was shown as reactive, instinctual, or perfunctory, and psychological story lines emphasizing Anglo American characters' inner turmoil and motivation (Bertellini, "Black Hands").

☆☆★★★ Picturesque Pathos

Beban's films grew out of these aesthetic, theatrical, and cinematic practices. Before examining the aforementioned *The Alien*, however, we must turn to another film, *The Italian*, which was also released in 1915 but produced a year earlier. *The Italian* initiated Beban into cinema and specifically into representations of Italian characters defined by melodramatic pathos rather than criminal association.[2]

In 1914, at the invitation of Thomas Ince, Beban took part in the Los Angeles and San Francisco filming of what today is generally considered his most famous film. Written by the veteran C. Gardner Sullivan, who had scripted *The Wop*, and directed by the often-uncredited Reginald Barker, *The Italian* was a sentimental melodrama of love and revenge set in Italy and New York's Lower East Side. Beban insisted on changing the film's title from the original, *The Dago*, into *The Italian*, apparently not out of sensitivity. Given the film's feature length and commercial ambitions, Beban desired to be associated with a Special Feature, for which the neutral title was more appropriate (*Motion Picture Magazine*, April 1916, 141). As the *New York Dramatic Mirror* emphasized, Ince's film was a notable example of "plot expansion." As a Paramount release, the six-reel film belonged to a "programme confessedly aimed at a more cultivated public than has been reached by that useful trinity, bathos, sentimentality and melodrama" (30 December 1914, 26).

The Italian starts, as it will end, with a theatrically rendered framework that reveals the ideological positioning and the aesthetic ambitions of Beban's work. In the film's opening image, curtains open onto the library room of a private residence. Sporting an elegant evening robe, Beban appears as an upper-middle-class book lover, quietly sitting in his book-filled studio, reading a novel entitled *The Italian*. The first part of the film is set in Old Italy, amid romantic monasteries, lush countrysides, and Venetian canals. Here, the title character, picturesque gondolier Beppo Donnetti, is in love with Annette, but he cannot yet afford to marry her. He then decides to emigrate to America. Landing in New York's Lower East Side, he finds work as a bootblack, saves his money, and a year later sends for Annette, whom he immediately marries. The birth of his first child, Tony, becomes an occasion for histrionic outbursts of happiness and communal celebrations. One intolerably hot summer, little Tony becomes sick and threatens to die without pasteurized milk. Beppo begs everybody for help, including Mr. Corrigan, a heartless local boss who feels disrespected and has him beaten and incarcerated. Lacking appropriate nutrition, his child dies.

Beppo (George Beban, right, raising glass) spiritedly celebrates the birth of his first child. *The Italian* (1915) Courtesy of Kevin Brownlow.

Plotting revenge, a deranged Beppo enters Corrigan's home with a strata-gem: he intends to kill the boss's daughter. His posture, movements, and facial expressions are beast-like, but not utterly atypical of his character's racial background. A visual regime of dramatic close-ups reveals a threat-ening physiognomy of primitive violence. He repents only after noticing that the little girl sleeps with the same baby-like posture he had loved in his own child. The last image is that of Beppo at his son's grave while the inter-title reads: "At the eternal bedside of his baby where hate, revenge and bit-terness melt to nothing in the crucible of sorrow." Despite his earlier rage, the humanity of his inner character ultimately prevails.

At the film's end, the library scene with which the film opened reap-pears. This time Beban closes the book as stage curtains signal the end of the picture. The scene may be interpreted as a generic desire to pair cinema with higher entertainment traditions such as theater and literature. Yet Beban also intended to dissociate himself from the negative, highly stereo-typed characterizations that one- or two-reelers had broadly created about Italians (and immigrants in general) and that duplicated the racial type-casting of the vaudeville scene. By expanding the story to six reels, Beban explicitly signaled his engagement with the traditions of realist and sentimental literature and legitimate theater which, best embodied by the countless theatrical representations of *Uncle Tom's Cabin* that Linda Williams has recently examined, staged complex forms of identification that conveyed "racial sympathy" and a "melodramatic crossracial recognition of virtue" (Williams, *Playing* 46–47). By echoing such respectable ideology of universal humanism, *The Italian* could aestheticize racialized characters and settings through sentimental touches of moral unanimity (Keil 37–38).

Such a universal humanism, however, had limits. Beppo's various misfortunes, particularly the loss of his child, are explicitly rendered as the result of the environment in which he lives, not as the result of his own personal failures. Yet the injustice and ill treatments he has to endure are not narratively transformed into punishment for his abusers. The film denies him not only the right to express his rebellion and avenge himself, but also his right to justice. After all, he remains an immigrant, not an American citizen, and one whose command of the English language remains always deficient—as the many intertitles written in broken English clearly display. What the film exacts from its audience is not *com*-passion for a peer, but a purely sentimental pity, kept at a distance by a stoic and ultimately mortifying narrative conclusion. In its melodramatic combination of realism, pathos, and commiseration, *The Italian* carefully preserves a racialized legal and ideological distinction between Italian and American individuals.

Beban's reputation as a virtuoso actor, established on stage with his long-running interpretation of Pietro in *The Sign of the Rose*, significantly increased with the creative filming of his signature stage play. The film opened as *The Sign of the Rose* at Clune's Auditorium in Los Angeles on 12 April 1915 (where *The Birth of a Nation* had just completed a nine-week run) and was released in New York a month later, on 31 May 1915, under the title *The Alien*. At both premieres, Beban capitalized on his crossover stardom in theater and film. *The Sign of the Rose/The Alien* was presented as a "Combination of Silent and Spoken Drama," because its denouement was a thirty-minute stage act, played by the same film actors, with impressive musical accompaniment that "ranged from popular songs of this and other days to the selections from well-known operas" (Blaisdell, "The Sign of the Rose," *Motion Picture World*, 1 May 1915, 740). At nine reels, the film was a racial melodrama of shocking adversity and cruelty, displaying the perverse outcome of racial prejudices, sentimentalizing along the way the miserable Italian protagonist. A financial dispute between two American brothers ends with one of them kidnapping the other's daughter and accidentally running over and killing Rosina, the only daughter of a humble and lively Italian widower, Pietro (Beban). Distressed over her death, Pietro is arrested as the kidnapper simply because he happens to be in the flower shop where the ransom was supposed to be paid to a man identified by "the sign of the rose." Despite his vivacious protests, nobody believes his innocence. As in *The Italian*, tragedy is the result of environmental and circumstantial factors, not of personal crimes or failures.

The Sign of the Rose's ideological address openly sympathizes with the Italian character's emotional outbursts, following his family tragedy and his unjust accusation. Yet, once more, the film narratively and visually racializes the protagonist: through the realism of costumes and setting, the "authenticity" of Beban's unrestrained acting performance, and, quite prominently, the lack of a narrative closure that would grant him some form of justice. Once racialized, in fact, Pietro's legal standing falls to substandard levels: nobody is indicted for the death of his daughter. The audience's emotional response is reduced to inconsequential compassion. Pietro appears as an imperfect, deficient, and "pathetic figure": no *full* identification is possible with him. Not only does the story deny him justice, but the film's social system also requests from him a sense of childish and fatalistic submissiveness to the authority that failed to protect him. As the alternate title indicates, Pietro is and remains an "alien." By (allegedly) mimicking Italian stage performers and real life individuals, Beban emphasized racial mannerisms through a skillful, widely appreciated, and almost obsessive attention to props, settings, costumes, and facial expressions. But the entire film achieved a carefully thought out *realistic effect*, further enhanced by mass scenes featuring extras brought in from New York City and trained to look like "an excited, surging, crowding crowd" (*Moving Picture World*, 24 April 1915, 561).

Between 1915 and 1928, the year of his sudden death due to a riding accident, Beban impersonated Italian characters in more than a dozen films that he regularly scripted and, in a few instances, directed. While contributing substantially to the scenario of his films, Beban initially worked within the studio rules set by Thomas Ince and the Oliver Morosco Photoplay Company, whose films were distributed by Paramount. In 1918, however, he decided to exercise full control over his productions. *Hearts of Men* (Hiram Abrams Production, 1919), in which he played the role of a humble Italian florist (Nicolò Rosetti) who relocates from New York to Arizona and strikes oil, was his first film as both producer and director ("Beban Makes Debut as Cinema Producer," *Los Angeles Express*, 8 March 1919, n.p.). His cinematic roles did not change. Although the majority of these productions are now lost, available reviews and plot synopses reveal a striking consistency of his characterizations of Italian immigrants—with the exception of *The Bond Between* (Pallas Pictures, 1917), where he interpreted the role of Pierre "Papa" Duval, a Frenchman living in New York.[3] Beban played an Italian grocer who is loyal both to Italy and his Italian American sweetheart in *Pasquale* (Oliver Morosco Photoplay, 1916), an Italian iceman in *His Sweetheart* (Oliver Morosco Photoplay, 1917) and *The Greatest Love of All* (George Beban Productions, 1924), and characters named Guido Bartelli in *The Marcellini Millions* (Oliver Morosco Photoplay, 1917), Luigi Riccardo in *One More American* (Famous Players-Lasky Corp., 1918), Nicolò Rosetti in *Hearts of Men* (Hiram Abrams Production, 1919), Lupino Delchini in *One Man in a Million* (Sol Lesser, 1921), Pietro Balletti in the remake of *The Sign of the Rose* (George Beban Productions, 1922), and Ricardo Bitelli in *The Loves of Ricardo* (George Beban Productions, 1926). In the acting manual he wrote in 1921 for the Palmer Photoplay Corporation, Beban himself explained quite eloquently why he kept playing Italian characters: "I like to play the Italian because his costume, his mannerisms, his gestures, and his unlikeness to the everyday people of the street make him stand out as a romantic and picturesque person" (*Photoplay Characterization*, 9). Although Beban's work is still relatively unknown and underappreciated, it is possible to argue that, while looking for the greatest emotional consensus, his feature-length stories of high dramatic and sentimental enticement played a crucial role in marginalizing earlier, unsympathetic representations of Italians as criminals and violent individuals. This was quite clear at the time. A *New York Dramatic Mirror* review of Beban's *His Sweetheart* (1917), for instance, praised his constant ambition to produce more authentic versions of temperamental Italian heroes instead of "the individual with a long black moustache and a bandana handkerchief, armed with a stiletto" (3 February 1917, 27). Pathos replaced unlawfulness, at least until, more than a decade later, Prohibition and the Depression would identify Italians as "the shame of a nation," to quote the aftertitle of Howard Hawks's *Scarface* (1932).

In the American cinema of the mid-1910s, and specifically at the time of D. W. Griffith's intense psychological characterizations, Beban's stardom was both rare and significant. Years before Richard Barthelmess's performance in *Broken Blossoms* (1919), Beban fostered an unprecedented intimacy and solidarity with racialized, non-American, characters. Still, Beban's films did not fully question contemporary Anglo American prejudices about Italian racial traits. Instead, they capitalized on Italians' conventional racial attributions, including childlike emotional excess, aggressive tendencies, limited intellectual faculty, and intense family bonds. Furthermore, Beban's interest in displaying the melodramatic turmoil of Italian immigrants was often kept within the safe narrative and ideological distance of an American point of

Luigi Riccardo (Beban) argues animatedly with an Ellis Island physician who has declared the Italian immigrant's wife and daughter unfit to enter the country, from *One More American* (1918). Courtesy of Kevin Brownlow.

view and within the respectable exhibitory boundaries of America's legitimate theaters. By relying on Italians' white racial status, Beban's racial urban melodramas stifled both nativist antagonism and newcomers' grievances by pasting "unanimous" and sentimental ideals of universal brotherhood and solidarity onto stories of indigence, exploitation, and injustice.

Despite the consistency of Beban's popular characterizations, his films about earnest and sentimental immigrants were not overall exceptional productions in American film culture. Responding to the industry's realization of the crucial role of female moviegoing, several films in the second half of the decade cast female protagonists in tenement stories of abuse, dislocation, and final redemption. In 1916 alone, Thomas H. Ince and Reginald Barker, respectively producer and director of *The Italian*, collaborated on two productions centered on young Italian women, *Three of Many* and *The Criminal*, both produced by NYMP Co./Kay-Bee Pictures. Special attention should be reserved here for another production company, the Oliver Morosco Photoplay Co. Its founder, Oliver Morosco (born Oliver Mitchell in Utah in 1876), a successful Los Angeles–based producer and theater owner, entered the film business at full speed in the mid-1910s and specialized in productions of tenement dramas. In addition to producing *Pasquale* (1916) and *His Sweetheart* (1917), both written by and starring Beban, between 1916 and 1917 Morosco Photoplay released *The Making of Maddalena* (1916), *Redeeming Love* (1916), *An International Marriage* (1916), *The Happiness of Three Women* (1917), and *Out of Wreck* (1917), all centered on battered female immigrants. While more research needs to be done on the Morosco Photoplay Co., it is safe to recognize that, despite its exotic name, the company operated in the mainstream of the U.S. media, particularly theater and motion pictures (Morosco and Dugger 250–58). Consider the story of Francis Marion. Before becoming one of Hollywood's chief screenwriters, she started her career in 1912 as a poster artist for Oliver Morosco's theater (Beauchamp 26). Possibly receptive to Beban's contributions, she wrote *Poor Little Peppina* (1916), about an American girl who grows up in Italy among bandits, and *The Love Light* (1921), a love story set in Italy during World War I, both starring America's sweetheart, Mary Pickford.

Another trajectory links the maverick Beban to both the popularization of immigrant narratives and the emergence of star-like racialized characterizations. The interest for dramas of oceanic migration and tenement life that

M. J. Moriarty Movie Souvenir Card, *George Beban*, ca. 1916. From the author's collection.

8 ☆☆☆☆☆☆☆☆☆★

Pearl White and Grace Cunard
The Serial Queen's Volatile Present

MARK GARRETT COOPER

After her 1914 appearance in *The Perils of Pauline*, Pearl White's tremendous celebrity established her as the definitive serial queen. There were numerous other examples of the type, but none so widely associated with the title or with the risk-taking antics demanded by serial adventures. Week after week, the serial heroine narrowly escaped one fiendish plot only to end up facing another. Through repetition, this structure defined peril as persistent but punctual, omnipresent but extraordi-

Pearl White. Courtesy of Museum of Modern Art Film Stills Archive.

nary, inevitable yet unexpected. The dangerous moment ended only to be renewed. As White's fans surely felt, to be enthralled by a serial queen means inhabiting a volatile present. Created by and for fictional characters, this paradoxical present came, *mutatis mutandis*, to define the serial stars' private lives. Through the many renditions of work and home life manufactured by the burgeoning star system, fans discovered women decidedly modern in their independence, fashion sense, athleticism, proficiency with machines, and worldwide fame. These altogether "modern" women, however, also experienced the tug of tradition. Especially onscreen, tradition asserted itself in scenarios that opposed a married, domestic woman to a working, public one. Despite spectacular feats of daring, the serial heroine often requires a hero's rescue, and marriage inevitably brings her adventures to a close. Precisely because she seems up-to-the-minute in some respects and tied to the past in others, one might well ask when the serial queen's moment began and if, in fact, it has ended.

On 22 March 1914, the *Cedar Rapids Daily Republican* announced, "It is becoming a fad among the great companies to film a serial picture that will interest the multitude of picture patrons in every city" ("Perils of Pauline at the Palace" 17). This was news not only in Cedar Rapids but also across the United States. At that moment, two strong precursors defined what would soon be a thriving genre. In July 1912, Thomas Edison's motion picture company began releasing monthly the twelve chapters of *What Happened to Mary?* in which Mary Dangerfield (Mary Fuller) travels to New York City in search of work, finds herself beset by a wicked uncle and his henchmen, and eventually discovers that she has come into a sizable inheritance. A prose version of Mary's adventures appeared concurrently in *The Ladies' World*, a monthly magazine with a very large circulation among working-class women; this tie-in apparently succeeded in luring a substantial portion of the magazine's readers into movie theaters (see Enstad; Stamp; Singer, *Melodrama*). The Selig Polyscope Co. repeated Edison's success beginning on 29 December 1913 when it teamed with the *Chicago Tribune* newspaper syndicate to present *The Adventures of Kathlyn* biweekly: Kathlyn Hare (Kathlyn Williams) travels to India to rescue her kidnapped father and has many thrilling encounters with big cats as well as locals, both wicked and benign. She serves briefly as queen of Allahah before restoring native administration and returning home with her father and newly acquired big-game-hunter husband.

In consequence of the success of *Kathlyn*, almost all the major film-making companies (except Biograph) began producing serials of around fifteen one- or two-reel chapters with a newspaper tie-in.[1] Interest in action series increased as well, and the genres cross-pollinated one another, the

technical difference being that a series features recurring characters and sit-
uations but completes a story in each episode, whereas a serial continues a
narrative arc across the episode breaks. By 1915, the suspenseful cliffhanger
had evolved into the serials' default chapter-ender. The audience would
have to return to the theater to see the heroine survive her newest, presumably lethal predicament. Thanhouser found early success with *The Million Dollar Mystery* starring Florence LaBadie (1914). The Kalem series
Hazards of Helen (1914–1917) and *The Girl Detective* (1915) established Helen
Holmes and Ruth Roland, respectively, as major stars.[2] But the decades'
most prolific producers of serials were Mutual, Vitagraph, Universal, and
the New Jersey–based branch of the French firm Pathé Frères. Beginning in
1914, Pathé and Universal each released no fewer than two serials every
year for the remainder of the decade (see Singer, *Melodrama* 213–24).
Accordingly, by 1920 the fad anticipated in Cedar Rapids had produced a
long list of serial queens (see Bean "Technologies").

   The Perils of Pauline, with Pearl White in the titular role, opened in cities
across the United States in the week following the *Daily Republican* story. At
the time, local theater owners largely controlled their own programming
and marketing. Because of the need to coordinate film releases with print
publication, serials began to shift such control to producers. This change
encouraged and drew strength from the developing star system. As early as
1910, White had been noticed as a "picture personality" for her work in
short films ("Picture Personalities," *Moving Picture World*, 3 December 1910,
1281; see also Abel in this volume), but her star persona congealed around
Pauline, an orphaned heiress and aspiring fiction writer who declares her
wish "to be absolutely free for a year," puts off her marriage to Harry Mar-
vin, and inspires the treacherous trustee of her estate to plot her destruction in hopes of seizing her fortune for himself. Developing the precedent
set by *What Happened to Mary* and *The Adventures of Kathlyn*, Pathé publicist
P. A. Parsons arranged a "hook up" with Eddie McMannus of the Hearst
newspaper syndicate. The Hearst papers published the prose version of
Pauline's perils and helped coordinate a massive advertising campaign,
including a $25,000 prize contest for fans eager to supplement Pauline's
adventures (and mimic her writing ambitions). Leading questions urged
them to fill in plot points not elaborated in print or onscreen (see Stamp).
As P. A. Parsons relates, this effort made "'The Perils of Pauline' . . . so well
known that it passed into a figure of speech." Commodifiers proliferated. "A
very popular song called 'Poor Pauline' was voluntarily composed by a
music publishing house," Parsons recalls, "and could be heard in almost any
vaudeville theater" ("A History of Motion Pictures Advertising," *Moving Pic-*

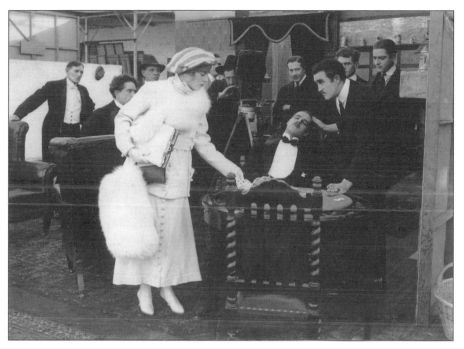

Grace Cunard and Francis Ford on the set of *The Broken Coin* (1915). Courtesy of the Academy of Motion Picture Arts and Sciences.

ture World, 26 March 1927, 308). Pathé and White worked diligently to extend the success of *The Perils*. By decade's end they had released nine chapter plays in the United States, plus multiple spin-offs abroad.

The Universal Film Manufacturing Company followed Pauline to the screen by just under a month with episode one of *Lucille Love, the Girl of Mystery*, in which Grace Cunard's Lucille commandeers a hydroplane and sets off on a globe-spanning pursuit of Francis Ford's Hugo Loubeque, who absconds with secret government papers entrusted to her father. Already popular for their work in short westerns, mysteries, and adventure films, Cunard and Ford became major stars through a total of four successful serials for Universal, the last of which appeared in 1917. Since Cunard and White portrayed similar sorts of characters onscreen, it only makes sense that their star personae would share certain features. Fans of both performers were urged to marvel at their hazardous stunt work (doubles were not typically used). In addition to their risk-taking, the global popularity of these serial stars also awed commentators. Reports established, for example, that to be a Cunard fan in Racine, Wisconsin, United States of America, gave one something in common with residents of Poona City, Bombay Presidency, India. This raises the question of what exactly such commonality entails. If admiration of serial queens made one modern in the 1910s, did this modernity confirm or contradict traditional affiliations of class, gender, race, and nation? Cunard's celebrity, like White's, encouraged discussion of the risks of modern life and of the new web of social connections movie-going created. Her fame differed, however, due to her sustained collabora-tion with Ford. Cunard and Ford were co-directors as well as co-stars, and she also wrote their scenarios. Their characters often married, but the stars never did. To consider these filmmaking partners alongside White thus fore-grounds a third problematic defining the serial queen's "now," namely, that of a changing division of labor, with all that entailed for women's prospects at work and for the organization of married life.

☆★★★★ Risk

In a February 1921 interview called "The Ninety-Nine Lives of Pearl White" for *The Picturegoer*, a fan magazine, Alice Hall stages her visit to White's Long Island home as if she were entering a serial episode:

> "A harmless-looking house enough," I thought, as I walked up the broad drive-way leading to Pearl's palatial home. But if you know anything about serials and their makers, you will remember that it is just these seemingly innocent abodes which prove to be the lair of dynamiting gangs, Black Han-ders, and criminals of the deepest dye. So I did not relax my vigilance. . . . I stood ready to make my escape the moment [the butler] began to exhibit those disquieting tendencies indulged in by the serial butler—who is invari-ably the villain in disguise.   (31)

Hall turns out to be perfectly safe, of course. The butler poses no threat, and the star hosts a not-at-all-poisonous, "super-feature" tea, despite the "3,750 attempts against her life" reported in a sidebar. Although White claims to have "renounced serials in favor of features" (she would in fact make one more serial, *Plunder*, in 1923), the persona established by her work in seri-als of the 1910s structures the interview. Echoing a trend established by journalists as early as 1914, Hall discovers a White more ordinary than one might imagine (cf. Mabel Condon, "Sans Grease Paint and Wig," *Motogra-phy*, 22 August 1914, 279–80; Condon, "The Real Perils of Pauline," *Photo-play*, October 1914, 59–64). Readers learn of her humble upbringing in the Ozarks, her work ethic, and her forthright good humor. Yet the star also turns out to be every bit as extraordinary as one expects: "golden-haired, rosy-cheeked, lovelier than I had ever seen her on the screen" (31). She also confronts death with a sangfroid exceeding that of her characters. White tells a wide-eyed Hall how she fought with villains on the narrow girders of unfinished buildings, high above the streets, and dangled from ropes that were severed to the last strand; how she was thrown upstairs by the villain, and downstairs by his accomplice; how, in one scene, a big china vase was smashed in pieces against her head; how climbing down a 300-foot flag-pole, or being cut loose in a drifting balloon, were but insignificant episodes in a day's work.   (34)

This recitation of perils—truly a set piece of writing on serial queens—conflates character with performer only to end up neatly distinguishing them. Like her characters, the star repeatedly defies death, but whereas each life-threatening predicament catches her character by surprise, for the performer the risk is part of the daily routine, hence "insignificant." Made quotidian, the most implausible hazards can be shrugged off with blithe disregard.

Poised for flight on White's threshold, Hall poses briefly as a naïve fan who mistakes fiction for real life. This is a ruse. The author playfully disavows her knowledge that villains do not infest the star's Long Island home in order to allow readers the satisfaction of believing they can tell the difference between fiction and real life. In so doing, Hall defines what real life is and offers the star, rather than her character, as a point of identification. Like White and the soon-to-be-enlightened reporter, fans know that the star only pretends to be menaced by "dynamiting gangs, Black Handers, and criminals of the deepest dye." If such threats perpetually catch Pauline unawares, the fan (and the star) expects them. Readers may therefore anticipate Hall's discovery of White's workaday nonchalance and come to see something of themselves in the star who gets up every morning, risks life and limb, and returns home only to repeat the process. Identification with the star thus invites a sense of vicarious mastery over the world of omnipresent danger serials depict.

In her encouragement of this identification, Hall enacts a knowledge game the rewards of which lie not in winning so much as in continuing to play. At first, readers might assume that discovering the true nature of a threat will suffice to defuse it. When Hall hovers cautiously on White's doorstep as if she were a serial heroine, she anticipates a danger that does not in fact exist. Her readers are wise to this and may take satisfaction in knowing what the mock-naïve reporter seems not to know. As the article proceeds to replace the character's fictional hazards with the real perils experienced by the star, however, the rhetorical strategy stresses the degree to which uncertainty and danger define White's daily routine, and lures the reader to anticipate learning more about the star's ongoing antics from publicity and press releases. Not only does Hall imply that she learns more from White than she situation in urban modernity" (*Melodrama* 262). "Urban modernity" refers to a cluster of changes coinciding with the extraordinarily rapid growth of cities worldwide in the late nineteenth century. In the United States, for example, the urban population quadrupled between 1870 and 1910. Expanding cities created jobs that brought women into the public arena, a situation that allowed greater independence but also created fears about sexual promiscuity and predation, which inspired new efforts to regulate women's conduct. Sexuality, like everything else, was increasingly commodified. The shop window and ubiquitous advertising hailed women as the ideal consumers for all manner of mass-produced commodities. Meanwhile, new communications and transportation technologies circulated people, information, and goods with increasing rapidity so that, while the city was the locus of change, its growth also affected the farms and smalls towns linked to it by means of, first, railroads, telegraphs, and magazines, and, soon thereafter, automobiles, telephones, and motion pictures. The new velocities and their concomitant dislocations often struck contemporary commentators as enervating: the thrill of mobility could prove excessively stimulating and also aroused fears of catastrophic technological failure. Just so, the cars, planes, speedboats, locomotives, and submarines that promised the serial heroine a thrilling escape are also liable to explode, spring leaks, or career out of control. Thus, when the serial queen launched herself out of a domestic setting into a more thrilling and dangerous public arena, she joined the women in her audience as they entered an urban traffic flow that united peril and empowerment in uncertain relation.

Where Singer understands the serial queen to express the paradoxes of a newly urban society, Shelley Stamp sees her tentatively revising the rules of courtship. Stamp emphasizes a difference between serial plots themselves and the fan culture that developed around the respective stars. Although, she argues, serials did "promote a kind of modern femininity clearly tailored to appeal to their cadre of female fans," their plots also obsessively told "alarmist tales in which independence is always circumscribed by the shadow of danger, the determinacy of familial ties, and the inevitability of marriage" (*Movie-Struck* 126). Pauline's case is prototypical in equating independence with the postponement of marriage, while associating wealth and security with its acceptance. Here, as elsewhere, wealth comes in the form of inheritance-with-strings-attached from an absent father. Pauline must marry to come into her father's money, so that in delivering a husband the ending also continues the father's estate. Let America's daughters have their adventures, serials might seem to say, but in the end they remain daddy's girls.

Matters look a bit different, Stamp argues, if one considers the types of marriages serial queens helped fans envision. For instance, when the New York Federation of Women's Clubs complained of the movies' "'degenerating influence upon the young' by encouraging women to be 'pals' with men," White responded by endorsing just that program: "'Why not give our men the same comradeship that many of them never find outside their clubs?'" she asked (qtd. in Stamp 147–48). Such comradeship, and the gender confusion it entailed, was a defining element of White's persona. For example, her publicist, Frank Bruner, characterized the "real Pearl White" as, first, "a rattling good fellow," and then, "a human, likeable person" ("The Real Pearl White," *Motion Picture Magazine*, July 1919, 33–34). More broadly, coverage in newspapers and fan magazines depicted the serial queen's private life as according with expectations for women in some ways while defying tradition in others. Visits to their (always impressive and tasteful) homes, attention paid to their (always plentiful and lovely) gowns, and reminders of their devotion to relatives and pets appeared alongside indications that those relatives depended on the stars' salaries, descriptions of the serial queens' characteristic passions such as motoring and outdoor sports, and notices that they lacked enthusiasm for domestic chores. While serials conducted their heroines' adventures in a way that appeared to restore patriarchal order, the serial queen herself arguably modeled a new kind of woman within broader fan culture: she appeared a talented shopper and homemaker, perhaps, but also an adventuresome, and equal, companion for a modern man.

Singer and Stamp both situate the serial queen amidst the social upheavals of turn-of-the-century modernity in order to argue for her particular relevance to the changing social circumstances of women in her audience. Jennifer M. Bean reverses that impulse. In her account, the serial queen figures for the possibility that *anyone* might survive the perilous pleasures of modern life, and in so doing secures cinema's claim to represent it. Looking back in 1932, Cunard slighted then-current stars as fussy and pampered, pointing out that in her day, in addition to working long hours, "We did all the stunts and went to the hospital regularly. They used to call the Good Samaritan Hospital in Los Angeles, 'Grace Cunard's Hotel'" ("Crowded out of Stardom," *New Movie Magazine*, February 1932, 117). Her cohort's performances were authentic, Cunard implies, because they put their bodies on the line. This same conceit established the serial stars' appeal in the first place, argues Bean. Celebration of the physical hazards of motion picture performance proclaimed a defiant, bodily reality in the face of modernity's rationalization not only of work, but also of increasingly come across one of them." The scrapbooks also include stars' replies to her letters and a few bits of correspondence from her friends about their shared movie obsessions. Crane Wilbur, White's co-star in *Perils of Pauline*, receives almost as much attention as White herself, and a letter from Vercoe's friend Flossie insinuates that Vercoe has a crush on him. Less expected, perhaps, is Vercoe's interest in Lubin actor Romaine Fielding. Among the letters from actors that survive in the scrapbooks, Fielding's reply is exceptional both in its length and in his request for a response: he asks for a photograph from Vercoe in return. For White—whose letter to Vercoe is unfortunately missing, although the envelope remains carefully pasted into volume six—one-way communications were clearly the norm (Edna G. Vercoe Scrapbooks, Margaret Herrick Library, Beverly Hills, California).

In "The Ninety-Nine Lives of Pearl White" (*The Picturegoer*, February 1921), White explains that a team of stenographers handles her voluminous fan mail. This does not mean she undervalues it. On the contrary, her 1919 autobiography, *Just Me*, describes fan mail as "one of the greatest mediums through which we [movie actors] can judge our popularity," because, unlike in live theater, the performers and audience are not co-present. She receives as many as ten thousand letters a month and confesses that, "although I don't have time to read them all, I should be heartbroken if they ceased, because the bundles of letters that are handed to me each day cheer me on a whole lot" (106). Fans familiar with the protocol limited themselves to the pro-forma request for an autograph and photograph. Thus, we may assume that Vercoe's letter mattered to White (and Pathé) primarily as aggregated into a bundle. That it came from a particular teenager in Highland Park, with a friend named Flossie, a crush on Crane Wilbur, and a keen eye for the inconsistent and ironic, can have made little difference to the star, because she almost certainly did not have this information.

Filmmakers developed their understandings of fans through processes of sampling and counting that defined groups of individuals as types. For example, U.S. fan magazines' decisions to publish certain kinds of information contributed to the conviction, by the end of the 1910s, that "movie fans" were young people and especially young, middle-class women (see Fuller). Vercoe's scrapbooks confirm that she can indeed be typed in this manner. In addition, they point to a constellation of preferences and talents invisible to publicists, editors, and filmmakers. From the vantage they provide, we see clearly that fandom does not homogenize so much as manage multiplicities. It makes the conduct of diverse individuals predictable by hitching them to a common star. Cunard and White provide striking early examples of how such a mechanism could be extended globally.

The 9 September 1916 issue of the Japanese fan magazine *Katsudō no sekai* (The Japanese Movie Magazine) devoted its cover and an entire section to Grace Cunard, including articles promising "Gossip of Cunard's Real Life," "The Psychological Explanation of Cunard's Expression," and a comparison of "Grace Cunard and Pearl White." The following month, Universal's house organ, *Moving Picture Weekly*, reported on the story, claiming Cunard as the most popular actress in Japan, followed by White. The previous May, it had headlined "Ford-Cunard Popularity Wave Hits India" (27 May 1916, 31), and in July, Daisy Dean reported for the *Racine Journal News* that Cunard and Ford films had inspired "Vishwanath Chintman Bhide, who lives in Poona City, Bombay Presidency, India . . . to 'hazard' himself in the films"; he had written Universal for advice on becoming an actor ("News Notes from Movieland," 18 July 1916, 6). In November, lavish advertisements for Cunard and Ford in *The Broken Coin* (1915) promised Puerto Ricans an experience that had stirred Europe (Rodríguez). In Gretna, southwest Scotland, and Carlisle, Cumbria, England, mostly female, most teenage, mostly single workers in munitions factories flocked to White's *The Exploits of Elaine* in 1915. They were spurred on by an aggressive publicity campaign that featured a giveaway of a thousand "Elaine" hats (see Brader). In Mexico, White's serials led a "yanqui invasion" of the market that nonetheless inspired a self-consciously national fan culture (see Serna). In France, White's "almost ferocious smile announced the upheavals of the new world" to surrealists (Soupault 61). White herself found it "really marvelous to get letters from all the different countries . . . even from far away places like Iceland, Siam, Finland, Guatemala, the Colonies of South Africa, etc." (106).

Importantly, the serial queens' global popularity defined their fame for locals around the world: they were famous for being internationally famous. This nonetheless entailed local modifications. Bao Weihong provides a salient example of how the serial queen's moment contains a problem of geopolitical difference when she explains how Pearl White returns to U.S. audiences as the Chinese prototype for The Bride (Uma Thurman) in *Kill Bill: Volumes 1 and 2* (2003 and 2004). Although Quentin Tarantino's epic explicitly acknowledges its debt to the popular *nüxiapian* (female knight-errant films) made by the Shaw Brothers in the 1960s and 1970s, it is imperative to recognize that the *nüxiapian* genre emerged in the late 1920s as an amalgam of traditional Chinese literary and theatrical forms, western-looking Chinese modernisms, and tremendously popular U.S. serials, especially those of Baolian (White's Chinese name, derived from Pauline).

Grace Cunard appears on the cover of the Japanese fan magazine *Katsudō no sekai* (The Japanese Movie Magazine), September 1916.

As Bao explains, and Qin Xiqing elaborates, the serial queens found themselves embroiled in discussions of what it would mean for post-Imperial China (the Qing Dynasty fell in 1911) to become a modern nation-state, an argument that inevitably entailed the question of what it would mean for Chinese women to become modern. As in the United States, the serial queen's heroism and her fashion sense together proclaimed a new order in which women's movements and sexuality would be differently regulated, particularly in that they themselves would seem to have more control over them. The question of whether this type of woman would remain American, or might become Chinese, posed an additional complication. In 1920, movie critic Zhou Shoujuan wrote in the *Shun Pao* (Chinese Daily News): "What Baolian does is only acting of an actress, but her braving untold dangers on the screen is something beyond any ordinary women. I would like to ask if there are any sisters of our country who can do that?"[5] The answer, it turned out, was yes. Far from remaining essentially American, Baolian was so successfully translated by the host culture that her heroic legacy might well strike Tarantino's audiences as unambiguously Chinese.

Such a process of translation is evident even in White's initial popularity in the United States. Monica Dall'Asta reminds us that Pauline's adventures, directed by a young Frenchman (Louis Gasnier) for Pathé, were a centerpiece of the French company's effort to maintain a dominant position in the international market by Americanizing its product for U.S. audiences (see also Abel, *Red*; Dahlquist). The French firm turned out to be so good at making American serials that they felt the need to revise them for release in their homeland. To present the first White serial shown to French audiences (in the winter of 1915–1916), the company compiled twenty-two episodes from the three serials that featured her as Elaine Dodge (*The Exploits of Elaine* [1914], *The New Exploits of Elaine* [1915], and *The Romance of Elaine* [1915]), rewrote intertitles to transform American scientific detective Craig Kennedy into French patriot Justin Clarel, and created a new prose version for the *feuilleton*, the more elliptical French counterpart of American newspaper and magazine fiction. Thus domesticated as *Les Mystères de New York*, Elaine's exploits offered a prototype for what Dall'Asta assesses as the first major French serial, *Judex* (1917), and gave impetus to the *"serialomanie"* that gripped the nation after the war.[6] Dall'Asta sums up the lesson taught by these feats of translation and retranslation: "As soon as the initial outline of an international-popular culture begins to take shape, identities show themselves for what they are and always have been, dynamic formulations in a field of relations" (167).

Chinese identities no more precede this field of relations than French or American identities do, but they are not positioned equally. As Dall'Asta notes, Pathé's transnational distribution network, by far the most robust of its kind before the start of World War I, uniquely positioned the French filmmaker to conduct the serial's internationalization. Universal was hot on Pathé's heels, however, and Cunard would not have won popularity contests in Japan and India if not for the company's aggressive movement into Asian markets.[7] Like Pathé, Universal had far more power to outline an "international-popular culture" than any of the Japanese, Chinese, and Indian firms that drew inspiration from the serial fictions they made and distributed. That such asymmetrical power often entails fear and ignorance of others is certainly evident in the stereotypes serials circulated as a matter of course. Judging by English-language plot summaries, advertisements, and (relatively few) surviving prints, labyrinthine Chinatowns, despotic rajas, and typically inscrutable Oriental villains were part of serials' stock-in-trade. Although there remains much to learn about local reception, the fact that Japanese, Chinese, and Indian audiences and filmmakers took up serials despite their Orientalist iconography doubtlessly testifies, in part, to the genius of the locals responsible for appropriating and promoting them (see Bao; Bernardi; Hughes; Vitali).[8] Features of the form itself may also help to explain it. The "dangerous stranger" trope unites characters that a racist optic might view as profoundly different. The stereotypical Chinatown thugs who kidnap Pauline, for example, do not seem substantially more devious than the old sailor who lures her out to sea with tales of hidden treasure, more diabolical than the western outlaws who bury her alive, or more perverse than the dope-fiend doctor hired to botch her appendectomy. Above all, serials plots required that the heroine's adventures bring her into proximity with someone new (or newly disguised) and more dangerous than she expects. Even as it reprises racist caricatures to define the foreign as threatening, this structure also makes the foreign intensely interesting, since every stranger may harbor a murderous secret—or be a friend in disguise. In a similar way, one might argue, the serial queen brought the world's audiences closer together and made them more curious about one another, without making them less divided or suspicious.

☆☆☆☆★ Work

Before a series of high-profile scandals in the 1920s established the movie star's private life as a tragic nexus of substance abuse and sexual promiscuity, the star system of the 1910s policed itself in ways calculated to counter the image of the actor's life created by theatrical stars (see deCordova; Fuller). Rather than being part of a nocturnal demimonde, movie stars engaged in wholesome and exhausting work during the day and retired to normal family lives in the evening. The serial queen's athleticism perfectly harmonized with this orientation. In 1916, Cunard recommended rope climbing both as a corrective for the "underdeveloped arms" that menace any woman's beauty and as a practical necessity for the stunts required by her serial work ("Rope Climbing Keeps Grace Cunard Fit," *Moving Picture Weekly*, 10 June 1916, 31). White echoed the sentiment, advising aspiring actresses in 1917 to "Be strong. Exercise. Live in the open if possible. Go to bed early and get up earlier. Ride horseback, dance, swim, do everything that makes for health and steady nerves. Even beauty and ability cannot exist without them" (John Ten Eyck, "Speaking of Pearls," *Photoplay*, September 1917, 117). On the other hand, White's 1914 pronouncement in *Cosmopolitan Magazine* that movie work "solves . . . the problem of women's economic independence . . . for she may earn as much as two hundred dollars a week, and for fifty-two weeks in the year" may have been greeted with ambivalence by the contemporary "family values" crowd ("A Model of the Movies," July 1914, 263). If so, they could find solace in White's later declaration that she envied the domestic life of her married sister because "the woman who seeks a public career is bound to have an empty old age" (Hazel Simpson Naylor, "All Over the Plot at Pathé," *Motion Picture Magazine*, May 1918, 48).

A married woman working in motion pictures in 1914 could be considered a demographic trendsetter. In the United States, the percentage of married women in the civilian labor force roughly doubled from under 6 percent in 1900 to just under 11 percent in 1910, at which point about a quarter of all women and about half of single women over sixteen worked for wages. To be more precise, 1,122,000 married women joined the civilian workforce through the course of the decade. Despite periods of reversal, the percentage of working married women remained relatively constant through 1930, when it began to grow by 4 to 8 percent each decade. Meanwhile, the proportion of single women who worked remained far more stable, fluctuating between 43 and 51 percent from 1900 to 1970, so that the doubling of the proportion of women in the workforce overall (from 21 to 42 percent) may be attributed largely to the growing numbers of employed married women (U.S. Census Bureau). While it seems safe to say that White voiced contemporary commonsense in opposing the financial independence of work to her sister's married life, it also seems likely that her audience was beginning to wonder about the possibility (or necessity) of combining the two. Far from merely indicating a change of attitudes, the shift altered an established division of a labor in which a wife's uncompensated domestic work supported her husband's wage-earning activities. The change had broad socioeconomic causes and consequences (see Cott; Blackwelder; Livingston).

The question of whether or not stars were married—certainly among the most common of published fan queries—concerned not only romance, then, but also the possibility of combining it with work. Universal's publicists seemed to surmise this early on. White largely succeeded in keeping her 1914 divorce and her second marriage in 1919 out of the papers and therefore appeared decidedly single at the height of her fame. In contrast, newspaper movie columns and fan magazines kept the news that Cunard and Ford might be married to each other alive by constantly denying it. Only rarely did replies to fans note Ford's marriage to writer Elsie Van Name. Rather than emphasize his domestic commitment, publicity underscored his working partnership with Cunard. In a typical 1916 interview, Ford explained: "Miss Cunard and I are an ideal team. We even work out the story together. Sometimes one of us, sometimes the other, has the original idea, and then she usually puts it into scenario form. She can dream scenarios. We play into each others' hands. She is a very capable director herself, you know" (Mlle. Chic, "Talking to Francis Ford," *Moving Picture Weekly*, 13 May 1916, 9). Describing the arrangement as incredibly efficient, *Photoplay* declared: "Both Ford and Miss Cunard are able to write, direct, and act with equal brilliance" (William M. Henry, "Her Grace and Francis," April 1916, 28). In all their serials except *Lucille Love*, competition between the characters establishes them as equally matched and eventually develops into a romance. When it celebrated their professional collaboration, then, publicity not only extended their onscreen personae offscreen but likely fueled speculation that the actors had a similar romantic destiny. Interestingly, when Cunard married Joseph Moore in late summer 1917, Universal publicist H. H. Van Loan presented the arrangement to readers of *Motion Picture Classic* as an extension of her frenetic production schedule. Over dinner at Levy's Café after work, she bets fellow stars that she "can be introduced, wooed and married within twenty-four hours"—and wins despite five hours of sleep and a full morning shooting exteriors ("Here Comes the Bride," August 1917, 46).

Cunard was not the only serial queen to acquire significant creative control over her productions. Kathlyn Williams directed herself in *The Leopard's Foundling* (1914), for instance, and Ruth Roland produced a popular set of serials in which she starred, beginning with *Adventures of Ruth*

(1919). Holmes co-directed "Escape on the Fast Freight," although she was not credited onscreen—a not uncommon situation judging by contemporary accounts (see "Helen Holmes," *Moving Picture World*, 16 January 1915, 382; "Escape on the Fast Freight," *New York Dramatic Mirror*, 3 February 1915, 27). In general, the occupation of motion picture director was open to women in the 1910s (a window of opportunity that narrows considerably in the 1920s). Universal in particular distinguished itself for the numbers of women it credited as director (see Cooper; Mahar). Even so, Cunard was the only woman it entrusted with serials.[9] This had everything to do with the fact that Universal tended to interpret the genre in ways that emphasized organizational hierarchy at the expense of professional collaboration. The company's 1910s serials without Cunard and Ford tend to cast their heroines as talented amateurs who assist a male professional—he is a mine foreman, detective, military officer, etc. In contrast, Cunard and Ford often work for competing organizations. In *The Broken Coin*, for instance, he is the unacknowledged heir to a Balkan throne while she is a newspaper reporter in search of what turns out to be his story. Each holds half of a coin necessary to solve the mystery and save the kingdom. Similarly, in *The Purple Mask* she plays socialite Patsy Montez, who disguises herself as the eponymous bandit and, at the head of a gang from the Paris sewers, robs from the greedy to give to the needy. Ford's Detective Kelley uses all the resources at his command in his efforts to apprehend her. In the end, however, they join forces to foil a bomb plot hatched by anarchists and abetted by river pirates. Whereas the development of the genre overall proposed that organizations worked best with clear, male-headed hierarchies, Cunard's and Ford's productions, consistent with their reputation as co-writers and co-directors, emphasized that the collaboration of professional equals was as effective and even more fun.

Although Cunard and Ford achieved unusual authority, a perhaps inevitable clash with management did result (see Birchard). White seems to have fit more neatly into the corporate machinery responsible for planning and directing her performances onscreen and off: "When fate picks out a girl for the photoplay career, it is liable to do all sorts of unexpected things with her life," she told *Cosmopolitan* readers, "exactly as the director does with her work" ("A Model of the Movies," July 1914, 263).

Pathé's manner of organizing White's work, always directed by someone else in a story written for her, anticipates what would quickly become the industrial norm: men decide, women perform. Cunard and Ford's success, however, suggested a different arrangement in which men and women might be equal work partners. In the publicity that linked these different approaches to the interests of fans, consideration of work was often explicitly connected with concern over stars' marital status. In this way, serial stardom organized an early, if still inchoate and inconclusive, discussion of what would replace the traditional household headed by a male breadwinner. At the same time, it raised the question of what it would mean for men and women to compete at the office.

☆☆☆★★ Conclusion

The serial queen's volatile moment cannot be precisely placed on any calendar; it is not a time period but a problem. Without a doubt, White, Cunard, and their imitators and rivals played a decisive role in the development of the global moving image culture of the 1910s. These "nervy" heroines gripped the imagination of diverse audiences worldwide, and corporate filmmakers developed robust new mechanisms to circulate and commodify them. In tandem with formulaic serial narratives, multimedia marketing strategies succeeded in sustaining audience interest over a period of months. This provided an ideal platform for the development of star personae, which could in turn be used to manage the risks entailed by future production. If the resultant serials craze struck contemporary commentators as a decided novelty, however, the figure of the serial queen herself had clear precedents in magazine fiction, dime novels, and theatrical melodrama. In this sense, serials may be regarded as reassembling and enthusiastically repackaging well-tested cultural materials.

Whereas noting precedents drags the serial queen's moment into the past, attention to her problems propels her into the future. Her fans wanted to know—or were expected to want to know—whether women could successfully combine marriage with work; whether being a woman necessitated subordination within a decision-making hierarchy; whether adventurous women had something in common with the potentially dangerous people on the other side of the globe and, if so, whether this made everyone more modern and substantially less like their parents; whether modern life demanded "nerve," an unthinking and spontaneous approach to hazard; whether men and women could be "pals" as well as romantic partners; and whether it was possible to survive the numbing routines and surmount the shocking brutalities of modern life while still enjoying its proliferating pleasures—and all without damaging one's reputation. For some early-twenty-first-century readers, these matters doubtlessly seem settled. For others, perhaps, they abide. The issue is less the existence of historical distinctions than their significance. One might feel the enthusiastic curiosity of

Pearl White's contemporaries to have long passed, but it is equally plausible to think of such enthusiasm living on among the contemporaries of Uma Thurman, Angelina Jolie, Jennifer Garner, and other luminaries who have recently given new life to serial adventure. Perhaps the serial queen's moment is, indeed, now.

NOTES

Many thanks to Val Almendarez, Jennifer Bean, Barbara Hall, and Meeghan Kane for their help with research for this article.

1. Some were extended to twenty episodes or more and others had as few as eight.

2. In 1915, Rose (renamed Helen) Gibson took over from Holmes in the role.

3. Based on a European release, the nine-chapter version available on DVD differs substantially from the twenty-chapter version first released in the United States.

4. Using the Consumer Price Index, $200 in 1914 had the value in 2007 of $4,300.

5. Thanks to Qiu Xiqing for the translation and reference: Zhou Shoujuan, "A Movie Review," *Shun Pao*, 4 July 1920.

6. The term is George Sadoul's (qtd. in Dall'Asta 161).

7. By the end of 1917, Universal had offices in London (through which it distributed to Africa and Australia), Paris, Berlin, Copenhagen, Vienna, Budapest, Barcelona, Vilna, Petrograd, Rio de Janeiro, Buenos Aires, Havana, Manila, Bombay, Calcutta, Singapore, Tokyo, and China (see Cooper). According to Hughes, Universal dominated the Indian market by the late 1910s and was the main supplier of serials to southern India after 1917 (38).

8. I know of no instance of local genius rivaling that of Félix and Edmundo Padilla, who reedited the 1916 Marie Walcamp serial vehicle *Liberty, A Daughter of the U.S.A.* as the heroic epic of Pancho Villa, on whom the villain of the serial was based. See Gregorio Rocha's film *Los Rollos Peridos de Pancho Villa* (2003).

9. Universal credited a total of eleven women as director before 1919. Although Madison became famous for her role in the serial *Trey o' Hearts*, she never directed serials.

movies under the auspices of Will Hays. "The massive system could not permit unregulated individual massiveness," writes historian Neda Ulady of the star. "The individual had to fit, neatly and thinly, into a regulated slot" (Ulady 163). The scapegoating of a fat man became the bedrock of a modern culture industry.

This perception of the relationship linking Arbuckle's stardom to his body has nonetheless produced complex critical problems. The portrait of Arbuckle that we have inherited from star profiles and news reports, as well as from some later scholarship, is simply that of a creature of fascinating excess—whether sympathetically evoked as, for example, the "Falstaff of the screen"; or condemned, after 1921, as an impotent rapist; or even, finally, theorized as a metonymy for the movies' "low" cultural origins. Yet none of this enables us to come to grips with what film scholar J. P. Telotte has astutely described as the "pattern of escape" in Arbuckle's career, his efforts to transcend the implications of his size in his screen performances, to resist the comic type to which his body condemned him (Telotte). Nor do we necessarily understand why he became one of the most acclaimed comic talents of his era, the "best comedian on the screen" according to Paramount head Adolph Zukor (Neibaur 25). At his peak, Arbuckle was paid the highest salary of any actor at the time. In the years between leaving the legendary Keystone Film Company in late 1916 and shifting to feature-length comedies for Paramount in 1919, he not only commanded his own studio, the Comique Film Corporation, but also enjoyed full artistic control of his films, which he wrote, directed, and starred in. This success was not achieved simply by being fat.

What needs to be insisted upon, rather, is the way that Arbuckle's stardom drew energy from some of the founding tensions within the formation of early American mass culture, and, in particular, the ambiguous role of the body within that constellation. Thus, whereas other scholars have theorized early stardom chiefly as a form of epistemology—whether as an expansion of the kind of knowledge available about film actors (deCordova) or as the discursive construction of a "realness" associated with daring performers and their athletic stunts (Bean "Technologies")—this chapter situates Arbuckle's meaning within the dynamics of cinema's emergence as a cross-class culture industry. As identified by Max Weber, those dynamics required the declassification of cultural categories, a mixing and hybridizing of genres and meanings capable of producing a diversified appeal (Weber 937). Arbuckle himself thus became a hybrid figure, a sign of the liquidation of cultural categories that was at once the condition of his success and a focus of the eventual scandal. Arbuckle's body may have been key to his star identity, but it represented only one pole in a complex dialectic of cultural meanings, of bodily presence *and* absence, that defined his stardom as a component of the new mass culture.

☆☆☆★★ Fatty versus Roscoe: The Body as Comic Signifier

"Fatty"—rather than sidestepping Arbuckle's problematic moniker, why not begin with it? Arbuckle hated the nickname and would politely correct fans who used it: "I've got a name, you know," was supposedly his response (Young 33). Yet the label "Fatty," and its variable prominence in discourse on the comedian, also offers insight into the changing parameters of Arbuckle's stardom. On the Keystone lot, for instance, the nickname was rarely used; instead, he was variously known as Roscoe, Bucky, or, after graduating to directing, Chief. Mabel Normand teasingly dubbed him "Big Otto" after the elephant at the Selig zoo, while Charlie Murray mysteriously christened him "My Child, the Fat" (Young 33). Within trade journals and fan magazines, meanwhile, Arbuckle's screen name charted a very clear evolution in tandem with his emergent stardom. Initially, after joining Keystone in the spring of 1913, he was little more than a category, commonly referred to as the "fat boy" or the "Keystone fat boy"; for example, "the fat boy . . . appears in this," from *Moving Picture World's* synopsis of Keystone's June release, *Passions, He Had Three* ("Comments on the Films," 7 June 1913, 1033). Soon, there was a short-lived attempt to personalize him as "the fat boy, Bob" (in publicity for *For the Love of Mabel* and *A Noise from the Deep*); but, by the fall of 1913, his screen personality had coalesced around the moniker "Fatty," which began appearing in the title of his movies with the September release of *Fatty's Day Off*. Within a few months, magazines also began using the comedian's real name, particularly in profiles celebrating his performative virtuosity: "Roscoe Arbuckle, the 'heavy' comedian with Keystone, is one of the most nimble footed men in the world" ("Doings at Los Angeles," *Moving Picture World*, 30 May 1914, 1248). This use of "Roscoe" became especially common after he started directing his own comedies (his first was *Barnyard Flirtations*, March 1914). Indeed, star profiles focusing on his achievements as a filmmaker—rather than solely as a performer—were conspicuous for almost never using the nickname "Fatty": "Mr. Arbuckle is one of the greatest of comedy directors" or "Roscoe Arbuckle, now . . . the most prolific and reliable director in Sennett's college of clowns" ("Plays and Players," *Photoplay* December 1915, 160; "The Shadow Stage," *Photoplay* May 1916, 109). By the time of his first Comique release, *The Butcher Boy* (April 1917), newspaper ads billed him as

"Roscoe ('Fatty') Arbuckle," relegating his established nickname to a parenthetical addendum, offset by scare quotes (Neibaur 32).

In an enormously suggestive reading of star discourses during the 1910s, Jennifer M. Bean has argued that the emergence of the star system entailed a shift in audience fascination along the axis of production, from the mechanical base of the cinematic apparatus to the body of the star; thus, "the player's body supersede[d] the body of the machine" as the foundation of the industry's appeal (a process that she sees exemplified in the acrobatic derring-do of early serial queens like Pearl White and Helen Holmes) (Bean, "Technologies" 21). Yet the evolution of language traced through Arbuckle's name suggests that this development was more inconsistent in practice, and that a fascination with the body could be complicated by pressures seeking to locate a star's meaning elsewhere. "Fatty" Arbuckle may have been fat; still, a significant trajectory of his star discourse labored to resist such physicality, to assert his identity as "Roscoe," and to seek alternate, less immediately carnal, meanings for comic stardom. For Arbuckle, this meant defining his comic talent not simply in terms of his onscreen slapstick performances but also through his behind-the-camera abilities as a director, a redefinition of comic "authorship" with lasting implications for how later silent comedians would be (and still are) evaluated. As a 1915 *New York Telegraph* profile put it, Arbuckle's "high pedestal in laugh filmology" did not merely reflect his extraordinary girth, but had been achieved "by reason of his brain *as well as* his weight-ridden physique," both through his "act[ing] foolish before the camera" *and* through "the success of many of the films in which he does not appear . . . but has directed" (Rapf 342). Body versus brain, performance versus direction, "Fatty" versus "Roscoe": these were the contradictory coordinates from which would emerge new parameters for comic stardom.

It is part of the wager of the present argument that this tension articulates conflicting cultural registers within the context of early-twentieth-century America. The distinction separating Arbuckle's star identity between (clown's) body and (artist's) brain corresponded to broader, well-established cultural hierarchies that had long differentiated the "embodied" realm of popular, working-class sensationalism from a more "sacralized" aesthetic of genteel transcendence. As a number of historians have suggested, those distinctions had first emerged in the late nineteenth century when America's genteel middle class sought to maintain social and cultural order by segregating "high" from "low" culture: a process of sacralization took place, endowing genteel aesthetics with quasi-spiritual status while actively denigrating the tastes and practices of the lower orders (DiMaggio;

Levine). During roughly the same period, however, the rapid growth of cheap commercial amusements supported an opposed idiom of popular sensationalism that emphasized materiality and corporeality, not transcendence, and that observers came to interpret as a response to the deprivations of working-class life.[1] From the belly laugh of variety entertainment to the "blood and thunder" scenes of cheap melodrama, from the thrills of the amusement park ride to the physical contact of knockabout comedy, popular forms reflected a hunger for intense bodily stimulation that, for genteel taste, was the very definition of vulgarity. To be both "body" and "brain," clown and artist, was, from this perspective, necessarily to conflate cultural registers—a productive and, as it would prove, dangerous position. At one time praised for inaugurating a "higher standard" of slapstick, Arbuckle would eventually be condemned as an interloping vulgarian, "the result of ignorance and too much money," to quote the post-scandal indictment of comedy director Henry Lehrman ("Miss Rappe's Fiancé Threatens Vengeance," *New York Times*, 13 September 1921, 2).

Still, it was simply as a rotund clown that Arbuckle began his film career, first in two brief stints at Selig in 1909 and early 1913, before joining the Keystone Film Company in April of the latter year. When Arbuckle first arrived at Keystone, the resident "fat" comic was Fred Mace; following the latter's departure for Majestic in May, Arbuckle quickly took over his mantle. "I had been there four weeks, when Fred Mace left Keystone, and I was taken to fill the vacancy," Arbuckle explained in a 1914 interview (George A. Posner, "Roscoe Arbuckle of the Keystone Company," *Motion Pictures*, September 1914, n.p.). His identity as the "fat boy" was swiftly established in his earliest Keystone appearances, many of which surely fueled the studio's growing reputation for intensely physical farce. His debut film, *The Gangsters*, was criticized as "a little rough for presentation in some houses," while his subsequent picture, *Help! Help! Hydrophobia*, was described as simply "a series of wild happenings" (see *Moving Picture World*, 31 May 1913, 922; *Moving Picture World*, 7 June 1913, 1033). It was also during these early months that Arbuckle was apocryphally the recipient of the first-ever pie in the face, in his ninth Keystone film, *A Noise from the Deep*, in June 1913 (Young 40–41; Oderman 64). Whether or not the comic pie in fact originates here, the heaving of pastries certainly attracted critics' notice ("It begins with throwing pies," noted one review), as did a subsequent pie fight in the October release, *A Quiet Little Wedding* ("a lemon meringue pie battle ensues") (*Moving Picture World*, 26 July 1913, 430; *Moving Picture World*, 23 October 1913, 422). Other early Arbuckle pictures meanwhile saw the "fat boy" falling around in drag (*Peeping Pete*, June 1913), dangling from telephone wires (*Mother's Boy*,

September 1913), and running around in torn-up pants (*Fatty Joins the Force*, November 1913, in which he again receives a pie in the face).

The purely physical focus of these early films inevitably wedded Arbuckle's screen persona to the popular logic of spectacular, rough-and-tumble bodies.[2] This was, of course, characteristic of slapstick, which commonly defined comic identity through bodily particularity (other performers' nicknames of the 1910s included "Baldy" Belmont, "Shorty" Hamilton, "Skinny" Dee Lampton, and "Slim" Summerville). But, crucially, it was not enough to make him a star. If, as Richard deCordova has argued, the emergence of a star system involved a "marked expansion of the type of knowledge that could be produced about the player," then, in the case of Arbuckle, this would require going beyond that which was most obviously knowable in the comedian's identity—namely, his fat (deCordova 98). It would mean transcending the physicality that dictated his early knockabout roles and a significant "disembodying" of his persona. Fatty's stardom entailed a redefinition of slapstick that ultimately emerged not through a discourse of physicality but through its refutation.

☆☆☆☆★ Comedian versus Director: Strategies of Respectability

To understand Arbuckle's ascent, it is necessary first to place it within a series of major transformations in film comedy's cultural status in the mid-1910s, each establishing dilemmas that Arbuckle—like all comedians of his generation—had to confront. During this period, for instance, slapstick's dominant format had remained the one- or two-reel short, placing the genre out of step with an industry increasingly geared to multiple-reel (or "feature") dramas. Feature production between 1913 and 1914 increased in America more than 500 percent, from 56 features of four reels or more to well over 300 (Singer 80); yet, during the same period, production of multiple-reel slapstick failed to develop beyond an occasional novelty, such as the Ramo Company's three-reel *This Is the Life* (1914) or Keystone's more celebrated six-reel experiment, *Tillie's Punctured Romance* (1914). Of course, one of the reasons for the emergence of the dramatic feature film, in America as elsewhere, was its cultural prestige; but here, too, slapstick countered prevailing trends, widely regarded as a throwback to the movies' disreputable, nickelodeon-era past. Throughout the decade, *Moving Picture World* and its leading critic, Epes Winthrop Sargent, consistently called for an evolution in screen comedy from the physical humor of "water throwing and senseless chases" toward more sophisticated fare appealing to audiences of "more discriminating taste" ("The Photoplaywright," 12 April 1913, 157). "Slapstick must be taboo" was the frank declaration of one such editorial in 1919 (Neale and Krutnik 110). Such gentrifying attitudes were even shared by many of the era's leading comedians, who offered numerous pronouncements declaring their support for what was variously termed "higher," "sophisticated," or just "clean" comedy. Upon arriving in Fort Lee, New Jersey, at the end of 1915 to establish a new Keystone unit, Arbuckle himself boldly asserted that "my ideas are along the newer lines of screen comedy," adding as a statement of intent: "I believe in comedy that makes you think, and I believe that the time has come to put it on— and that's what I am going to do" (Young 127). In a later interview, Arbuckle restated his intent in more explicitly moral terms: "I shall produce nothing that will offend the proprieties, whether applied to children or grown-ups. . . . My pictures are turned out with clean hands and therefore with a clear conscience which, like virtue, is its own reward" ("Clean Pictures That Will Please Children, Arbuckle's Aim," *Motion Picture News*, 12 May 1917, 2999).

Arbuckle's attempt to define a "newer line" of comedy was thus no unique effort in the mid-1910s, although his comedies, like Charlie Chaplin's, arguably provide notable landmarks. More significant than the shared intent, however, were the varied directions in which these ambitions led different comedians. An unmistakably "low" physical clown, Arbuckle was also a filmmaker who innovated a range of distinctive strategies for "clean" comedy; in consequence, his films offer rich testimony to the dilemmas and contradictions wrought by a modern mass culture predicated in part on the gentrification of popular forms. The following paragraphs point to three ways in which Arbuckle's later work at Keystone can be related to an awareness of questions of cultural status: narrative form, comic persona, and visual style.[3]

1. *Slapstick and Narrative Form*: In what has been among the most influential historical accounts of screen comedy's development during the 1910s, Henry Jenkins's *What Made Pistachio Nuts?* (1992) identifies two distinct, socially defined comic aesthetics in turn-of-the-century America—a genteel tradition of "thoughtful laughter" (associated with classical narrative values and exemplified in film by Sidney Drew's "situation" comedies), and the popular sensationalism of the "new humor" (associated with vaudeville and exemplified in film by Keystone-style slapstick). Efforts to refine screen comedy during the 1910s, Jenkins argues, need to be understood as a series of attempts to negotiate between these traditions, to merge the gag-based immediacy of the new humor with the greater respectability and narrative complexity of the "thoughtful laughter" tradition, ultimately

Keystone publicity flaunts Arbuckle's various characterizations. Courtesy of the Academy of Motion Picture Arts and Sciences.

Arbuckle's "country boy" persona, and here too a link can be made with discourses of comic respectability.

Arbuckle's interest in rural characterizations dates to the very beginning of his directing career—his first film as a director, *Barnyard Flirtations*, although no longer extant, was reviewed as a "rough and tumble" farmer's daughter comedy—and would recur in several of his early self-directed films, such as *Those Country Kids* (August 1914) and *Lovers' Post Office* (November 1914) (*Moving Picture World*, 4 April 1914, 58). Such settings and character types were, of course, no innovation of Arbuckle's: the rural clown or "rube" had long been a stock figure of vaudeville and comic strips, and early filmmakers had seized upon the encounter of rural folk with modern technology as one of their earliest comic themes (as in Edison's *Uncle Josh at the Moving Picture Show* [1902] or *Rube and Mandy at Coney Island* [1903]). This tension between country life and technological modernity carries through into Arbuckle's rural comedies, particularly in the "Fatty and Mabel" series that began in early 1915, pairing Arbuckle with Keystone's leading comedienne, Mabel Normand. Repeatedly, in that series, a young, often rural couple enters into farcical negotiation with the forces of progress, whether in the form of their comic encounters with world's fair exhibits in *Fatty and Mabel at the San Diego Exposition* (January 1915), with an errant and uncontrollable automobile in *Fatty and Mabel's Simple Life* (January 1915), or with the modern conveniences of their new cottage in *Fatty and Mabel Adrift* (January 1916) (Keeler).

More uniquely characteristic of Arbuckle's work in this tradition, however, was his ability to transform the rube, a stock figure of fun, into a more complex character, capable of mobilizing shifting patterns of empathy and ridicule, compassion and derision. "The secret of Arbuckle's popularity," commented *Motion Picture News*, "is the fact that he makes his audiences laugh at him as well as with him, never fearing to be made the victim of a joke himself, instead of insisting upon always being the one who plays the tricks upon others" ("Arbuckle to Act and Direct for Paramount," 7 January 1917, 541). Applied to rural settings, the trajectory of Arbuckle's comedy was thus to reverse the dynamics of rube humor for urban audiences, to present the country boy less as a figure of social maladjustment than as a vehicle for identification, even for a kind of preindustrial nostalgia. *Fatty and Mabel's Simple Life*, for instance, begins as a lightly comic idyll of young love: "She was happy," declares the opening intertitle that introduces Mabel, who is seen playing with a calf; "Poor but honest," announces the next, as Fatty comically endeavors to protect his milk pail from a thirsty cow. The opening of *Fatty and Mabel Adrift* (January 1916) similarly establishes an idealized bucolic setting, while also exhibiting the formal playfulness characteristic of Arbuckle's work from this period. The film begins with a (literally) rose-tinted shot of rolling hills, over which the image of a heart is superimposed. Before the narrative proper commences, a prologue depicts the romance as sentimental abstraction: Fatty and Mabel are introduced

In *Fatty and Mabel Adrift* (1916), the characters are introduced through heart-framed, cameo-style close-ups. Courtesy of the Academy of Motion Picture Arts and Sciences.

through heart-framed, cameo-style close-ups, their heads isolated against black backgrounds, and Cupid's arrow is shown bringing the two lovers together. "It was ingenious," commented *Photoplay*'s review of the film, "it was sensational, it was clean, and it was always funny" ("The Shadow Stage," April 1916, 148).

Biographers have hypothesized that this bucolic strain might be traced to Arbuckle's memories of his childhood in Smith Center, Kansas. (As an adult, he wistfully recalled the "tin soldiers, toy locomotives, candy, ice cream cones and popcorn balls" that made Christmas in Kansas, "when I was only five or six years of age, a good little boy," beyond compare [Young 8].) However, Arbuckle's rural comedies signified more than merely personal nostalgia. In a way that characterized other developments in film comedy from the mid-1910s onward—in, for instance, Selig's *Chronicles of Bloom Center* series (1915–1916) or the Betzwood Company's later *Toonerville Trolley* films (1920–1922)—the bucolic evocation of rural settings served Arbuckle's films as a token of refinement, substituting the ideological systems of small-town nostalgia for the "vulgar," plebeian dynamics of knockabout comedy. The obvious sentimentalism implicit in Arbuckle's pastoral retrospect thus positioned his comedies at odds with the sensationalism more typical of Keystone's output and brought them closer to genteel, literary standards of

humor. Arbuckle himself seems to have realized this, explaining in a syndicated interview that "the rural atmosphere is one that never fails to have its
humorous appeal," while middlebrow critics responded in kind, celebrating
his rural comedies for a "genuine humanity" that transcended "tried and
true slapstick." "Fatty belongs in subjects of rural life," declared the fan magazine *Motion Picture* in the late fall of 1919. "He is supreme in delineating the
country yokel and in his treatment of the character he has always
approached the bull's eye of truth" (Neibaur 71, 155).

    3. *Visual Style and Pictorialism:* "Do you know that . . . Mr. Arbuckle is one
of the greatest of comedy directors?" ("Plays and Players," *Photoplay*, December 1915, 160). This question, posed shortly before the comedian's move to
Fort Lee at the end of 1915, is one of several indications that Arbuckle's stardom was gradually being redefined to include his talents behind the camera,
as well as in front. While fan magazines still happily ran feature profiles on
Arbuckle's fatness, they now also insisted on his creative authority as simultaneously director, writer, and performer. "'Fatty' Arbuckle ranks today
uniquely in the field of comic productions and possesses the added faculty
of directing the pictures in which he stars," noted *Motion Picture News*, continuing: "The fact that Arbuckle directs his own pictures is important
because he will set tasks for himself to do that no other director would have
the moral courage to ask him to perform" ("Arbuckle to Act and Direct for
Paramount," 7 January 1917, 541).
    Of course, Arbuckle was hardly unique as a comic star who also directed;
among his peers, Chaplin was already gaining a reputation by mid-decade as
a "serious, systematic" director, notorious for extensive retakes and his total
control over actors (Harry Carr, "Charlie Chaplin's Story—Conclusion,"
Photoplay, October 1915, 97–98). Still, there were differences: whereas Chaplin's authorship was understood at this stage primarily in terms of his distinction as a *performer*, Arbuckle defined the validity of his directorial signature
through a distinctive visual *pictorialism*, shaping a mise-en-scène that
accorded with traditional, painterly standards of art. A brief consideration of
contemporary reviews clearly illustrates the centrality of lighting effects in
Arbuckle's attempts to legitimize himself as a director: beginning in the fall of
1914, critics for *Moving Picture World* frequently singled out Arbuckle's films
for praise in this respect, pointing out that particular titles were "well photographed" (*Fatty's Debut*, September 1914) and describing the cinematography
as "very fine" (*That Little Band of Gold*, 13 March 1915, 1615) and "excellent"
(*Fatty and Minnie-He-Haw*, 12 December 1914, 1525). Arbuckle likewise
insisted on the value of a pictorial approach, as he reflected in one interview:

"I have always thought there was room for beautiful scenic achievements in comedy as well as the kick and the custard pie" (Neibaur 15). By late 1915, he was giving full rein to visual aestheticism, experimenting with staging in depth, color tinting and toning, and low-key lighting and shadow play.[5] There can be few examples of Arbuckle's pictorial artistry as evocative as the famous "shadow kiss" from *Fatty and Mabel Adrift*—in which the comedian's shadow falls over Mabel and "kisses" her on the lips—a scene that prompted producer Hobart Bosworth to write the comedian:

> You manage to infuse these things with a genuine and very pure sentiment that leavens all the mass of farcical action, and I don't know how you do it. I lay much of it to your own personality which is wholesome and decent. Your touch is so sure, and right in the midst of some uproarious situation, you give a touch that is as full of poetry and sentiment as anything I ever saw. Many times since I saw "Adrift" I have said that the business of the shadowy good-night kiss was the most touchingly poetic thing I have ever seen in a motion picture.   (Oderman 92)

Two aspects of this remarkable passage should be emphasized. First, the terms of Bosworth's praise overtly align Arbuckle's pictorialism with established concepts of artistry. "Pure sentiment," "full of poetry and sentiment," "touchingly poetic": these are terms commensurate with the sacralized realm of genteel aesthetics. Second, and perhaps more significantly, we begin to see how Arbuckle's directing style was provoking a substantive redefinition of comic creativity in film. As Henry Jenkins has shown, the tradition of vaudeville comedy from which slapstick derived typically prioritized the *performer* as the chief creative force, emphasizing the individual comic actor's ability to "stop the show" or "command the stage" (Jenkins 63–69). Arbuckle's authorship, by contrast, uniquely relocated comic creativity *away* from the performing body, making him arguably the first film comedian to be discussed seriously as a director.

By the time Arbuckle announced his decision to leave Keystone in late 1916, his stardom was situated ambiguously between cultural vectors. His interest in the cerebral pleasures of narrative games ("comedies that make you think"), the pastoralist nostalgia of his rural comedies ("the bull's eye of truth"), and his developing pictorialism as a director ("very pure sentiment") stood in tension with his identity as "Fatty," binding his stardom to competing regimes, the fully embodied realm of popular comedy versus the quintessentially *dis*embodied realm of "true" culture—again, "Roscoe" versus "Fatty." For some writers at the time, Arbuckle became an object of fascination precisely as such a hybrid, a conflation of cultural categories that, as noted earlier, led commentators to frame his work in terms of a brain/body distinction. It was at this point, for instance, that interviewers began to speak of the "size of his brains" as well as the "size of his stomach," of his "brains as well as bulk," or, as previously quoted, of his "brain as well as his weight-ridden physique."

☆☆★★★ Star versus Scapegoat: Arbuckle at Paramount and Beyond

Arbuckle was thus able to play a catalytic role in slapstick's broadening popularity because he managed to fuse low comedy with genteel cultural registers. As 1916 came to an end, those efforts were rewarded when he was approached by Joseph Schenck to enter into a contract with the Paramount Pictures Corporation. According to that arrangement, Arbuckle would take the reins as head of his own producing company, the Comique Film Corporation, with total artistic control over his pictures and a salary of $1,000 per day plus 25 percent of the gross profits. Since the two-reel comedies would be distributed on the open market—allowing all exhibitors to book the films regardless of contract—a nationwide banquet tour was scheduled to introduce the comedian to theater owners in person. The Paramount Pictures Corporation had, from its founding in 1914, preached the rhetoric of film industry uplift, and Arbuckle wasted no time reminding exhibitors of his commitment to similar values: "Nothing has ever pleased me so much as has the signing of the contract for the distribution of my future pictures by Paramount," Arbuckle commented in January. "I can only assure you and Paramount that my future pictures will be of a far higher caliber and funnier than ever" ("Arbuckle Leaves Keystone," *Motion Picture News*, 3 February 1917, 745). Exhibitor requests for the films flooded Paramount's exchanges. Shortly before the release of the first Comique production, *The Butcher Boy*, on April 23, it was reported that two thousand contracts had already been signed, with 150 for first-run rights to the films. "Where it had originally been thought seventy-five prints for the production would be needed," said *Motion Picture News*, "there is expectation that over two hundred prints will be necessary by time of first release" ("Arbuckle Comedy Contracts Flood Paramount," 28 April 1917, 2661). Indeed, so popular did the films prove that, by the time Arbuckle released *Back Stage* (1919), some exhibitors were playing the Comiques as their feature attractions, not simply as comic support (Neibaur 139).

Arbuckle's series of nineteen shorts for Paramount have been described, with good reason, as the culmination of his filmic achievement (Neibaur 4). Yet, rather than marking a major paradigm shift in his output—equivalent departure from Keystone, Arbuckle had declared his intent to "develop new people" in his Comique productions, and the films were soon recognized as much for their co-starring talent as for Arbuckle's individual star turns ("Arbuckle to Leave Keystone," *Motography*, 7 October 1916, 832). "Roscoe Arbuckle, like Charlie Chaplin, likes to dope out his funny stunts right in front of the camera," *Photoplay* declared in 1918, "but 'Fatty' is more generous with his footage so far as his colleagues are concerned—he lets them 'get' the laugh if it improves the completed product" (Neibaur 86). Those colleagues included his nephew and fellow former Keystoner Al St. John, female leads Corinne Parquet and Alice Lake, the eccentric dancer Jackie Coogan Sr. (father of the future child star), and, most notably, the knockabout vaudevillian Buster Keaton in his screen debuts. Arbuckle clearly appreciated the security of a stock company of performers and filmmaking personnel—something that he had previously developed at Keystone's Fort Lee unit—but it was only at Comique that this approach significantly impacted the form of the films themselves. Despite Arbuckle's ongoing efforts to elaborate comic narrative, a number of the Comique films move in a quite different direction, offering a thinly plotted, modular structure akin to that of a vaudeville performance, with different comedians doing their "bits" for the camera. Notable examples include *The Bell Boy* (1918), *The Garage*, and, above all, *The Cook* (1918), whose first reel unfolds as a virtually plotless series of comic turns set in a beach café: Roscoe, in the titular role of cook, offers one of his trademark displays of juggling, flipping pancakes in the air and catching them behind his back; Buster Keaton, the waiter, performs a parody of Orientalist choreography; next, Al St. John, "the toughest guy in the world," sashays into a spectacularly rough "grizzly bear" dance with cashier Alice Lake.

Ironically, in his efforts to "develop new people," Arbuckle unwittingly prepared the way for his eventual disappearance as a star of slapstick shorts. There is no question that the Comique productions gave Buster Keaton crucial early exposure while playing a formative role in his filmmaking prowess. Keaton recalled how Arbuckle "took the camera apart for me so I would understand how it worked and what it could do. He showed me how film was developed, cut, and then spliced together. . . . I could not have found a better-natured man to teach me the movie business, or a more knowledgeable one" (Keaton 93, 95). Nor did Keaton's contributions to these films go unnoticed by other studios. In 1919, lucrative offers arrived from other production companies, with Jack Warner and William Fox each offering contracts of $1,000 per week for his services. Keaton's loyalty to Arbuckle prevented him from taking those offers, but Joseph Schenck and Paramount head Adolph Zukor soon masterminded an arrangement that would turn the situation to mutual advantage: Zukor approached Arbuckle with an offer to graduate him to feature-length movies for Paramount Pictures, at a salary of $3,000 a week for three years, plus 25 percent of the Comique Film Corporation's continuing profits; Schenck, meanwhile, promoted Keaton to Comique's creative head, for a scheduled eight two-reelers per year to be released through Metro.

Arbuckle thus became the first of the major comedians to break into features, although it was a move that drastically altered the coordinates of his stardom. At a time when the slapstick feature was not yet a proven commodity, Arbuckle's talents were employed simply as an actor in light comedy dramas. Reviews of the first of these, *The Round-Up*—a relatively "straight" western released in October 1920—struck an understandably perplexed note. "It is evident Fatty Arbuckle of the mammoth breaches and slapstick funnies has given way to Roscoe Arbuckle in a regular hero role, entirely serious in personation with but a modicum of comedy for relief," *Variety* noted ("The Round-Up," 10 September 1920, 35). Others, however, seem to have recognized this deferral of knockabout as a necessary gambit in further solidifying Arbuckle's claims for artistry. "Unlike most comedians, [Arbuckle] is an artist," one critic observed of the acting in his new features, "and his artistry is manifested with pleasing frequency" (Young 63); Arbuckle's performances, chimed another, suggested that it was now "not at all necessary for him to interpolate any of the horseplay of the farce in order to win pure comedy" ("Brewster's Millions," *Moving Picture World*, 5 February 1921, 725). With the move to features, Arbuckle at last seemed to have secured the mantle of respectability, but only by fully divesting himself of his slapstick physicality. His success would prove short-lived.

☆★★★★ Conclusion

In what sense, finally, might Arbuckle have been paradigmatic of the operations of film stardom during its first decade? Not simply as a sensational body, to be sure, but rather as a field of tension in which his "fat" was but one pole in a continuous dialectic of cultural meanings. This is where it becomes possible, however briefly, to offer some closing observations on the scandal that has forever dogged critical readings of Arbuckle's career. Whereas most of those readings have understood the scandal as a policing of the excess symbolized in Arbuckle's body (e.g., "the massive system could not permit unregulated individual massiveness"), the context of meanings traced in this chapter suggests precisely the reverse. What the

10 ★★★★★★★★★★★★

Douglas Fairbanks
Icon of Americanism

SCOTT CURTIS

The rise of Douglas Fairbanks (1883–1939) in the late 1910s was nothing short of spectacular. In a variety of films for Triangle, Artcraft, and United Artists, Fairbanks played cheery, athletic young men who bounded their way over obstacles and rivals to get the girl and the prize. His first film debuted in September 1915, but in a fan survey three years later, Fairbanks already ranked third in a long list of popular stars behind Mary Pickford and Marguerite Clark (*Motion Picture Magazine*, September 1918, 6). By the end of the decade, after only four years in the industry, Fairbanks was the most popular male star in Hollywood, second only to Pickford in fame and fortune. Among the reasons for this quick ascent we can count a

Douglas Fairbanks, circa 1919. Courtesy of the Academy of Motion Picture Arts and Sciences.

successful filmmaking formula that displayed Fairbanks's sound business sense and his ability to surround himself with top talent, as well as a well-oiled publicity machine that kept him constantly in the public eye. We can also count hard work: from the fall of 1915 to the end of 1919, Fairbanks made nearly thirty films, published two books and countless articles, formed his own production company, criss-crossed the nation several times selling Liberty Bonds for the war effort, and co-founded United Artists. We must also not underestimate the vigor and flexibility of the Fairbanks star persona, which he trained and developed on Broadway, adding bulk, definition, and endurance in Hollywood. Everybody liked "Doug," it seemed, and this amiability was certainly a key to his success. But there was something deeper and more meaningful in the Fairbanks persona. Perhaps this energetic, even indefatigable star became so popular because he projected an image of Americans as they wanted to see themselves, and as they still want to see themselves: as youthful and athletic, optimistic and adventurous, decisive and democratic. Ultimately, at a crucial point in the nation's entry on the world stage, Fairbanks gave his domestic and worldwide audience a pleasing vision of what it meant to be American.

Surveying the films and press about Fairbanks reveals a remarkably consistent picture, an almost seamless identity between private actor and public character. To be sure, this is the goal of all early star discourse—to present the actor as the embodiment of his or her roles, and to emphasize the compatibility of these roles with the "real" life of the actor (see de Cordova). In Fairbanks's case, however, the discourse is unusually insistent in this regard. Even from his days on the theatrical stage, reviewers noted that "off the stage, one imagines, Mr. Fairbanks must be very much the sort of young man he is called upon to play" (*New York Times*, 23 August 1908, 9). When plays were written especially for him, as in this case, we can imagine this fit to be particularly apt, but throughout his career Fairbanks insisted that he was not a great actor, instead emphasizing the importance of "personality" for his success. Early serial characters were often named after the actors who played them (Kathlyn Williams in *The Adventures of Kathlyn* [1913], for example) in order to stress the identity of actor and character; in an interesting twist on that strategy, many of Fairbanks's early films have characters with such obviously contrived names (Sunny Wiggins, Passin' Through, Steve O'Dare, Blaze Derringer) that it has the same effect, with a sly, satirical wink: Fairbanks is just playing himself.

For our purposes, this "self" is, ironically, an effect of his representations in film and in the written discourse about him. Any screen persona is an amalgam of different qualities in various measures. If we were to melt down and separate Fairbanks's winning alloy, forged by his numerous appearances onscreen and in the press, we would find at least four distinct but related elements. Foremost, the films and publicity emphasize his *youthfulness*. Even though he was thirty-two years old when he started making films, he is nearly always portrayed as carefree and adventurous, as someone who brings boundless enthusiasm and energy to whatever tasks he faces. Gaylyn Studlar argues persuasively that there is something Peter Pan–like in this fantasy; Fairbanks's boyishness means that he was never weighed down by commitments or responsibilities (*This Mad Masquerade* 50). Work is not work for Fairbanks or his characters—it is play. This manifests itself most obviously in his extraordinary *athleticism*. Fairbanks runs, leaps, rides, tumbles, and climbs his way through his films as if they were pentathlons. Every piece written about him stresses his incredible physical prowess, and his sheer joy in physical activity is palpable on screen. Physical vigor is more than a healthy attitude for Fairbanks; it is a moral imperative akin to (even borrowed from) Theodore Roosevelt's concept of "the strenuous life."[1]

Yet he does it all with a smile so infectious that they called him "Old Doc Cheerful." His smile was, like Buster Keaton's lack thereof, a trademark. It signals his ready *optimism*, his confidence, and his good humor. "Doug" lets nothing get him down. There is a purity to this optimism, a straightforwardness, and a guilelessness that allows him to be comfortable in any situation. Whether in the East or in the West, with men or with women, at a society dinner or in a working-class pub, Fairbanks is at home. One commentator wrote, "Take my word for it, he is every inch all that he looks . . . a regular fellow, one who 'belongs' in any company" (*Moving Picture World*, 24 June 1916, 2213). This ability to belong in any social situation is absolutely central to the Fairbanks persona. He is able to move freely among the classes, as if he belongs to all of them; he has a uniquely unfettered social mobility. Confidence is not his only means here; there is something inherently *democratic* about the Fairbanks persona. Fairbanks is represented as transparent, sincere, and unpretentious—he is just a "regular fellow." Yet he is also often represented as a member of the upper classes. This dual citizenship is not contradictory or adversarial in his films. The true democrat presumes equality wherever he goes, and this is exactly the Fairbanks attitude. It is not simply that he has the equipment and background to move freely among different social milieux—although he does, as we shall see. Unique among the characters in any of his films, Fairbanks has skills that accommodate—or as Studlar argues, reconcile—opposite worlds. He can ride a horse with as much assurance as he wears a tuxedo, and he can do both better than anybody else in the film. But, again, the "democratic" aspect of his persona depends not on confidence alone—it would be more accurate to say that barriers between milieux mean nothing to him. Anyone who has seen a Fairbanks film knows that fences are for leaping over; he vaults social barriers with equal grace.

Fairbanks represents a boyish fantasy of mastery, which no other star of his day put over with as much pluck and skill. All these qualities—youthfulness, athleticism, optimism, and a democratic instinct—were in place by the time Fairbanks left the stage in 1915. Despite Alistair Cooke's claim that Fairbanks's "theatrical record had very little to do with his startling Hollywood fame and with the creation of the screen character 'Doug'" (13), the opposite is true. Limiting an assessment of his persona to his film work disrespects the ten years or more he spent crafting and developing this marketable "personality" on stage. This is not to say that his persona did not adjust to motion pictures. On the contrary, his extraordinary success is due as much to his ability to modulate his stage persona to the new medium as to his likeability. Unlike many of his Broadway colleagues who were not able to navigate the transition, and true to his persona, Fairbanks was as comfortable on a Hollywood backlot as on a New York stage.

☆★★★★ Broadway

Fairbanks came to the stage at a fairly young age. He grew up in Denver, Colorado, where his father apparently enjoyed reading Shakespeare to his children and Douglas, in turn, enjoyed reciting soliloquies in school as another way—besides acrobatics and practical jokes—to be the center of attention (the best-researched account of Fairbanks's early life is Vance). While he was in high school, Douglas also attended drama school in Denver, so when he was expelled from high school for a prank shortly before his sixteenth birthday, he felt he was not without options. Soon thereafter, he met Frederick Warde, a prominent British actor-manager, who was in Denver for a week-long engagement. Impressed by the boy's personality and determination, and with the mother's blessing, Warde hired Fairbanks for his traveling company. Fairbanks made his stage debut in 1900 in Richmond, Virginia, but stayed with the company only briefly, since he was apparently not a very good actor. Even so, Fairbanks moved to New York with his mother and made his Broadway debut in February 1902 with a small part in *Her Lord and Master* (Vance 12–16).

Not yet nineteen years old when he got his Broadway start, Fairbanks naturally attracted juvenile roles. But this was not the only reason that critics emphasized his youthfulness in their reviews. They consistently mentioned his appealing, lighthearted personality. By 1906, critics were already noting a pattern as he played "his now familiar, breezy, attractive youth" (*New York Times*, 5 December 1906, 11). Audiences and critics loved this combination of youth, energy, and enthusiasm: "His genial boyishness and merry suggestion of irresponsible impudence are quite irresistible," wrote one critic (*Boston Daily Globe*, 21 September 1910, 9). Early in his career, "boyishness" became a trope to describe Fairbanks, and when he was in his late twenties, "the casual observer might mistake him for thirty. That is, while he is silent. Everyone looks older when his features are in repose. But when the Fairbanks smile is turned on full power—the sudden, illuminating, sincere smile, which makes friends and keeps them—and the black eyes sparkle with Fairbanks fun and enjoyment of living, the Fairbanks arms fling about in their vigorous fashion, the most casual might suppose him twenty-two. Youth is a dynamic state" (*Theatre Magazine*, November 1911, 178). This description contains many of the themes common to his publicity during his Broadway days, which would carry over to his film career: the focus on youthfulness, optimism, enthusiasm, athleticism, sincerity—all signaled by his high-wattage smile.

Fairbanks began to attract critical notice in 1905, with his role as Bennie the bellhop in the short-lived but acclaimed *A Case of Frenzied Finance*; critics said he played his part with "animation, glibness and assurance" (*Theatre Magazine*, May 1905, 110). More parts followed, and in December 1906 he was cast in the political melodrama *The Man of the Hour*, which was a big hit. During this play's run, Fairbanks courted and married (in July 1907) Anna Beth Sully, daughter of "Cotton King" Daniel J. Sully. With Sully he had his only child, Douglas Jr. (born 1909). His first starring role was in *All for a Girl* in the fall of 1908, after which he co-starred in another huge hit, *The Gentleman from Mississippi*. This ran for a couple of years, until he snagged the starring role in *The Cub* in 1910. He toured and played in revivals for the next two years until he starred in a string of successes: *Hawthorne of the U.S.A.* (1912), *The New Henrietta* (1913), *He Comes Up Smiling* (1914), and *The Show Shop* (1915). By the time he left for film, he was considered one of the top light-comedy actors of the stage, having worked in theater continuously from 1902 to 1915.

Fairbanks's "boyishness" also referred to his acrobatics, which were on display even in the theater. His manager and producer, William Brady, recalled a rehearsal of *The Cub*, during which Fairbanks elected to jump and climb up a two-level set rather than run up the stairs—a decision that "made a tremendous hit with the audience" (Vance 19). Publicity pieces at the time also emphasize his athleticism: "He can box, row, swim and ride, all in championship form" (*Boston Daily Globe*, 2 March 1908, 12). Or gossip columns might tell stories about his over-enthusiastic participation in a fight scene (*Los Angeles Times*, 29 August 1912, 3:4). Fairbanks was indeed portrayed as a "big" personality whose energy spilled off the stage into a thrilled and grateful audience.

But throughout this period, the publicity, reviews, and interviews all insist that there is something more to Fairbanks than boyish athleticism. Yes, he can box, row, swim, and ride, but wait, he can also cook, and "his cooking has been elevated to the dignity of a fine art. If Mr. Fairbanks ever desires to abandon histrionic endeavors he can always play a successful engagement as a French chef" (*Boston Daily Globe*, 2 March 1908, 12). Similarly, he often tells the story of taking time off from the stage to work in Wall Street, whether as a clerk or another minor position (see *Theatre Magazine*, November 1911, 178, or *Boston Daily Globe*, 9 April 1913, 17). The number of times this story surfaces in interviews speaks to its importance in establishing his ability to straddle boundaries between apparently opposing worlds. He is not just an actor but a businessman, not just an athlete but a chef.[2]

Despite this duality, Fairbanks plays his roles, as critics often noted, "without artifice" (*Theatre Magazine*, November 1908, 288). Fairbanks's democratic instinct, his ability to move easily between worlds, is often framed in terms of his "sincerity," as in this publicity piece: "There is nothing 'stagey,' nothing artificial or affected about this young American player. . . . He is not addicted to mannerisms, he does not cultivate any eccentricities, nor get rid of his talent to make room for his temperament. He is just a sincere, natural, good-naturedly frank, young man with gracious manners and an air of being always at ease in any situation" (*Theatre Magazine*, April 1913, 116). "Sincerity," then, is the glue that binds actor and character into a seamless unit and allows Fairbanks to move freely between opposing worlds without the penalty of affectation. Moreover, to be "at ease in any situation" requires an honesty and democratic sensibility that, in Fairbanks's case, is tagged early on as uniquely American. Indeed, during this period commentators start to connect his optimism, honesty, and youthful demeanor to an American outlook, as in this early review: "Mr. Fairbanks, the star of the occasion, symbolizes the very best type of clean-limbed, well-bred American young man, wholesome, self-reliant, and ingratiating" (*New York Times*, 25 August 1911, 7).

Nowhere is this connection between Fairbanks and Americanism more explicit than in the reviews and publicity for *Hawthorne of the U.S.A.* This play, which anticipates *His Majesty the American* (1919), his first film for United Artists, tells the story of a young American tourist who stumbles into the aristocratic plots of a decaying Balkan monarchy and "by the introduction of American methods and money, effects the rehabilitation and

"Doug" leaps over all obstacles with equal ease. Courtesy of the Academy of Motion Picture Arts and Sciences.

development of a decadent nation" (*Washington Post*, 20 October 1912, MS2). Broadway audiences reacted positively to this idea of rehabilitating decadence through "American" methods. The *New York Times* declared, "And in it Douglas Fairbanks, that young man with a smile that invites confidence and muscles that enforce it, finds himself perfectly suited as the conquering young man from America" (7 November 1912, 13), while *Theatre Magazine* exclaimed, "The star is Douglas Fairbanks, and he enacts the title role with rollicking good nature, dramatic fire, and true American hurrah!" (December 1912, 164). With *Hawthorne*, a familiar pattern emerges: Fairbanks represents the best America has to offer, or, more precisely, he represents how America wants to represent itself.

Already by 1912 Fairbanks had spent ten years on Broadway and, with the help of a press agent, was becoming quite adept at garnering and directing his publicity. He solidified his persona as a youthful, athletic, light-comedy actor whose optimistic and unaffected personality uniquely represented American sensibilities. He was doing quite well with this approach. So when Harry Aitken, the founder of Triangle Films, approached Fairbanks in 1915 with an offer of $2,000 a week to star in films, Fairbanks was initially hesitant. It was, after all, the *movies*, which were not a thrilling prospect at the time for an established stage actor. But $100,000 a year can buy a measure of legitimacy, and motion pictures presented new possibilities; they represented "wide open spaces," economically, socially, and aesthetically. And Fairbanks was prepared: he had a press agent, a marketable persona, and years of experience managing that persona in the public eye. Now it was just a matter of adapting his "personality" to film.

☆☆☆☆☆ Triangle and Artcraft

Fairbanks was not the only stage star to sign with Triangle Film Corp. in 1915, nor was his high salary exceptional. Harry Aitken, flush with Wall Street cash for his new company, wooed as many as sixty stage actors, including Billie Burke, Frank Keenan, H. B. Warner, comic opera star DeWolf Hopper, and the British Shakespearean Sir Herbert Beerbohm-Tree. Aitken spent flamboyantly in order to attract a more genteel crowd to his films. The high salaries offered to stage actors were part of a strategy—which included bringing directors D. W. Griffith, Thomas Ince, and Mack Sennett together under one corporation; securing top theaters exclusively for Triangle films; and charging higher admission prices—to make films "for the masses with an appeal to the classes." This project failed miserably. By mid-1917, Triangle's books were hemorrhaging red ink, Griffith and the others had fled, and most of the theatrical imports found themselves back on Broadway (King; Slide). Of all of Triangle's stage stars, Fairbanks made the most significant impact on the movie-going public. With his emphasis on youth, action, and movement, his stage persona was certainly more screen-ready than that of, say, Beerbohm-Tree. But Fairbanks was also willing to adjust his stage style to the screen. Rob King argues persuasively that part of the problem with Aitken's stage-stars experiment lay in "the difficulties

Triangle's producers encountered in harmonizing the performances of the stage stars with existing filmmaking practice" (12). For example, to accommodate hyperbolic, mannered, theatrical acting styles, Triangle directors found themselves relying on static long takes and sluggish editing, which were a disappointment to movie audiences already accustomed to the more up-tempo styles of Ince and Griffith.

Fairbanks, on the other hand, demonstrated a savvy cinematographic presence as early as his first feature, *The Lamb* (1915). Here he plays Gerald the Lamb, an eastern mama's boy with a crush on a well-bred young lady. During an outing to the beach, his party comes across a drowning woman and, in a moment of weakness and indecisiveness, Gerald is shown up by his rival—a tough, "cactus-fed" westerner—who saves the woman and wins Gerald's beloved. Determined to win her back, Gerald starts a physical training regimen and then follows her and his rival to Arizona, where he is comically out of place and subject to predators of all sorts. But Gerald's good nature disguises an inner grit that comes in handy when he and his young lady are captured by renegade natives; Gerald wreaks havoc on the enemy camp, rescuing and winning her back. The climatic scenes feature Fairbanksian acrobatics and a last-minute, Griffithian cavalry rescue, complete with parallel editing. Just as impressive, however, is his nuanced performance for the camera. The film includes a number of medium shots and Fairbanks knows what to do with them: his unassuming, slightly unsteady characterization of Gerald recalls Charlie Chaplin's similar gestures as the Little Tramp. For someone new to film, Fairbanks was a quick study. Critics appreciated his talents as well: "A new star has appeared in the motion-picture constellation, a comedian who wins through interesting personality and delightful characterization. . . . He holds the eye so strongly, and without apparent effort, that he is the whole play from beginning to end" (*Moving Picture World*, 9 October 1915, 233). Fairbanks was not a great actor, by any means, but unlike some of his Broadway colleagues, his acting style perfectly suited motion pictures, both in its attentiveness to small gestures for the camera and in its rousing displays of athleticism. With its up-to-date filmmaking techniques and its thrills, *The Lamb* was a hit that set the stylistic pattern for later Fairbanks films.

The Lamb established another pattern as well. Five of his Triangle films were set in the West or had significant western themes. These included *The Lamb, Double Trouble, The Good Bad Man, The Half-Breed,* and *Manhattan Madness* (all 1916). (From summer 1915 to December 1916, Fairbanks made twelve features and one short for Triangle, a pace that even *Moving Picture World* thought was record-breaking [22 April 1916, 624].) Two of these, *The*

Good Bad Man and *The Half-Breed*, are straight-up westerns, the first a tale of cowboy vengeance and the second a sensitive drama of racial hatred, with Fairbanks playing a mixed-blood Indian outcast. There is a distinct tendency toward duality in Fairbanks's films, characters, and persona. If *The Good Bad Man* is about cowboys, *The Half-Breed* is about Indians (and *The Half-Breed*, of course, makes duality an explicit theme). This penchant for dual personalities is especially pronounced in *The Lamb*, *Double Trouble*, and *Manhattan Madness*. In *The Lamb*, as we have seen, Fairbanks's character is quite meek until he finds his spine out west, as if drawing gumption from the land itself. In *Double Trouble*, Fairbanks plays an eastern fop who, after a blow to the head, becomes an outspoken, rowdy mayoral candidate for a western boomtown. In *Manhattan Madness*, the duality is expressed in more subtle ways: Fairbanks plays Steve O'Dare, a former New Yorker who returns from Wyoming to sell horses, only to be bored by the big city. His friends oblige by concocting a thrill-packed mystery. O'Dare has two worlds: he is equally comfortable in the exclusive clubs of Manhattan and on the range in the West, but he clearly prefers the latter. This duality extended even to Fairbanks's production schedule; he traveled back and forth between Hollywood and New York, eventually making nine films in California and four in New York. Perhaps because of this bi-coastal schedule, a number of his films draw a sharp distinction between East and West (Tibbetts and Welsh).

But this distinction was also a shrewd publicity move. Like his hero, Theodore Roosevelt, who transformed his public image from a "Jane-Dandy" New York assemblyman to a manly "Rough Rider" by going west, Fairbanks also sought to realign his persona by emphasizing his investment in the region. If we believe his publicity, his move to California was not just a business trip, but also a journey of rejuvenation, an educational rite of passage that amounted to his personal "Grand Tour" of the West. Taking his cues from Roosevelt, Frederic Remington, and Owen Wister, Fairbanks painted his move to Hollywood as a story of masculinity reborn (White, *Eastern Establishment*; Studlar, *This Mad Masquerade*). Fairbanks achieved this revitalized masculinity primarily by renouncing his Broadway career—as if his success in film depended on it. With the righteousness of a new convert, he proselytized for the Cowboy Way, which was presented as synonymous with Hollywood. "Fairbanks really is the Fairbanks of *Manhattan Madness*," reported the *Los Angeles Times*, "that is, he prefers a wild horseback trip through the mountains of Wyoming to a wild night on New York's Broadway" (8 October 1916, 3: 20). The *New York Times* agreed that his move to cinema meant more elbow room: "The movies were made for the great outdoors; so was Mr. Fairbanks. The four walls of a studio cramp the cinematograph; the four

appeal. Everybody loves "Doug" as just a "regular guy," not as an "actor." For example, Fairbanks recruits for his films "riders and ropers and cowboys of the old school. 'He men'—every one of them, and for a time they looked with dislike and suspicion upon the 'star,' but when they saw that Fairbanks did not ask for any 'double,' and took the hardest tumble with a grin, they received him into their fellowship with a heartfelt yell" ("A 'Close-Up' of Douglas Fairbanks," 735). Even the toughest among us cannot resist his down-to-earth optimism and honesty.

This portrayal of Fairbanks as a man's man definitely fits into larger cultural trends expressing the anxieties of white, middle-class males at the turn of the century, as Studlar argues (see also Lears). But for Fairbanks there was a personal stake in this portrayal as well. At a moment when Triangle was trying unsuccessfully to sell stage stars to the masses, Fairbanks differentiated himself from his theatrical colleagues by adjusting and emphasizing certain aspects of his established persona in order to appeal to movie-going audiences. Even though he returned often to New York, he made it clear through his movies and press that he preferred California. He forsakes the soft life of the stage for the hard, strenuous life of film. He turns his considerable athletic talents toward exuberant and authentic fight scenes for the benefit of a thrill-seeking audience. He makes sure that this audience sees and knows exactly who he is—a straight shooter who would never lie or use a "double." This adjustment was wildly successful. In fact, at the end of an interview one journalist laments, "I could not help but wish, after spending an hour and a half with Mr. Fairbanks, that there were more real red-blooded actors like him on the screen and less dolled-up beauties with neatly pressed suits and a 'How charmed' expression" (*Motion Picture Magazine*, December 1916, 68). And as George Creel would conclude, "Let no one quarrel with this popularity. It is a good sign, a healthful sign, a token that the blood of America still runs warm and red, and that chalk has not yet softened our bones" ("A 'Close-Up' of Douglas Fairbanks," 738). In the Artcraft era, from 1917 through 1918, which coincided with U.S. involvement in World War I, Fairbanks would indeed become the symbol of "red-blooded" Americanism. During this period, other aspects of his persona also became prominent. Although he still alternated his western-themed films with modern comedies, the discourse around Fairbanks emphasized roles other than rowdy cowboy: businessman, author, popular philosopher, patriot. Youthfulness and optimism were emphasized more in the feature stories and films than his western-edged manliness. This western masculinity did not disappear, but the investment in it was not quite so insistent or obviously compensatory. Youthfulness and optimism, of course, were impor-

Fairbanks was the foundation of the alliance between "The Big Three": Mary Pickford, Fairbanks, and Charles Chaplin on location during the filming of *Rebecca of Sunnybrook Farm* (1917). Courtesy of the Academy of Motion Picture Arts and Sciences.

tant facets of his persona since his Broadway days, but those characteristics took on a special resonance as Fairbanks's health, success, and sunny determination were mobilized in service of wartime "preparedness."

By the end of 1916, the writing was on the wall at Triangle. Aitken's enthusiastic spending was catching up to him and the receipts from his company's films, even including the Fairbanks features, were not nearly enough to soak up all the red ink. Fairbanks left for New York in mid-December 1916 and it was fairly clear that he was not coming back to Triangle. The publication that month of two high-profile feature stories on him now looks less than coincidental—he was probably promoting himself in preparation for free agency, even though he was making $10,000 a week with Triangle. Sure enough, in early January he sent out press releases indicating he was dissatisfied with his Triangle contract and was opening the bidding for his services, aiming for a phenomenal $15,000 weekly salary (*Variety*, 12 January 1917, 1; *Moving Picture World*, 27 January 1917, 537). His existing contract posed less of a problem than one might expect, since the agreement stipulated that D. W. Griffith would "supervise" all the Fairbanks films and it was easily proved that Griffith had nothing to do with them. Assured that he was on safe ground legally, he was ready to strike out on his own, advised by the savvy Mary Pickford. They had met in New York in 1915 and now Fairbanks followed her business model exactly: he set up his own production company and negotiated a distribution deal with Adolph Zukor's Famous Players–Lasky under the Artcraft label, which had been established in July 1916 to distribute Pickford's films (*New York Times*, 7 February 1917, 11; *Variety*, 9 February 1917, 18). After a final brief legal back-and-forth with Triangle, Fairbanks was making his first film for Artcraft by the beginning of March.

At Artcraft, Fairbanks continued to enjoy a bi-coastal lifestyle that allowed him to make most of his films in Hollywood while returning to New York occasionally to make one or two. In fact, even though the West played an important role in shaping his film persona, most of his features were modern urban comedies. In these, Fairbanks plays two types of characters. In films such as *The Habit of Happiness*, *Reggie Mixes In*, *The Matrimaniac*, *The Americano* (all Triangle, 1916), or *Down to Earth* and *A Modern Musketeer* (both Artcraft, 1917), Fairbanks plays a "regular fellow": a capable, exuberant young man who is presented with a problem and sets about solving it with pluck and resolve (see Thompson, "Fairbanks"). Unlike many of his western-themed films, in which the contrast between East and West is written into the character's eventual transformation, there is very little duality in "Sunny Wiggins" of *Habit* or "Ned Thacker" of *Musketeer*. Instead we have, in such cases as Sunny and Ned, a character whose main traits are optimism, youthful athleticism, determination, and an ability to move freely among vastly different social milieux. Sunny Wiggins, for example, comes from a wealthy family but rejects the exclusivity of the upper class—the film opens with him sharing his bedroom with a dozen or so homeless men he ran into the night before. Sunny is something of a professional optimist who believes that anyone's life can be improved by the power of laughter. He tests his theory successfully at a flophouse, and is eventually engaged to cheer up a morose industrialist. Meanwhile, he uses his good humor to quell a potential riot in a company town. Sunny's success among the different classes rests with his disarming smile: it is his main tool in attaining his goals and deflecting class hostility. *Habit*'s Sunny thus sets a pattern for many of Fairbanks's later goal-oriented protagonists.

In films such as *His Picture in the Papers, Flirting with Fate, American Aristocracy* (all Triangle, 1916), or *Reaching for the Moon* (Artcraft, 1917), Fairbanks plays another kind of character, one who possesses many of the same traits discussed above, but with a subtle duality similar but not identical to that found in Gerald of *The Lamb*. Here the character starts off not weak or foppish, as Gerald is, but instead distracted or directionless. Sometimes the character is obsessed with something, such as self-help books or his possible royal lineage in *Reaching*. At other times, as in *Picture*, he is just bored, especially with corporate culture (Osterman). In *Picture*, Fairbanks plays Pete, the son of Proteus Prindle, a publicity-friendly health-food mogul and producer of "Prindle's 27 Vegetarian Varieties," such as "Prindle's Macerated Morsels," "Prindle's Perforated Peas," or "Prindle's Dessicated Dumplings." Pete has a job with the company, but he is unenthusiastic about selling the Prindle line or buying the Prindle philosophy. Instead, he enjoys sleeping until noon and taking a cocktail or steak on the side. If he wants the girl, however, her father demands that he have half-interest in the Prindle company; in order for him to get that company interest, Prindle the elder demands that young Pete stir up some good publicity. The rest of the film reveals Pete's unsuccessful attempts to get "his picture in the papers." There are plenty of occasions for the usual Fairbanks stunts, but ultimately he gets the girl and the attention he needs by winning a boxing match against "Battling Burke" and by overpowering a group of ruffians who have plotted against the girl's father. In *Picture, Reaching,* and others, the Fairbanks character displays dissolution or distractedness that is transformed into focused and relentless determination, another common pattern in his films. In fact, Fairbanks's films of the teens—whether western or eastern, Triangle, Artcraft, or early United Artists—mix and match different character traits and narrative trajectories established in his first films for Triangle, *The Lamb, His Picture in the Papers,* and *The Habit of Happiness.*

We should also note *Picture*'s parody of publicity and the health-food craze, a gentle satire of modern fads that would continue with some of the Artcraft films, especially those written by Anita Loos and directed by John

Emerson. Emerson and Loos worked on *Picture* while they were employed at Triangle, and Fairbanks enjoyed collaborating with them. Loos wrote seven of Fairbanks's thirteen Triangle films and Emerson co-wrote and directed three of those seven. In late 1916, after their work on his final Triangle feature, *The Americano*, Fairbanks announced that he would demand that Loos write the titles for all his films (*Moving Picture World*, 2 December 1916, 1337). At that point, of course, he was almost done with Triangle, but he was able to keep his promise when he created his own production company. He signed Loos and Emerson immediately (although he had to buy out Emerson's Triangle contract) and the three of them collaborated on four of his first five features for Artcraft. Loos was known for her witty titles and satirical stories, which sometimes even poked fun at the Fairbanks persona—Doug was never one to take himself too seriously. Emerson and Loos left the Fairbanks company in late 1917 (*Moving Picture World*, 29 December 1917, 1948), but the collaboration produced some of Fairbanks' most memorable early films.[3] Perhaps the best example of a film that simultaneously promotes and parodies the Fairbanks persona is *Wild and Woolly* (1917).[4] Fairbanks plays Jeff Hillington, a rambunctious easterner with an enthusiasm for the Wild West. The son of a New York–based railroad tycoon, Jeff enjoys the trappings of upper-class life, but he wants none of the corporate culture that makes it possible. Instead, he likes camping with a teepee and saddle—in his bedroom. The residents of Bitter Creek, Arizona, are so eager to get a railroad spur through their town that they transform their modern village into a replica of the Old West just to please Jeff, who visits as the railroad's emissary. Recalling *Manhattan Madness*, the townspeople give Jeff a hero's role to play, a mystery to solve, and, thankfully, a gun loaded with blanks. When local villains cause the plan to go awry, Jeff is ready with western skills and a suitcase full of real bullets. Part of the film's considerable charm comes from the pleasing echo between Jeff's role in the town's plot and Fairbanks's movie stunts: both Jeff and the stunts have been set up to succeed, but still require real talent to pull off in the end.

Similarly, in *Reaching for the Moon* Fairbanks plays a sincere young man inspired by self-help books and taken with his quasi-aristocratic heritage (his mother was a member of the banished court of fictional Vulgaria). Fairbanks was intrigued by royalty and this is the first film of many to flirt with the idea of Doug-as-monarch. In *Reaching*, royal genealogy turns out to be a dream, but the fantasy will recur in later films and publicity in the 1920s. The earnestness with which Doug's character takes advice from self-help books is especially fun, particularly since early in his Artcraft era Fairbanks developed another dimension of his persona: author and popular philosopher of precisely these kinds of motivational volumes. Probably again inspired by Roosevelt, who was a prolific author, Fairbanks published two titles in quick succession: *Laugh and Live* in April 1917 and *Making Life Worthwhile* in 1918.[5] These books outline, in Fairbanks's voice, his recipe for success and his personal philosophy of life. *Laugh and Live* was particularly popular, reportedly selling 400,000 copies in a year (*Moving Picture World*, 2 November 1918, 607). These were not the first words to appear under the Fairbanks name, however. As early as 1912 he had been publishing stories and articles from his point of view (see "Those Guileless Ruralites," *Green Book Magazine*, August 1912, or "Styles in Farce," *Theatre Magazine*, January 1913). After the move to Artcraft, the number of essays and columns published under his name steadily increased. Most Fairbanks biographers agree, however, that he could not sit still long enough to read a book, much less write one, and that the articles and books were the work of his trusted secretary, Kenneth Davenport (Schickel, *His Picture* 48; Vance 42).[6] Nevertheless, the books provide an even more interesting view of the Fairbanks persona, since now we can hear them as the voice of someone who *imagines* who "Doug" is. That is, if "Doug" is an entity comprising all the representations of Fairbanks, then the ghostwritten articles and books neatly fit that category.

They also neatly fit the war effort. Indeed, Fairbanks was one of the most prominent and most frequently called-upon celebrities in the effort to stir up money and domestic fervor for an initially unpopular conflict. Behind this we can count his own enthusiastic patriotism, but also his connection to George Creel, a journalist who wrote an important early feature article on Fairbanks ("A 'Close-Up' of Douglas Fairbanks") and who became one of the chief architects of the domestic propaganda machine in his capacity as chairman of the Committee on Public Information (see also Creel, *How We Advertised America*). Fairbanks worked especially hard as a fund-raiser for the war, first by sponsoring a number of rodeos around the West designed to raise money for the Red Cross, and second as an active member of the "Liberty Loan" tours, during which he became acquainted with Secretary of the Treasury William McAdoo, one of the other principal planners of the domestic effort (see Kennedy 98–106). Fairbanks also made films to advertise the Liberty Loan bond drives: *Swat the Kaiser* and *Sic 'em, Sam* (both 1918) were allegorical shorts starring Fairbanks and his crew. In addition, his first Artcraft film, *In Again—Out Again* (April 1917), toyed with wartime themes (such as pacifism and munitions-factory sabotage), even if it is the only Fairbanks film to do so. So the appearance of *Laugh and Live* in April 1917 not only coincides with—and is intended to publicize—his

Chaplin, Fairbanks, Pickford, and Griffith sign the United Artists articles of incorporation. Courtesy of the Academy of Motion Picture Arts and Sciences.

Chaplin, who were always rather cool to one another, but his Liberty Loan connection brought William McAdoo aboard as company counsel and McAdoo's long-time assistant, Oscar Price, as the company's first president. The McAdoo-Price experiment failed after one year, but as Chaplin later admitted, they were brought in to lend prestige and legitimacy to the company, not film industry savvy (Balio 35). He also carried United Artists for its first year; because the other three were still tied to contracts with other companies, Fairbanks made the company's first films in 1919, *His Majesty the American* (released in September) and *When the Clouds Roll By* (December).

United Artists was, in many respects, the next logical step for "The Big Four," since each had been taking strides toward greater autonomy. For Fairbanks, this autonomy and success brought changes in his persona as well. On one hand, in the immediate postwar era, his status as an icon of Americanism was completely secure. For example, in January 1919 Fairbanks received a telegram from the Office of the President and the Liberty Loan people asking him to make another film that would be "used as propaganda to stem the tide of popular criticism" of the administration after the war. Fairbanks was instructed to be a "foolkiller," who would give critics "a lecture on real Americanism and then wallop them as you did the Kaiser [in 1918's *Swat the Kaiser*]. . . . This request goes to you alone" (*Los Angeles Times*, 10 January 1919, 2:8). This was to be one in a series of pictures by Fairbanks that would boost morale and promote four principles: "'Purity of purpose,' 'cheerfulness,' 'steadfastness,' and 'willingness to sacrifice'" (*Moving Picture World*, 25 January 1919, 456). There is no indication that these pictures were ever produced, but the government's faith in Fairbanks's image was clear. Even *His Majesty the American* was initially planned to extol President Woodrow Wilson's famous 14 Points for prosecution of the impending armistice, but that plan was changed in production when the Senate refused to ratify U.S. membership in the League of Nations (Vance 78). All this led one fan magazine writer to remark, "Restless endeavor, energetic ambition, indefatigable energy, whether for work or play, pictures or politics, humanity or himself, these are the things Douglas Fairbanks typifies. He is typically American—the Fairbanks scale of Americanism is 100 per cent perfect" (*Motion Picture Magazine*, February 1919, 32).

But his first films for United Artists also hint at changes to his persona that would become dominant in the 1920s. With the reputation of the new company on the line, Fairbanks spared no expense to mount the largest productions of his career to date; *His Majesty* cost $175,000 to produce, for example. *When the Clouds Roll By* included the most spectacular effects and set pieces in his films so far, such as a scene in which Doug walks on the ceiling of a room (à la Fred Astaire in *Royal Wedding* [1951]) and a conclusion that featured an actual flood! These two films were only tastes of what was to come—in the 1920s, Fairbanks's films would become larger, more expensive, and more grandiose, to the point that the discourse on Doug as producer almost eclipsed the discussion of his star persona.

In the same way, *His Majesty the American* hints at a new trend in the Fairbanks persona: Doug's aristocratic leanings. Like *Reaching for the Moon*, *His Majesty* tells the story of an energetic American who finds that he has blood ties to royalty in a fictional Balkan state. Looking forward, this fascination with nobility is a strong theme in his films and persona of the 1920s. After his marriage to Pickford, they were crowned Hollywood royalty and their home was often a way station for visiting dignitaries and aristocrats. His swashbuckling characters of the later films were usually noblemen intent on helping the common man. In fact, it could be argued that the tension between aristocracy and Americanism that the title of *His Majesty the American* implies has always been in the Fairbanks oeuvre in some form or another. After all, nearly all his characters from the teens are comfortably middle or upper class. In the 1910s, Fairbanks negotiated this tension in a uniquely American way. Just as nineteenth-century western heroes achieved manliness by being "like" their Indian counterparts while remaining unmistakably white, the Fairbanks character achieves a democratic effect by being "like" his plebian compatriots while remaining unmistakably noble. He replaces the racial politics of the western hero with class politics, while maintaining the familiar pattern of "simultaneous kinship and superiority" (Bederman 173). In the 1910s, Fairbanks put considerable effort into maintaining this kinship. In *His Majesty*, his highborn character goes out of his way to entertain the chambermaids and smoke a cigar with the hansom driver, actions perfectly in keeping with the character's "American" roots. But as the 1920s wore on and Fairbanks became the unrivaled "King of Hollywood," this democratic kinship would give way to something more like *noblesse oblige*. Making only one huge film a year, traveling around the world for months at a time, greeted by crowds of fans the world had never before witnessed, it would be harder and harder for Douglas Fairbanks to pretend to his audience and to himself that he was just a "regular fellow."

NOTES

My thanks to The Alumnae of Northwestern for a research grant; to Alla Gadassik for her thorough and timely research assistance; to Jeffrey Vance and Mary Francis for a pre-publication copy of Vance's important biography of Fairbanks; and to Val Almendarez, Barbara Hall, Doug Johnson, Matt Severson, and the rest of the staff of the Margaret Herrick Library, Academy of Motion Picture Arts and Sciences, Beverly Hills, California.

1. In an 1899 speech, Theodore Roosevelt advocated "the strenuous life" as an antidote to individual and national "over-civilization" and effeminacy. Roosevelt contrasted "timid peace" with the "virile qualities" required for the nation to take its place on the global stage. Hence "the strenuous life" was originally linked with Roosevelt's imperialism, but by the mid-1900s it had become more broadly associated with any ambitious masculine endeavor. See Roosevelt *Strenuous*, and "Mr. Roosevelt's Views on the Strenuous Life," *Ladies' Home Journal*, May 1906, 17.

2. The range of abilities in stories such as this may also be another Rooseveltian influence, since Roosevelt was often portrayed as a "renaissance man" of many talents. In any case, as Vance notes, "Doug" was an invention—even Douglas Jr. said of his father, "He designed the living of his life, almost from the start, coloring it as he went along. He did it so successfully that his best friends and biographers were seldom able to see him accurately" (Vance 6). We should look at all Fairbanks stories, interviews, and films equally as fiction—not as a judgment on their validity or truth value, but as works to be read for unifying patterns.

3. In her autobiography, Loos claims that she and Emerson split with Fairbanks because Doug was jealous of the critical attention they were receiving (Loos 178). There may be some truth to this, since critics did indeed lavish praise on Loos's contributions, especially, and lamented her later absence from Fairbanks's films.

4. For an interesting discussion of *Wild and Woolly* as an example of early Hollywood narrative, see Bordwell 166–68, 201–04.

5. Fairbanks also published *Youth Points the Way* in 1924 in association with the Boy Scouts of America. Some historians have listed other titles, such as *Taking Stock of Ourselves*, *Initiative and Self-Reliance*, or *Profiting by Experience*, but these were merely excerpts from *Laugh and Live* reprinted and sold in pamphlet form.

6. Fairbanks is also credited with a number of scenarios for his films, which no one disputes, since his films were very collaborative ventures and he was acknowledged to be the guiding hand behind them. For a humorous parody about his scenario-writing skills, see "'Doug' Writes Plays," *Los Angeles Times*, 19 August 1917, 3:3.

11 ☆☆☆☆☆☆☆☆☆☆☆

Charles Chaplin
The Object Life of Mass Culture

JENNIFER M. BEAN

If the state of being "known" determines the scale of stardom, then Charles Chaplin's superlative status emerged early. In 1916, a mere two years after his first appearance before the Keystone camera, a reporter for the *Chicago Daily Tribune* known only as Mae Tinnee sighed to her readers: "It is not much use to try to tell you anything about Charles Chaplin. You know all about him . . . enough has been printed to start a Chaplin encyclopedia well on its way" ("Right Off the Reel," 28 May 1916, D3). By now, that comprehensive compendium of information has been written several times over, each incarnation flush with a reverent nod of praise. "Charles Chaplin is arguably the single most important artist produced by the cinema," observed film critic Andrew Sarris, "certainly its

Charles Chaplin. Courtesy of Photofest.

most extraordinary performer and probably still its most universal icon" (45). George Bernard Shaw lauded him as "the only genius developed in motion pictures," while James Agee honored him as "the first man to give the silent language a soul. . . . His rivals," Agee added, "speak of him no more jealously than they might of God" (see Schickel, "Charles" 17; Agee, "Comedy's" 18–19). Deities of sundry sorts might have been jealous too, given J. Hoberman's recent estimation of the clown as "the most popular man on earth, the icon of the twentieth century, Jesus Christ's rival as the best known person on earth" (Hoberman 37).

In the reverences quoted above, one cannot help but notice a slippage between Chaplin's status as a "man" and the popularity of an "icon," an indeterminate ontology of sorts, somewhere between what it means to be a person and what it means to adopt a persona. What makes Chaplin's startling ascension to global stardom in the 1910s truly unique, as critic Gilbert Seldes aptly assessed in the early 1920s, is "that unlike many excellent and many second-rate people who played in the movies he was *not playing himself*" (105). For this reason, Seldes opts to use the French name "Charlot" when referring to the universally recognized icon, since "Charlot was a figure existing only on the screen and the great critical error was in confusing him with the man whose imagination brought him to life there."

Taking a cue from Seldes's formulation, this chapter reframes Chaplin's rapid rise to global celebrity status in the 1910s as the inverse of more familiar tales, most precisely as the story of a subject who transforms into an object. This object has a distinctive relationship to mass culture and is—contrary to so many invocations—not really modernist, because modernism's antagonistic relationship to imitation in favor of originality and authenticity precludes the nearly *endless* imitations through which the tramp's phenomenal life emerges, travels, and continues to depend.[1] The story I tell thus begins—and ends—with a funny kind of walk.

⭐⭐⭐⭐⭐ The Charlie Chaplin Walk

"In a Chaplin film," wrote Rudolf Arnheim in a 1929 retrospective celebration of the comedian's early work, "no face, no motion of the hand is true to nature" (312). He might more aptly have said no motion of the *feet*. Garbed in dusty and rather gargantuan brogans, those feet can kick, most often backward, usually as a gesture of defiance or retribution, and they run forward at a decidedly quick pace. They can take a corner in geometrically intricate patterns, like a 90-degree angle balanced on one leg, replete with several skids, an occasional hop, and even, for good measure,

While Lane's lyrics offer yet another simile for the Tramp's funny walk—"acting like a rabbit"—they do so by way of describing a transnational phenomenon, a near global "habit," something "ev'rybody does." Nor is it a stretch to speculate that Lane "shuffled," too, incorporating a variation of the movement in his stage performance, while his audience undoubtedly stumbled about that year to the tune of a popular fox trot, also titled "The Charlie Chaplin Walk," as well as to a broader array of musical numbers in the United States such as "The Charlie Chaplin Glide" and "Charlie Chaplin—March Grotesque" (or to the "Charlot One Step" in France).

Whether shuffling, gliding, marching, stepping, or trotting, "Chaplinitis" was afoot by almost any account. In the summer of 1915, the numbers mounting in Cleveland, Ohio, astonished the *Cleveland Plain Dealer*, which announced that the city "has been getting so full of imitators of Charlie Chaplin that the management of Luna Park decided to offer a prize to the best imitator and out they flocked," competing among themselves, if not with the thirty theaters in New York City that, according to the *New York World*, were also sponsoring "Charlie" amateur nights (Maland 10–11). While organized venues were harder to come by in the trenches of the Great War, Kevin Brownlow recalls that "British soldiers with a sense of humor would cultivate Chaplin mustaches, and in prison camps, every hut had its imitators" (Hoberman 40). Female soldiers with a sense of humor imitated the Tramp with equal aplomb, or so one might glean from the marvelous impersonation performed by a female cadet in the Women's Army Auxiliary Corps for her off-duty colleagues in the 1918 documentary *Life of a WAAC*. In 1916 high school students in Madrid painted the Tramp's iconic mustache on their faces, surprising their teachers in school one day, while the surprising fact breathlessly announced by *Illustrated World* in 1917, that "Charlie Chaplin has *countless* impersonators in real life," implied a mass body that defied statistical enumeration. Even so, reporter Ernest A. Dench could not resist describing the specific antics of a "Finnish sailor on shore leave" who "was hailed [*sic*] before a magistrate for knocking a young woman down in Battery Park, New York, while pulling off Chaplin stunts." This sailor then replayed these stunts as a unique mode of legal defense: "He demonstrated before the magistrate by kicking his left foot in the air and manipulating a pencil like a cane. The magistrate laughed and ordered the culprit's release" ("Strange Effects of Photo-Plays on Spectators," *Illustrated World*, July 1917, 788).

It seemed the funniest thing in the world was to "pull off" a few Chaplinesque stunts, a phenomenon noisily disparaged by the Illinois Congress of Mothers who convened in Chicago on 13 April 1916, where "pie, licorice, snakes, Charlie Chaplin, and the lard dinner pail were classified as among the evils to which childhood is heir." "No one," intoned the *Chicago Daily Tribune*, "voiced a protest against the proposals to abolish them all" ("Point to Perils Children Face," 14 April 1916, 12). Although these mothers restrained from describing the "atrocities committed by Mr. Chaplin's cane," even a cursory glance at the thirteen Essanay films released the previous year reveal the cane's artful capacity to initiate a teasing flirtation, to swipe, hook, crank, probe, or trip any object that enters its orbit. It can also lift a lady's skirt, a thoroughly déclassé act that tickled Rufus, the youthful protagonist of James Agee's last novel, *A Death in the Family*. Set in Knoxville, Tennessee, in the summer of 1915, the story begins when Rufus and his father, Jay, plan a trip to the "picture show," a proposal that prompts an immediate, and transparently repetitive, response from his mother: " 'He's so *nasty*!' She said, as she always did. 'So *vulgar*! With his nasty little cane; hooking up skirts and things, and that nasty little walk' " (11). It would be impossible, even ludicrous, to recuperate Charlie's antics as anything other than "vulgar," a feature that critic Gilbert Adair aptly understood as "ubiquitous in Chaplin's work," as well as the "fundamental component of humor" (101) sadly effaced by other comedians' elaboration of "clever," "lovely," and brilliantly polished gags (think Buster Keaton and Harold Lloyd). While Adair's primary interest lies in assessing Chaplin's performance as resonant with the "*deepest* common denominator" of crude vulgarity (rather than the "lowest common denominator"), the primary interest of reporters like Helen Duey was to defend "Chaplinitis" as "a safety valve for children's crude sense of humor." As she explained to readers of *Woman's Home Companion* in 1917: "They imitate his funny walk with the little swinging cane, and the stiff hat topping sober face. He is a kind of clown-hero" ("Why Do We Like Them?" 26).

Regardless of how one evaluates the propriety of such behavior, there can be little doubt that the sudden profusion of Chaplin imitators heralds an unprecedented moment in the history of early stardom. This is not to say that the penchant for imitating film stars was limited to the Tramp. The fashionable lure exerted by Mary Pickford's "cute little short dress that goes bobbing and frou frouing just like the cute little curls," for instance, appeared equally pervasive ("They Are All Trying to Be Mary Pickfords," *Los Angeles Times*, 11 May 1915, 3:1). That such attempts "to be" like America's Sweetheart "fills one with alarm and dismay," "freezes your blood," and provides a spectacle "terrible to contemplate" emerges from the tension between women who are older and noticeably more ample in girth than Pickford's short and slender figure (3:1). Extrapolating from this example, it is reasonable to conclude that it is the flaunting of the grotesque that defining the novelties, trinkets, souvenirs, and effigies circulating in a newly commercialized commercial. Far from the effigy practice that Mark Sanderberg traces in wax museums at the turn of the century, for instance, that sought to produce perfect illusions of otherwise absent or immaterial bodies, these imitations of "Charlie" herald a mode of corporeal image production that shrieks of artifice. Crudely painted figurines miniaturize the tramp's body and magnify the scrunch of a mustache; baggy pants billow into dizzying folds on stylized silhouette cutouts, while gigantic brogans point outward.

That these things jettison the illusion of naturalism or authenticity, however, may be less interesting than the fact that the production and circulation of all things Chaplin in these early years jettison an organized model of commercial distribution and exploitation. According to David Robinson, Chaplin's most thoughtful biographer, Sydney Chaplin, Charles's half-brother who was finishing a contract at Keystone while working as Chaplin's manager, attempted to establish the Charles Chaplin Music Company and the Charles Chaplin Advertising Service Company in late 1915 in order to control the commercial exploitation of the various Chaplin by-products. The companies did not survive. In October of that year, Sydney received a letter from James Pershing, the man who had been appointed to run the advertising service:

> We find that things pertaining to royalties are in a very chaotic state. There seems to be hundreds of people making different things under the name of Charlie Chaplin. First we have to find out where they are, what they are making, and are notifying them as fast as possible to stop or arrange with us for royalties, which is about all we can do.
>
> (qtd. in Robinson 153)

Insofar as the "chaotic state" of all things Charlie suggests a rather unsystematic mode of production, one that belongs to the public (or "hundreds of people") rather than an individual person or authorizing agency, it could be seen as a "grotesque" interruption of capitalism's rationalized efficiency and systematic coordination of production relative to profit. As a marvelously ironic correlative to such festive disorder in the marketplace, Berton Bradley, a popular writer and social commentator, argued that the surplus of "Charlie's" presence in the public sphere devalued the icon's affective charge. In a ditty titled "Satiety" composed for *Green Book* magazine in late 1915, Bradley complained:

> Go where we will, we must happen upon
> Busts of you, statuettes, photographs various,
> Cartoons and comments and posters galore.

Honestly, Charlie, in way multifarious
You're getting more of a spread than the war!

Vaudeville is crowded with acts imitating you;
Every old movie has you on the screen.
We who were strong for you soon will be hating you
Simply because you're so constantly seen.   (J. McCabe 80)

☆★★★★ Charlie, Not Charles

It perhaps goes without saying that the fate of being "so constantly seen" conspicuously refers to Charlie, the icon, and not to Chaplin,
the man, whose face was handsome, evenly sculpted, and observably ordinary. His body was small—some would say tiny—but his feet appeared in
noticeably perfect proportion to the rest. It may very well be that the striking
disparity between Charlie and Charles proved useful for the comedian, insofar as it "protected his [Charles's] identity from fans." Or so muses Alistair
Cooke while lingering over his personal experience of coming out of a movie
theater with Chaplin, at which point a young fellow on the street "nudged
his girl and hissed, 'There's Charlie Chaplin!'" She made the obvious comment that it didn't look like him, to which the young man irritably snapped,
'You can't expect anybody to *look* like Charlie Chaplin'" ("Fame" 132).

Or can you? A closer look at the historical phenomenon we have been
tracing reverses that young man's terms, which is another way of saying that
everybody could look like Charlie. At the very least they could try. Some succeeded quite notably, among them talented comedians such as vaudeville
performer Minerva Courtney, who directed and starred in three Chaplin
impersonation films in 1915, while Stan Laurel, Billie Ritchie, Billy West,
and Harold Lloyd each took their turn at imitating the iconic tramp (see
Bean "Art"). It would be a gross overstatement to claim that these comedians' performances as variations of the "little fellow" trumped those of
Chaplin himself. Even so, when Betty Fleet exclaimed to readers of *Motion
Picture Magazine* in April 1918 that "the superb clown of the Silversheet
side-show is, without question, Charles Spencer Chaplin," a bit of corrosive
irony shaded her praise. For what settled the matter of Chaplin's superior
status is the fact that "like his fame, Charlie's mustache continues to grow—
not on Mr. Chaplin's upper lip, but on those of his imitators. Billie West,
chief among these, is so very clever, in his own way, that some cannot even
tell the difference" ("What Could Be Funnier Minerva?" 37).

The inability to "tell the difference" between Charlie's many imitators
and Chaplin himself arguably began on the comedian's trip back to Califor-

nia from New York in late 1915 to sign the Mutual Contract. Having boarded the Twentieth Century with his brother Sydney and Henry P. Caulfield, general manager of the new Mutual studios, the party stopped off for a few days in Chicago. According to David Robinson, "Chaplin was induced to do his funny walk outside a cinema where one of his films was playing, but the publicity stunt fell flat. No one recognized him and the cashier, bored to death with would-be Chaplin imitators, only sniffed haughtily" (163). Ironically, less haughty responses greeted Steve Duros, a local of Columbus, Ohio, whom theater owners hired that same year to dress like Charlie and walk the streets to advertise the Tramp's screen presence. Duros's remarkable likeness earned him momentary celebrity status in the mass media when the November issue of *Motion Picture Magazine* featured his impersonation. Although not every impersonator utilized to advertise a Chaplin film attained similar recognition, the confusion generated by the geometrical number of Tramps confused many. In August 1916 Chaplin recited for the *Los Angeles Times* a series of "funny experiences with my imitators," including his encounter with one man who thought he had seen Chaplin performing in front of a theater an hour ago, and asked: "Why do you do it? I think you lose prestige that way—cheapen yourself." Chaplin retorted: "Oh . . . I hardly know myself why I do it. It just helps keep me busy that's all—helps pass the time away" (20 August 1916, 2:10). Two years later, while working with a cast of children on the set of *Shoulder Arms*, Chaplin sounded a bit more plaintive when recalling how "one little boy walked up to me and told me timidly that he 'liked me better than he did any of the others Charlies'" (Grace Kingsley, "Chaplin's Funny Feet Walk into War Comedy," *Los Angeles Times*, 30 June 1918, 3:1).

Regardless of preferences, the implication that there are many Charlies, rather than one, raises questions peculiar to Chaplin's status as a mass cultural icon. What differentiates one incarnation of "Charlie" from another? How small or large must the differences between the "authentic" and the "copy" be for us to categorize and identify a unique entity known as "Charlie Chaplin"? One way is to distinguish between "Charles" and "Charlie," to reveal the offscreen artist as a comic genius whose rich inner reflections, spontaneous bursts of inspiration, and laborious work ethic give life to the capering fool onscreen. Such journalistic patter began in 1915 when a flurry of reports touted the comedian's ambitions, his interest in perfecting the art of comedy, his attentiveness to every detail on the set, and his obsessive work ethic. Such strategies, however, could also backfire, annihilating the promise of difference, nowhere more viciously than when reporter Epson Bowes observed that Chaplin's determination to be "the whole show," to function as "scenario writer," "director," "cameraman," "scene-shifter," and "leading man," meant that the comedian's investment in the originality of his productions encouraged a certain type of "sameness." "Charlie practically does the acting for all the other members of the company," Bowes explains, "for he always goes through their parts for them and shows them how he does it and they try to copy after him." Such mimicry means "he is getting together a whole bunch of imitation Charlie Chaplins on his staff" ("Chaplin as the Whole Show," *Los Angeles Times*, 8 June 1915, 3:1).

Bowes's barbed critique may have troubled Chaplin, especially if we believe the many reports accentuating the comedian's acute sensitivity to criticism. Chaplin's alleged inability to even watch his films in the company of others, and his altogether "serious" demeanor, appeared quite "strange" to reporter Grace Kingsley, who dryly observed that the "famous comedian" has "created a guffaw that is heard around the world, a ripple of laughter that ceaselessly encircles the globe" ("Witty, Wistful, Serious Is the Real Charlie Chaplin," *Los Angeles Times*, 20 August 1916, 2:10). However strange, both "sensitivity" and "seriousness" assumed familiar status in most every interview with the comedian in the course of the decade.

These combined features may be why Chaplin granted relatively few interviews in these years, relative at least to those offered by his friend Douglas Fairbanks, who functioned as a sort of spokesperson for the industry and for an "all American" spirit more generally. While the "real" Chaplin attained some prominence in the press and in the public eye when he traveled across the country with Fairbanks and Mary Pickford in a series of Liberty Loan Bond tours in 1917 and 1918, and while the three stars had been linked in the press by virtue of their enormous celebrity status, Chaplin was different. Strange, even. In part this was because his British citizenship means he was not American, a striking contrast to Fairbanks's enthronement as an all-American "Mr. Pep," or Pickford's iconic status as "America's Sweetheart." Moreover, rumors that Chaplin utilized his celebrity status to dodge the draft questioned even his allegiance to Britain. In March 1916, a special cable from London circulating in U.S. newspapers targeted the Mutual Film Company for incorporating a clause in Chaplin's contract that prohibited him from visiting Great Britain, where he might "run the risk of being conscripted" ("They'll Go to See Him Just the Same," *Chicago Daily Tribune*, 23 March 1916, 14). The following year London's *Weekly Dispatch* more specifically targeted Chaplin's patriotism, a bit of personal slander that enraged the comedian. He hotly retorted that he had invested "a quarter of a million dollars in the war activities of America and England," that he was "ready for military service under the Union Jack the minute England . . . officially calls him," and also that he had "registered for the U.S. draft" without requesting any "exemptions or favors" ("Chaplin Angry over Criticism in London Paper," *Chicago Daily Tribune*, 29 July 1917, 12).

It is certainly possible that insinuations such as these contributed to Chaplin's later profile as a radical leftist socialist, the likes of which accelerated through the Second World War, culminating in his active sponsorship of the "World Peace" movement in 1949 and subsequently his banishment/exile from an increasingly paranoid United States in 1952 (Maland 258–78). In the 1910s, however, the media's noisy defense of the comedian emerged somewhat circuitously, insofar as commentators lauded "Charlie"—the fictional persona—as "the greatest single lightener of the iron burden" in "a shrapnel-smashed world" (Julian Johnson, "The Immigrant," *Photoplay*, September 1917, 99). In August 1917, a writer for the *Chicago Daily Tribune* recounted the story of a young "American in the Canadian forces" who found himself in Boulogne, "waiting to be embarked for England" but miserably "homesick, deadly homesick." "He wanted something from home," which he found when arriving in England: "The first thing that met his eye was a figure of Charlie Chaplin, smoking a big cigar with an electric light at the tip." Thus, the writer merrily concludes: "The American's heart was made glad" ("English Become Movie Fans," 5 August 1917, C3). Exemplifying this type of acclaim, cartoonist E. Gale sketched a caricature of the tramp in early 1918, hyperbolizing even further the figure's notoriously gigantic shoes. Here those brogans flop upward, miniaturizing the tramp's Lilliputian stature and the grotesquely irregular body which a caption trumpets as "one of our best little anchors during these stormy days" (*Los Angeles Times*, 20 January 1918, 3:1). More than a figure of speech, and far from tongue-in-cheek, the sketch literalizes the little fellow's capacity to enable "our grip on sanity": hog-tied several times over and strung to an image of a hovering globe covered with smoking cannons (over which the acronym SOS spells out "Sick Of Slaughter"), the capricious tramp with his big shoes sways. But those feet hold him firm.

Charlie's capacity to generate laughter (the antidote to s-laughter) amounted to quite serious stuff. Indeed, the appearance of the Tramp on the screen, his imitators in the camps, or the silhouette cutouts of the iconic figure that soldiers would steal from theater marquees and stage in the trenches suggested itself to Blaise Cendrars as the decisive victory of the war. "Charlot was born on the front," he wrote. "The Germans lost the war because they didn't get to know Charlot in time" (Hoberman 40). In contrast, Chaplin's "serious" and "sensitive" backstage persona made relatively

The little fellow whose gargantuan feet anchor the public's "grip on sanity" in a war-torn world. Cartoon sketch by E. Gale, *Los Angeles Times*, 20 January 1918.

"Charlie" on the set of *Kid Auto Races in Venice* (1914), Chaplin's second Keystone film and the first screen appearance of the tramp's iconic costume. From the author's collection.

1919, fans could take in a revival of *Shoulder Arms* (First National, 1918) at the Plaza, or head over to the Rialto where *The Cure* (Essanay, 1917) featured as part of the evening's entertainment.

If there is something magnificently revealing in a reception history that mocks the linearity implied by Chaplin's successive contracts and stages of production, then it is all the more revealing to recognize that each of the films listed above interrupts the lexicon of development and growth so often associated with narrative structure. "The curve he plots is always the same," observed Gilbert Seldes in 1924 (105), a circular movement most transparent in films like *The Adventurer* (1917)—which opens with Charlie playing an ex-con evading the police and ends as he flees from the cops— or *The Tramp* (1915), in which he enters the screen as a wandering itinerant and exits walking down a country road alone, kicking his heels in the dust. Many films simply end with the Tramp's anarchic energy "all washed up," quite literally so in *One A.M.* (1916), where Charlie's inability to negotiate the workings of a Murphy Bed finds him sinking into sleep in a watery bathtub, just in the way that he sinks into a "spirit-filled" well in the final frame of *The Cure* (1917). Other endings find the Tramp tossed out of the house (*A Woman*, 1915), crashed in an elevator (*The Floorwalker*, 1916), or simply hooking his cane to the nearest automobile and skating away (*The Rink*, 1916).

Other endings hint at alternatives to the Tramp's status as eternal misfit, but a closer look suggests otherwise. In the climatic finale of *The Pawnshop* (1916), Charlie, a menial store employee, triumphantly rescues his employer and the girl (Edna Purviance) from the villainous crook, saving the day as he hops abruptly out of an old treasure-trunk and knocks the swarthy bully on the head. The timing is impeccable. Too impeccable, in fact, so much so that the morality emanating elsewhere from melodrama's suspenseful resolutions, as in D. W. Griffith's race-to-the-rescue dramas where good (at long last) triumphs over evil, flattens here into a single moment. It's a cheap imitation, one might say—hollowed of meaning and all the funnier for that. In films like *The Bank* and *Shoulder Arms*, Charlie again performs as a hero, respectively saving the banking corporation and the entire Allied forces while winning the heart of the girl. But these dreams of a happy ending, rich with the plenitude of closure and the Tramp's integration into the community, are revealed to be just that: "dreams." The Tramp wakes up alone. To be sure, Charlie's adventures occasionally end in the company of others, whether with an impoverished immigrant girl (*The Immigrant*) or with an exploited dancing girl *and* a mangy dog (*A Dog's Life*, 1918). Insofar as these stray waifs make strange companions, then they perfectly suit the Tramp, a figure repeatedly dislodged or estranged from any civilized, official, or organized world.

Charlie's refusal to adopt (or adapt to) any one recognizable tradition or cultural milieu has understandably generated a critical itch, an urge to explain what is meaningful about the Tramp's resistance to meaning-making codes. "His homeland is everywhere and nowhere," wrote Siegfried Kracauer, who assessed Charlie's endless perambulations as liberating: "Denomination, nationality, wealth and class affiliations erect barriers between people, and only the outcast, the person on the outside, lives untrammeled by restriction" (118). The Spanish orator Francisco Ayala, however, diagnosed Charlie as "an unmistakable product of the modern city and of modern restlessness," as "the man who belongs to the docks, the markets, the streets" (Morris 522). But even this restless "belonging" doesn't quite fit for the writer known as Vela, who described the Tramp as a figure "who has lost his way in this world. He lived in a different world, but one day, without realizing it, he half-opened a door and fell . . . into a world with fewer dimensions, where the mirrors cannot be stepped through, where every step is a stumble" (Morris 521).

the very moment his boss enters the room, just as he suddenly shifts from boxing movements to a waltz-like glide outside the store when a cop arrives on the scene. When a cop approaches him on the street in *A Dog's Life*, the brick Charlie has hefted and aimed at the "Green Lantern" pub suddenly becomes a toy he throws to the stray dog not far from his side. His rascally behavior in *The Rink* goes one better, if only because his deliberate (and successful) efforts to systematically trip his swarthy rival (Eric Campbell) remain perfectly in synch with his simultaneous (and successful) performance as the most graceful and courteous of gliding skaters. These seemingly minor moments reflect the major theme of many films in which Chaplin's persona, Charlie, adopts a persona, becoming someone who masquerades as someone else: a janitor masquerading as a dentist in *Laughing Gas* (1914); a masher masquerading as a seductive woman in *A Woman*; a lowly employee masquerading as a manager in *The Floorwalker*; an escaped convict masquerading as a wealthy yachtsman in *The Adventurer*.

The "essence" of mimetic play that uniquely characterizes the Tramp shimmers with farcical grandeur in *Easy Street* (1917), a film in which Charlie transforms from soup-kitchen idler to busy policeman, and exchanges his worn coat and little cane for an oversized uniform and billy club. Emphatically, this transformation is not another deceitful masquerade but an identity motivated by a plot that ultimately grants the itinerant-turned-policeman "star" status in the community when he clears the ghetto of Machiavellian thugs and vicious gangs, rendering the street safe for families and missionaries once again. While I agree with the many critics who endorse *Easy Street* as Chaplin's most thoughtful social commentary of the 1910s, it would not do to overlook the majestic irony lurking in the climactic scene when Charlie inadvertently sits on a syringe full of dope and thus defeats his massive foes in a drug-induced delirium. The twist whereby illegal opiates enable social peace is a funny bit of incongruity. It is also perfectly congruous with the incongruities that define the Tramp's persona: stoned on drugs, the policeman becomes something other than himself, and hence emblematic of the Tramp's capacity to mock what we usually mean when we speak of a "character" as the fictional reflection of a singular, unified self.

⭐⭐⭐⭐⭐ **Conclusion**

A fake, an impostor, a trickster, a plagiarist: call him what you will, the tramp derides the ideal of authenticity rooted in the singularity of the private person, the very ideal elsewhere assuming such a vivid sheen of glamour through the American film industry's nascent star system in the course of this decade. Herein lies the secret of Charlie's continued status as cinema's most universally recognized icon, which both exemplifies and disorients what cultural critic Susan Stewart more recently calls the "abstraction" of the film star from everyday life. The fact that stars become "'larger than life'" is the inevitable result, she argues, "of their medium of presentation; the representation fully effaces its referent; there is only a series of images related to each other in a chainlike, cumulative formation" (91). This is another way of saying that stars, by definition, are not proper subjects at all but more like objects—visual signs that accrue meaning through a process of duplication designed to entrance and deceive. Chaplin's stardom radicalizes and thereby mocks this abstraction. To speak of Charlie Chaplin is to *begin* with an image, with a sign that enters the economy of exchange and signification at a remove: there is no original or authentic referent; there is only the constructed and fictional persona, the chimerical little fellow with a funny walk.

Then again, to *speak* of Charlie Chaplin doesn't quite suffice. Quite frankly, for those of us who share the habit of waddling our way out of a Chaplin film, eyes rolling, manipulating sticks as if they were canes, we experience what is otherwise tough to explain. Put in the simplest terms, we, too, become stars. Not the kind that shimmer in the heavens above, but far more profoundly the fallen kind—the kind cut free from the despair of uniqueness and the cruelty of ideals, staggering one into another on our still ungainly feet.

NOTE

1. Critics have devoted considerable attention to Chaplin's lionization by avant-garde artists and thinkers. Recent work on this aspect of Chaplin's early stardom by, respectively, Sabine Hake, Susan McCabe, Amy Sargeant, and David Trotter are especially noteworthy.

1895 in Pisqua, Kansas. Unlike Lloyd, Keaton was not a true midwesterner. His parents were traveling vaudeville performers and "Buster" joined their act at the age of five, rapidly becoming the star attraction of the "Three Keatons" in a series of skits primarily based on mimicry and physical knockabout. It is well known that his father, Joe Keaton, often hurled his young son into the stage backdrop for the show's climactic finale in those early years; by the time he was eight, Buster's spectacular leaps and violent falls formed the centerpiece of the family's program. The extraordinary physical grace exhibited by the child undoubtedly astonished audiences. The child, in turn, was astounded by the sleight-of-hand physical feats performed by his family's friend Harry Houdini. "No one, by the by, ever worked harder than I did to figure out Houdini's tricks," he later wrote. "I watched him like a hawk every chance I got. I studied his act from all parts of the theatre. . . . I even climbed high up in the flies so I could look straight down on him as he worked" (Keaton 51). Although Keaton never did figure out those tricks, he learned a great deal about the art of exposure from the magician whose famous stunts began by revealing to the audience the foolproof function of every handcuff, manacle, trunk, iron chest, tank, and so on—before performing, in bathing suit or loincloth, a miraculously daring escape. Notwithstanding his debts to early family "training" and Houdini's influence, it was under the ample wing of director and star Roscoe Arbuckle that Keaton made his film debut, appearing in two-reel productions such as *The Bell Boy* (1918), *The Garage* (1918), and *The Cook* (1918). The ever-generous Arbuckle also taught Keaton the workings of the camera as well as the industry. "I could not have found a better-natured man to teach me the movie business," Keaton later recalled, "or a more knowledgeable one" (95). Keaton would ultimately "expose" the magic of cinema in modern masterpieces such as *Sherlock Jr.* (1924) and reveal his physical dexterity and mechanical genius in feature film vehicles such as *The Navigator* (1924), *The General* (1926), and *Steamboat Bill, Jr.* (1928), among others, where his narrow escapes from disaster generated astonishment from even the most jaded of jazz age audiences.

It is hardly coincidental that the ever-serious "Stone-Face" Keaton and the ever-earnest Harold Lloyd assumed pride of place in the 1920s as their comic counterparts, Arbuckle and Normand, suffered scandal's aftershocks. It may very well be that "the silent-comedy studio was about the best training school the movies have ever known," as James Agee reflected in the late 1940s, and not simply for producing the likes of Lloyd and Keaton. Rather, "some of the major stars of the twenties and since . . . also got their start in silent comedy" ("Comedy's" 17), a lengthy roster including talented directors such as Leo McCarey, George Stevens, and Frank Capra, as well as later stars such as Phyllis Haver and Carole Lombard. Nor should we overlook Gloria Swanson and Wallace Beery, whose careers began almost simultaneously at the Essanay Company in 1914 and where Beery earned some notoriety cross-dressing as a Swedish maid named "Sweedie." Among the fourteen "Sweedie" films that featured a capering Beery in 1914 was *Sweedie Goes to College*, in which Swanson plays a debutante in a girl's dormitory opposite Beery's burly Swedish maid. The two worked together again at Keystone, flanking "Teddy," the company's star dog, in two-reel farces such as *Teddy at the Throttle* (1917). Beery would perform in over forty more films in the 1910s alone, and in the early 1920s he began working alongside the likes of Douglas Fairbanks in *Mollycoddle* (1920) and *Robin Hood* (1922) as well as Rudolph Valentino in *The Four Horsemen of the Apocalypse* (1921). But Beery's ascension to the giddier heights of stardom was a slow and laborious one, perhaps not fully achieved until he played opposite Marie Dressler in the acclaimed wharf-side drama *Min and Bill* (1930). This may be the place to mention that Dressler, a well-known stage star in the early twentieth century, also made her film debut at Keystone in 1914, playing opposite Charles Chaplin and Mabel Normand in *Tillie's Punctured Romance* (1914).

While Dressler and Beery initially embraced, with varying degrees of intensity, their comic personae, Swanson emphatically did not. "I hated comedy, because I thought it was ruining my chance for dramatic parts," the actress explained in later interviews. "I didn't realize that comedy is the highest expression of the theatrical art and the best training in the world for other roles. . . . Comedy makes you think faster, and after Keystone I was a human lighting conductor" (Basinger 207). It took more than a flash of light for Swanson to assume her dramatic persona, which she reportedly modeled after the emerging Norma Talmadge when Swanson moved to Triangle Studios in 1918. Her first Triangle film, *Society for Sale* (1918), directed by Frank Borzage and co-starring William Desmond, undoubtedly enabled this onscreen identity. But it wasn't until she appeared in *Don't Change Your Husband* (1919), the first of six films she would make with director Cecil B. DeMille, that the Swanson "star" identity illuminated the screen: sophisticated, elegant, fashionable, and far from naïve.

With the benefit of hindsight, it might seem that Swanson's woman-of-the-world persona was a bit risky (if not simply too risqué) for an industry staving off the sour effects of scandal. But if we emphasize the "worldliness" of such an identity, we uncover a star-making strategy inaugurated in the early 1920s through which stars such as Pola Negri and Emil Jannings

Benjamin, Walter. "The Formula in Which the Dialectical Structure of Film Finds Expression." *The Work of Art in the Age of Its Technological Reproducibility and Other Writings on Media.* Ed. Michael W. Jennings, Brigid Doherty, and Thomas Y. Levin. Cambridge, Mass.: Harvard UP, 2008. 340–41.

Bernardi, Joanne. *Writing in Light: The Silent Scenario and the Japanese Pure Film Movement.* Detroit: Wayne State UP, 2001.

Bertellini, Giorgio. "Black Hands and White Hearts. Italian Immigrants as Urban Racial Types in Early 20th Century American Cinema." *Urban History* 31.3 (2004): 374–98.

———. "Duce/Divo: Displaced Rhetorics of Masculinity, Racial Identity, and Politics among Italian-Americans in 1920's New York City." *Journal of Urban History* 31.5 (2005): 685–726.

———. *Italy in Early American Cinema: Race, Landscape, and the Picturesque.* Bloomington: Indiana UP, 2009.

———, audio commentary. *The Italian* (DVD). *The Perils of the New Land: The Immigrant Experience (1910–1915)* (2 discs). Los Angeles: Flicker Alley/Film Preservation Associates, 2008.

Birchard, Robert S. "The Adventures of Francis Ford and Grace Cunard." *American Cinematographer* 74.7 (1993): 72–82.

———. "The (Continued) Adventures of Francis Ford and Grace Cunard." *American Cinematographer* 74.8 (1993): 64–86.

Blackwelder, Julia Kirk. *Now Hiring: The Feminization of Work in the United States, 1900–1995.* College Station: Texas A&M UP, 1997.

Blake, Angela. *How New York Became American, 1890–1924.* Baltimore: Johns Hopkins UP, 2006.

Bordwell, David. *Narration in the Fiction Film.* Madison: U of Wisconsin P, 1985.

Bowser, Eileen. *The Transformation of Cinema, 1907–1915.* New York: Scribner's, 1990.

Boyer, Paul S. *Urban Masses and Moral Order in America, 1820–1920.* Cambridge, Mass.: Harvard UP, 1978.

Brader, Chris. "'A World on Wings': Young Female Workers and Cinema in World War I." *Women's History Review* 14.1 (2005): 99–117.

Bramen, Carrie Tirado. "The Urban Picturesque and the Spectacle of Americanization." *American Quarterly* 52.3 (2000): 444–77.

Braudy, Leo. *The Frenzy of Renown: Fame and Its History.* New York: Oxford UP, 1986.

Brooks, Peter. *The Melodramatic Imagination: Balzac, Henry James, Melodrama and the Mode of Excess.* New Haven, Conn.: Yale UP, 1976.

Brownlow, Kevin. *Behind the Mask of Innocence.* New York: Knopf, 1990.

Burrows, Jon. "Girls on Film: The Musical Matrices of Film Stardom in Early British Cinema." *Screen* 44.3 (Autumn 2003): 314–25.

———. *Legitimate Cinema: Theatre Stars in Silent British Films 1908–1918.* Exeter: U of Exeter P, 2003.

Buszek, Maria Ellena. *Pin-Up Grrrls: Feminism, Sexuality, Popular Culture.* Durham, N.C.: Duke UP, 2006.

Butler, Judith. *Gender Trouble: Feminism and the Subversion of Identity.* London: Routledge, 1990.

Carson, Anne. *Eros: The Bittersweet.* Princeton, N.J.: Princeton UP, 1986.

Carroll, Noël. "Notes on the Sight Gag." *Comedy/Cinema/Theory.* Ed. Andrew S. Horton. Berkeley: U of California P, 1991. 25–42.

Chaplin, Charles. *My Autobiography.* New York: Simon & Schuster, 1964.

Conron, John. *American Picturesque.* University Park: Pennsylvania State UP, 2000.

Cook, David A. *A History of Narrative Film*. 4th ed. New York: W.W. Norton & Company, 2004.

Cooke, Alistair. *Douglas Fairbanks: The Making of a Screen Character*. New York: Museum of Modern Art, 1940.

———. "Fame." *The Essential Chaplin: Perspectives on the Life and Art of the Great Comedian*. Ed. Richard Schickel. Chicago: Ivan R. Dee, 2006. 120–49.

Cooper, Mark Garrett. *Universal Women: Filmmaking and Institutional Change in Early Hollywood*. Urbana: U of Illinois P, 2010.

Cott, Nancy. *The Grounding of Modern Feminism*. New Haven, Conn.: Yale UP, 1987.

Creel, George. *How We Advertised America: The First Telling of the Amazing Story of the Committee on Public Information That Carried the Gospel of Americanism to Every Corner of the Globe*. New York: Harper & Brothers, 1920.

Curtis, Scott. "Douglas Fairbanks: King of Hollywood." *Screen Stars of the 1920s*. Ed. Patrice Petro. New Brunswick, N.J.: Rutgers UP, 2010. 21–40.

Dahlquist, Marina. "Becoming American in 1910? Pathé Frères Settlement in New Jersey." *Quarterly Review of Film and Video* 22.3 (2005): 251–62.

Dall'Asta, Monica. "American Serials and the Identity of French Cinema, or How to Resist Colonization." *Cinegrafie* 9.14 (2001): 161–74.

Daniels, Roger. *Asian America: Chinese and Japanese in the United States since 1850*. Seattle: U of Washington P, 1988.

deCordova, Richard. *Picture Personalities: The Emergence of the Star System in America*. Urbana: U of Illinois P, 1990.

Deguchi, Takehito. "Nani ga hakujin konpurekkusu o umidashitaka [What caused Caucasian complex?]." *Nihon eiga to Modanizumu 1920–1930* [Japanese cinema and modernism 1920–30]. Ed. Iwamoto Kenji. Tokyo: Riburopôto, 1991. 104–23.

De Lauretis, Teresa. "The Technology of Gender." *Technologies of Gender*. Bloomington: Indiana UP, 1987. 1–30.

Deleuze, Gilles. *Cinema I: The Movement Image*. Trans. Hugh Tomlinson and Barbara Habberjam. Minneapolis: U of Minnesota P, 1986.

Delluc, Louis. "Beauty in the Cinema." *French Film Theory and Criticism: A History/Anthology 1907–1939*. Vol. 1: *1907–1929*. Ed. Richard Abel. Princeton, N.J.: Princeton UP, 1988. 137–39.

DeMille, Cecil B. *The Autobiography of Cecil B. DeMille*. Ed. Donald Hayne. Englewood Cliffs, N.J.: Prentice Hall, 1959.

de Mille, William C. *Hollywood Saga*. New York: E. P. Dutton, 1939.

DiMaggio, Paul. "Cultural Entrepreneurship in Nineteenth-Century Boston: The Creation of an Organizational Base for High Culture in America." *Media, Culture, and Society* 1 (January 1982): 33–50.

Dyer, Richard. "The Colour of Virtue: Lillian Gish, Whiteness and Femininity." *Women and Film: A Sight and Sound Reader*. Ed. Pam Cook and Philip Dodd. Philadelphia: Temple UP, 1993. 1–9.

———. "*A Star Is Born* and the Construction of Authenticity." *Stardom: Industry of Desire*. Ed. Christine Gledhill. London: Routledge, 1991. 132–40.

———. *Stars*. London: BFI Publishing, 1979; 1990.

Dyer, Thomas G. *Theodore Roosevelt and the Idea of Race*. Baton Rouge: Louisiana State UP, 1980.

Dykstra, Bram. *Evil Sisters: The Threat of Female Sexuality in Twentieth-Century Culture*. New York: Henry Holt, 1996.

Eagleton, Terry. *Holy Terror*. New York: Oxford UP, 2005.

Kimber, John. *The Art of Charlie Chaplin*. Sheffield: Sheffield Academic Press, 2000.

King, Rob. "'Made for the Masses with an Appeal to the Classes': The Triangle Film Corporation and the Failure of Highbrow Film Culture." *Cinema Journal* 44.2 (Winter 2005): 3–33.

Kline, Wendy. *Building a Better Race: Gender, Sexuality, and Eugenics from the Turn of the Century to the Baby Boom*. Berkeley: U of California P, 2005.

Koshy, Susan. "American Nationhood as Eugenic Romance." *Differences* 12.1 (2001): 50–78.

Koszarski, Richard. *An Evening's Entertainment: The Age of the Silent Feature Picture 1915–1928*. New York: Scribner's, 1990.

Kracauer, Siegfried. "Two Chaplin Sketches." Trans. John MacKay. *Yale Journal of Criticism* 10.1 (1997): 115–20.

Lahue, Kalton C., and Terry Brewer. *Kops and Custards: The Legend of Keystone Films*. Norman: U of Oklahoma P, 1968/1972.

Lant, Antonia. "The Curse of the Pharaoh, or How Cinema Contracted Egyptomania." *Visions of the East: Orientalism in Film*. Ed. Matthew Bernstein and Gaylyn Studlar. New Brunswick, N.J.: Rutgers UP, 1997. 69–98.

———, ed. With Ingrid Perez. *Red Velvet Seat: Women's Writing on the First Fifty Years of Cinema*. London: Verso Press, 2006.

Lasky, Jesse L. *I Blow My Own Horn*. Garden City, N.Y.: Doubleday, 1957.

Lears, T. J. Jackson. *No Place of Grace: Antimodernism and the Transformation of American Culture, 1880–1920*. Chicago: U of Chicago P, 1994.

Levin, Martin, ed. *Five Boyhoods: Howard Lindsay, Harry Golden, Walt Kelly, William K. Zusser, and John Updike*. Garden City, N.Y.: Doubleday, 1962.

Levine, Lawrence. *Highbrow/Lowbrow: The Emergence of Cultural Hierarchy in America*. Cambridge, Mass.: Harvard UP, 1988.

Livingston, James. *Pragmatism, Feminism, and Democracy: Rethinking the Politics of American History*. New York: Routledge, 2001.

Looby, Christopher. "Southworth and Seriality: 'The Hidden Hand' in the *New York Ledger*." *Nineteenth-Century Literature* 59.2 (2004): 179–211.

Loos, Anita. *A Girl Like I*. New York: Viking, 1966.

Mahar, Karen Ward. *Women Filmmakers in Early Hollywood*. Baltimore: Johns Hopkins UP, 2006.

Maland, Charles J. *Chaplin and American Culture: The Evolution of a Star Image*. Princeton, N.J.: Princeton UP, 1989.

Mann, William J. *The Biograph Girl: A Novel of Hollywood Then and Now*. New York: Kensington Publishing Corporation, 2000.

Marx, Karl. *Capital* (1887). Ed. Frederick Engels. Vol. 1. New York: International Publishers, 1967.

Mast, Gerald. *The Comic Mind: Comedy and the Movies*. Chicago: U of Chicago P, 1979.

Matsumoto, Yûko. "Amerika jin de arukoto, Amerika jin ni suru koto: 20seiki shotô no 'Amerika ka' undô ni okeru jendâ, jinshu, kaikyû [Being American, making American: Gender, class and race in the 'Americanization' movement in early twentieth century]." *Shisô* 884 (February 1998): 52–75.

May, Lary. *Screening Out the Past: The Birth of Mass Culture and the Motion Picture Industry*. Chicago: U of Chicago P, 1980.

McCabe, John. *Charlie Chaplin*. New York: Doubleday, 1978.

McCabe, Susan. "'Delight in Dislocation': The Cinematic Modernism of Stein, Chaplin, and Man Ray." *Modernism/Modernity* 8.3 (September 2001): 429–52.

Michaels, Walter Benn. *Our America: Nativism, Modernism, and Pluralism*. Durham, N.C.: Duke UP, 1995.

Miyao, Daisuke. *Sessue Hayakawa: Silent Cinema and Transnational Stardom*. Durham, N.C.: Duke UP, 2007.

Mori, Iwao. "Eiga Haiyû no hanashi (part 2) [A story about film actors]." *Katsudô Kurabu* (July 1922): 72–73.

———. *Hayakawa Sesshû*. Tokyo: Tôyô shuppan sha, 1922.

Morosco, Helen M., and Leonard Paul Dugger. *The Oracle of Broadway: Life or Oliver Morosco*. Caldwell, Oh.: Caxton Printers, 1944.

Morris, Brian C. "Charlie Chaplin's Tryst with Spain." *Journal of Contemporary History* 18 (1983): 517–31.

Muscio, Giuliana. "Girls, Ladies, Stars: Stars and Women Screenwriters in Twenties' America." *Cinegrafie* 13 (2000): 177–220.

Nash, Elizabeth. *Always First Class: The Career of Geraldine Farrar*. Washington, D.C.: UP of America, 1981.

Neale, Steve, and Frank Krutnik. *Popular Film and Television Comedy*. London: Routledge, 1990.

Neibaur, James, L. *Arbuckle and Keaton: Their 14 Film Collaborations*. Jefferson, N.C.: McFarland, 2007.

Newton, Isaac. *Opticks* (1717). Reprinted from the 4th ed. New York: McGraw-Hill, 1931.

Ockman, Carol, and Kenneth E. Silver. *Sarah Bernhardt: The Art of High Drama*. New Haven, Conn.: Yale UP, 2005.

Odell, George Clinton Densmore. *Annals of the New York Stage*. New York: Columbia UP, 1927–1949. Reprint, New York: AMS Press, 1970.

Oderman, Stuart. *Roscoe "Fatty" Arbuckle: A Biography of the Silent Film Comedian, 1887–1933*. Jefferson, N.C.: McFarland, 1994.

Okihiro, Gary Y. *Cane Fires: The Anti-Japanese Movement in Hawaii, 1865–1945*. Philadelphia: Temple UP, 1991.

Osterman, Anne Burri. "The Tramp, the Ingenue, and the Cowboy: Work, Authority, and the Mass-Mediation of Gender during the Silent Film Era." Ph.D. diss., U of Chicago, 2004.

Parker, Andrew, and Eve Kosofsky Sedgwick, eds. *Performativity and Performance*. London: Routledge, 1995.

Perez, Gilberto. "On Chaplin and Keaton." *Film Theory and Criticism*, 7th ed. Ed. Leo Braudy and Marshall Cohen. New York: Oxford UP, 2009. 474–79.

Pickford, Mary. *How to Act for the Screen*. London: Standard Art Books, 1919.

Qin, Xiqing. "Pearl White and the New Female Image in Chinese Early Silent Cinema." Unpublished manuscript, Institute of Film and TV Studies, Chinese National Academy of Arts.

Rapf, Joanna E. "Both Sides of the Camera: Roscoe Arbuckle's Evolution at Keystone." *Quarterly Review of Film & Television* 26.4 (2009): 339–52.

Robinson, David. *Chaplin: His Life and Art*. New York: McGraw-Hill, 1985.

Rodríguez, Clara E. "Film Viewing in Latino Communities, 1896–1934: Puerto Rico as Microcosm." *From Bananas to Buttocks: The Latina Body in Popular Film and Culture*. Ed. Myra Mendible. Austin: U of Texas P, 2007. 31–50.

Roosevelt, Theodore. *The Strenuous Life: Essays and Addresses*. New York: Century, 1901.

Rutherford, Susan. *The Prima Donna and Opera, 1815–1930*. Cambridge: Cambridge UP, 2006.

Sandberg, Mark B. *Living Pictures, Missing Persons: Mannequins, Museums, and Modernity.* Princeton, N.J.: Princeton UP, 2003.

Sargent, Amy. "Dancing on Fire and Water: Charlot and *l'esprit nouveau.*" *Slapstick Comedy.* Ed. Tom Paulus and Rob King. New York: Routledge, 2010. 193–206.

Sarris, Andrew. "The Most Harmonious Comedian." *The Essential Chaplin: Perspectives on the Life and Art of the Great Comedian.* Ed. Richard Schickel. Chicago: Ivan R. Dee, 2006. 45–58.

Schickel, Richard. "Charles Chaplin: An Unexamined Premise." *Richard Schickel on Film: Encounters—Critical and Personal—with Movie Immortals.* New York: William Morrow, 1989. 17–33.

———. *His Picture in the Papers: A Speculation on the Celebrity in America Based on the Life of Douglas Fairbanks, Sr.* New York: Charterhouse, 1973.

Seldes, Gilbert. *The Seven Lively Arts.* New York: Harper & Brothers, 1924.

Serna, Laura Isabel. *Making Cinelandia: American Films and Mexican Film Culture before the Golden Age, 1896–1936.* Durham, N.C.: Duke UP, forthcoming.

Shaviro, Steven. *The Cinematic Body.* Minneapolis: U of Minnesota P, 1993.

Sherman, William Thomas. *Mabel Normand: A Source Book to Her Life and Films.* Seattle: Cinema Books, 1994.

Shohat, Ella. "Gender and Culture of Empire." *Visions of the East: Orientalism in Film.* Ed. Matthew Bernstein and Gaylyn Studlar. New Brunswick, N.J.: Rutgers UP, 1997. 109–66.

Showalter, Elaine. *Sexual Anarchy: Gender and Culture at the Fin de Siècle.* New York: Viking, 1990.

Sinclair, Upton. *Upton Sinclair Presents William Fox.* Los Angeles: n.p., 1933.

Singer, Ben. "Feature Films, Variety Programs, and the Crisis of the Small Exhibitor." *American Cinema's Transitional Era: Audiences, Institutions, Practices.* Ed. Charlie Keil and Shelley Stamp. Berkeley: U of California P, 2004. 76–100.

———. *Melodrama and Modernity: Early Pulp Cinema and Its Contexts.* New York: Columbia UP, 2001.

Sklar, Robert. *F. Scott Fitzgerald: The Last Laocoon.* New York: Oxford UP, 1967.

Slide, Anthony. *The Kindergarten of the Movies: A History of the Fine Arts Company.* Metuchen, N.J.: Scarecrow Press, 1980.

Smith, Andrew Brodie. "'The Making of Broncho Billy': Gilbert M. Anderson Creates the Western-Film Hero." *Shooting Cowboys and Indians: Silent Western Films, American Culture, and the Birth of Hollywood.* Boulder: U of Colorado P, 2003. 133–56.

Sobchack, Vivian. *Carnal Thoughts: Embodiment and Moving Image Culture.* Berkeley: U of California P, 2004.

Soupault, Phillipe. "Cinema, U.S.A." (1924). *The Shadow and Its Shadow: Surrealist Writings on the Cinema.* 3rd ed. Ed. Paul Hammond. San Francisco: City Lights Books, 2000. 60–61.

Staiger, Janet. *Bad Women: Regulating Sexuality in Early American Cinema.* Minneapolis: U of Minnesota P, 1995.

———. "Seeing Stars." *Stardom: Industry of Desire.* Ed. Christine Gledhill. London: Routledge, 1991. 3–16.

Stamp, Shelley. *Movie-Struck Girls: Women and Motion Picture Culture after the Nickelodeon.* Princeton, N.J.: Princeton UP, 2000.

Stewart, Susan. *On Longing: Narratives of the Miniature, the Gigantic, the Souvenir, the Collection.* Durham, N.C.: Duke UP, 1993.

Stoloff, Sam. "Normalizing Stars: Roscoe 'Fatty' Arbuckle and Hollywood Consolidation." *American Silent Film: Discovering Marginalized Voices*. Ed. Gregg Bachman and Thomas J. Slater. Carbondale: Southern Illinois UP, 2002. 148–75.

Streeby, Shelley. *American Sensations: Class, Empire, and the Production of Popular Culture*. Berkeley: U of California P, 2002.

Studlar, Gaylyn. "'Out-Salomeing Salome': Dance, the New Woman, and Fan Magazine Orientalism." *Visions of the East: Orientalism in Film*. Ed. Gaylyn Studlar and Matthew Bernstein. New Brunswick, N.J.: Rutgers UP, 1997. 99–129.

———. "The Perils of Pleasure?: Fan Magazine Discourse as Women's Commodified Culture in the 1920s." *Silent Film*. Ed. Richard Abel. New Brunswick, N.J.: Rutgers UP, 1996. 263–97.

———. *This Mad Masquerade: Stardom and Masculinity in the Jazz Age*. New York: Columbia UP, 1996.

Takaki, Ronald. *Strangers from a Different Shore: A History of Asian Americans*. New York: Penguin, 1989.

Taranow, Gerda. *Sarah Bernhardt: The Art within the Legend*. Princeton, N.J.: Princeton UP, 1972.

Telotte, J. P. "Arbuckle Escapes: The Pattern of Fatty Arbuckle's Comedy." *Journal of Popular Film and Television* 15.4 (1988): 172–79.

Thompson, Jan. "The Role of Woman in the Iconography of Art Nouveau." *Art Journal* 31.2 (Winter 1971–72): 158–67.

Thompson, Kristin. "Fairbanks without the Moustache: A Case for the Early Films." *Sulla via di Hollywood, 1911–1920*. Ed. Paolo Cherchi Usai and Lorenzo Codelli. Pordenone, Italy: Biblioteca dell'Immagine, 1988. 156–93.

———. "The International Exploration of Cinematic Expressivity." *The Silent Cinema Reader*. Ed. Lee Grieveson and Peter Krämer. London: Routledge, 2004. 254–69.

Tibbetts, John C. "Mary Pickford and the American 'Growing Girl.'" *Journal of Popular Film and Television* 29.2 (Summer 2001): 50–62.

Tibbetts, John C., and James M. Welsh. *His Majesty the American: The Cinema of Douglas Fairbanks, Sr.* New York: A. S. Barnes, 1977.

Trotter, David. *Cinema and Modernism*. Oxford: Blackwell, 2007.

Ulady, Neda. "Roscoe Arbuckle and the Scandal of Fatness." *Bodies out of Bounds: Fatness and Transgression*. Ed. Jana Evans Braziel and Kathleen LeBesco. Berkeley: U of California P, 2001. 153–65.

U.S. Census Bureau. "No. HS-30 Marital Status of Women in the Civilian Labor Force: 1900 to 2002." *Statistical Abstract of the United States*. 2003. 52–53.

Vance, Jeffrey, with Tony Maietta. *Douglas Fairbanks*. Berkeley: U of California P, 2008.

Van Dyke, John C. *The New New York: A Commentary on the Place and the People*. New York: Macmillan, 1909.

Vitali, Valentina. *Hindi Action Cinema: Industries, Narratives, Bodies*. New Delhi: Oxford UP, 2008.

Wagenknecht, Edward. "Geraldine Farrar's Film Career." *Films in Review* 28 (January 1977): 23–38.

———. *Lillian Gish: An Interpretation*. Seattle: U of Washington Book Store, 1927.

Watkins, Fred. "Sessue Hayakawa Today." *Films in Review* 17.6 (June/July 1966): 391–92.

Weber, Max. *Economy and Society: An Outline of Interpretive Sociology* [1924]. Trans. Ephraim Fischoff. Vol. 2. New York: Bedminster Press, 1968.

Weitzel, Edward. *Intimate Talks with Movie Stars*. New York: Dale Publishing, 1921.

White, G. Edward. *The Eastern Establishment and the Western Experience: The West of Frederic Remington, Theodore Roosevelt, and Owen Wister*. New Haven, Conn.: Yale UP, 1968.

White, Pearl. *Just Me*. New York: George H. Doran Co., 1919.

Whitfield, Eileen. *Pickford: The Woman Who Made Hollywood*. Lexington: UP of Kentucky, 1997.

Williams, Linda. "Film Bodies: Gender, Genre, and Excess." *Film Theory and Criticism: Introductory Readings*. Ed. Leo Braudy and Marshall Cohen. 5th ed. New York: Oxford UP, 1999. 701–15.

———. *Playing the Race Card: Melodramas of Black and White from Uncle Tom to O.J. Simpson*. Princeton, N.J.: Princeton UP, 2001.

Wood, Houston. *Displacing Natives: The Rhetorical Production of Hawai'i*. Lanham, Md.: Rowman & Littlefield, 1999.

Wullschlager, Jackie. *Inventing Wonderland: the Lives and Fantasies of Lewis Carroll, Edward Lear, J. M. Barrie, Kenneth Grahame, and A. A. Milne*. London: Methuen, 1995.

Yoshiyuki, Junnosuke, "Sekai ni kakeru Nippon no hashi: Hayakawa Sesshû [Japanese bridge over the world: Sessue Hayakawa]." *Shûkan Gendai* 50 (19 December 1963): 46–49.

Young, Robert Jr. *Roscoe "Fatty" Arbuckle: A Bio-Bibliography*. Westport, Conn.: Greenwood Press, 1994.

CONTRIBUTORS
★★★★★★★★★★★

RICHARD ABEL is Robert Altman Collegiate Professor of Film Studies in Screen Arts & Cultures at the University of Michigan. Most recently he edited the award-winning *Encyclopedia of Early Cinema* (2005/2009/2010), published *Americanizing the Movies and "Movie-Mad" Audiences, 1910–1914* (2006), and co-edited (with Giorgio Bertellini and Rob King) *Early Cinema and the "National"* (2008). Currently he is writing *Menus for Movie Land: Newspapers and the Emergence of American Film Culture, 1913–1916*.

JENNIFER M. BEAN is the director of the Cinema Studies Program and an associate professor of comparative literature at the University of Washington. She is co-editor of *A Feminist Reader in Early Cinema* (2002) and of a special issue of *Camera Obscura* on "Early Women Stars." She is currently editing a collection entitled *Border Crossings: Silent Cinema and the Politics of Space*, and writing a book on the geopolitical imagination of early Hollywood and the formation of mass culture.

GIORGIO BERTELLINI is an associate professor of film studies in the Departments of Screen Arts & Cultures and Romance Languages and Literatures at the University of Michigan. He is the author of *Emir Dusturica* (1996; 2nd expanded ed. 2010) and the award-winning *Italy in Early American Cinema: Race, Landscape, and the Picturesque* (2009), editor of *Cinema of Italy* (2004; 2007), and co-editor (with Richard Abel and Rob King) of *Early Cinema and the "National"* (2008).

MARK GARRETT COOPER is the interim director of Moving Image Research Collections and an associate professor of film and media studies at the University of South Carolina. He is the author of *Love Rules: Silent Hollywood and the Rise of the Managerial Class* (2003) and *Universal Women: Filmmaking and Institutional Change in Early Hollywood* (2010). He is currently researching the history of motion picture accounting, and, with John Marx, is writing a book about cinema's role in the development of humanities disciplines.

SCOTT CURTIS is an associate professor in the Radio/Television/Film Department at Northwestern University, where he teaches film history and historiography. He has published on a wide variety of topics, including early film theory, film sound, animation, Alfred Hitchcock, the Motion Picture Patents Company, industrial film, medical cinematography, microcinematography,